Exposing Prejudice

Puerto Rican
Experiences of
Language, Race,
and Class

D0145784

INSTITUTIONAL STRUCTURES OF FEELING

George Marcus, Sharon Traweek, Richard Handler, and
Vera Zolberg, *Series Editors*

FORTHCOMING

Exposing Prejudice

Puerto Rican
Experiences of
Language, Race,
and Class

Bonnie Urciuoli

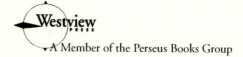

Westview
PRESS
A Member of the Perseus Books Group

Institutional Structures of Feeling

Copyright © 1996 by Westview Press, A Member of the Perseus Books Group

Published in 1996 in the United States of America by Westview Press, Inc., 5500 Central Avenue, Boulder, Colorado 80301-2877, and in the United Kingdom by Westview Press, 12 Hid's Copse Road, Cumnor Hill, Oxford OX2 9JJ

Library of Congress Cataloging-in-Publication Data
Urciuoli, Bonnie
Exposing Prejudice: Puerto Rican Experiences of Language, Race, and Class /Bonnie Urciuoli.
    p.   cm.
   Includes bibliographical references and index.
   ISBN 0-8133-1830-0 (alk. paper)—ISBN 0-8133-2967-1 (pbk.)
    1. Puerto Ricans—New York (State)—New York—Social conditions.   2. Puerto Ricans—New York (State)—New York—Languages.   3. Sociolinguistics—New York (State)—New York.
4. New York (N.Y.)—Languages.   5. New York (N.Y.)—Social conditions.   6. Prejudices—New York (State)—New York.   I. Title
F128.9.P85U73   1996
305.868'7295—dc20   98–10325
                                                    CIP

10   9   8   7   6   5   4   3   2   1

This book is dedicated to the people who speak through its pages

Contents

Tables

Acknowledgments

The 1978–1979 research was aided by a research award from the Ford Foundation Advisory Committee on the Movement of Caribbean People. The 1988 research was aided by the Spencer Foundation Small Grants Program. The 1991 research and much of the writing and editing was aided by research awards from Hamilton College, including a Margaret Bundy Scott leave award. The idea of metacommunication and the performance of social identity was developed in the 1990 National Endowment for the Humanities summer seminar, "Poetics and Social Life," directed by Michael Herzfeld at Indiana University.

I cannot begin to thank sufficiently the people who participated in this research. Those who took part in the 1978–1979 study alone appear only under pseudonyms. Those with whom I worked in 1988 (some of whom also took part in the 1978–1979 work) appear under their own names for reasons discussed in the introduction. My deepest thanks to all of you for your insight, patience, time, belief in this project despite all the time it took, and most of all, your friendship. You changed my life.

Over the past decade and a half, friends and colleagues from New York, Chicago, Bloomington, and Clinton have helped develop and clarify the ideas in this book. So thanks to John Attinasi, Cele Bucki, John Calagione, Steve Caton, Phyllis Pease Chock, Allison Dorsey, Brenda Farnell, Paula Girshick, Carol Greenhouse, Richard Handler, Richard Herrell, Michael Herzfeld, Gregory Jusdanis, Ruth Mandel, Susie McKinnon, Mercedes Niño-Murcia, Henry Rutz, Dan Segal, Jagna Sharff, Jim Wafer, and Tom Wilson. Thanks also to several of my Hamilton students: Rupert Maura, Teresita Romero, Gwen Sancherico, and Jackie Vargas, who transcribed and translated the Spanish interviews; Michelle Meade and Kate Taylor, who helped transcribe the English interviews; Jessica Che-

Mponda, Timna Genzlinger, Rob Marinovic, and Diane Uyar, who read and offered comments on portions of the manuscript. Thanks also to Chris Ingersoll for her help with the cover design.

Particular thanks to Ana Celia Zentella for sharing ideas and providing support at crucial intellectual points, Charlotte Beck for her endless encouragement, April Oswald for her careful editing, and Luis Molina and Gregory Jusdanis for helping me think up an intelligible title. Thanks to Paul Friedrich and Michael Silverstein for their guidance and encouragement in the complex world of language and culture and to Raymond Smith for insisting I think a little harder about class. Sadly I can only express posthumous gratitude to David Schneider for inspiring so much of my thinking about accents and other language "things." He is much more a part of this book than he ever knew.

Above all, thanks to my parents, Dee Andreani Urciuoli and Vincent Urciuoli, for their boundless love, support, and belief in me.

Bonnie Urciuoli
Clinton, New York

Chapter 1

Racialization and Language

Racializing and Ethnicizing

Language differences are routinely attributed to origin differences and in the United States origin differences are framed as race and ethnicity. Race and ethnicity are both about belonging to the nation, but belonging in different ways. When people are talked about as an ethnic group, as Italian-American, Polish-American, African American, Hispanic-American, Asian-American, the ideological emphasis is on national and/or cultural origins. This emphasis gives them a rightful place in the United States and their claim to language is seen as a point of pride. When people are talked about as a race (and every group now seen as ethnic was once or is still seen as a race as well as an ethnic group), the emphasis is on natural attributes that hierarchize them and, if they are not white, make their place in the nation provisional at best. When groups are seen in racial terms, language differences are ideologically problematic.[1]

Although Americans talk about race and ethnicity as if they were self-evident facts, I argue that they are constructions of difference that are opposed to each other in complex ways.[2] The current meanings of race and ethnicity emerge from decades of national discourse about difference, value, and belonging.[3] Race discourses, or racializing, frame group origin in natural terms; ethnic discourses, or ethnicizing, frame group origin in cultural terms.[4] Racializing is defined by a polarity between dominant and subordinate groups, the latter having minimal control over their position in the nation-state. Brackette Williams (1989, 1991) argues that race and ethnicity intertwine with class to grow from the processes which form the nation-state. Racial and ethnic discourses make up the myths of purity in the nation-state.[5] Racialized people are typified as human matter out of place: dirty, dangerous, unwilling, or unable to do their bit for the nation-state. In ethnic discourses, cultural difference is safe, ordered, a contribution to the nation-state offered by striving immigrants making their way up the ladder of class mobility. In these discourses, language difference is routinely racialized, typified as an impediment to class mobility.

These are U.S. hegemonic perceptions of difference. Raymond Williams (1977) explains "hegemony" as a body of practices that emerge in a system of unequal relations and that reproduce that system in ways that suit the interests of the dominant. Hegemony does not form a neatly articulated ideology and it is not monolithic. It is a system of influences that regularize and co-opt what people ordinarily do and say. Those influences are continually recreated through historically specific structures, resulting in:

> A saturation of the whole process of living—not only of political and economic activity, nor only of manifest social activity, but of the whole substance of lived identities and relationships. (Williams 1977:110)

In this process, the structural limits and pressures that shape race/ethnic experience seem natural, even common-sensical.[6]

At the base of U.S. assumptions about ethnicity and race is the idea of the normative or generic American, white, middle-class, English-speaking. This persona represents a cultural default setting, the automatic point of comparison for any kind of difference. It stands in opposition to all categories of origin difference, racialized or ethnicized, and stands furthest from racialized difference. Whiteness is unracialized so any kind of non-whiteness is subject to racialization. The racial polarity shapes perception of all language and cultural difference as problematic, often as parasitic—hence the intense reactions frequently expressed to public recognition of languages other than English, especially Spanish. Ethnicized difference is not racialized in that perception of cultural or language difference is not seen as evidence of racial inferiority or as a social problem. Instead difference is seen as evidence of a high-culture origin that legitimates the group's identity but does not interfere with the group making its proper contribution to the nation-state. Ethnicization is a kind of mediating discourse: if the chief polarities are white, middle-class Anglo versus non-white, poor and culturally/linguistically deficient, then being ethnicized is a way to mediate these extremes. Ethnicized people are not Anglo (they may or may not be white), but their origin is pedigreed by an external high culture that validates their difference because it somehow makes them act like Americans in crucial ways (i.e., their culture provides a work or education ethic, family values, and so forth). Foreign languages are justifiable in public places when they are used solely to reinforce the authenticity of a cultural performance. Singing folk songs in Spanish at a street fair is safe because translating the folk songs into English makes them less authentic. Speaking Spanish at work is dangerous because people are supposed to act like Americans at work: work settings are spaces that belong to English. Bilingual education or ballots are even more dangerous because by challenging the all-English nature of nationally defining public spaces (classrooms and voting booths) they threaten the integrity of the nation-state itself. Spanish in a folk song is interpreted in ethnicized terms; Spanish at work or in the classroom or on the ballot is interpreted in racialized terms.

Races and ethnicities are not primordial groups. They are powerful facts of day-to-day social life. The generic white American is, in semiotic terms, unmarked while the non-normative, the racialized or ethnicized person, is marked. Unmarked terms are relatively general and marked terms relatively specific. For example, in the vocabulary of color, unmarked terms include red, blue, or green whereas marked terms include fuschia, aquamarine, or blonde, all used in specialized contexts.[7] The distinction is relative: a term can be slightly or highly marked. In social life, the unmarked is typical and the marked is atypical. The contrast can be highly politicized. In the United States, where Anglo origins are unmarked, all other origins range along a sliding scale of slightly marked and safely different to highly marked and dangerous. Ethnicity is safely marked; race is dangerously marked.

This markedness develops cumulatively over decades, even centuries of discourse: public, private, face-to-face, written, proclaimed, printed, legislated, media-generated. Some discourses racialize, some ethnicize. Racializing discourses talk about unindividuated populations that differ fundamentally from whites in values, habits, language, character, and aspirations. Examples include the scientific racialism of the 1800s, the anti-immigrant writing of the early 1900s, and much of the writing on the culture of poverty and the underclass in the mid-late 1900s. In such discourses, racialized groups are seen as collectively, inherently, and unchangingly flawed. Ethnicizing discourses focus on the achievements of ethnic families and individuals. In such discourses, people who were once racialized are now able to unmark themselves to some degree by recasting cultural difference in positive terms—as warm and colorful, as a rich tradition, as family solidarity, as a drive to succeed. Such unmarking is never entirely complete but some groups are now only slightly marked (German-Americans, for example). The hyphenation -American is characteristic of ethnicizing discourse and the emergence of terms like African American, Hispanic-American, Native American, and Asian-American marks a degree of ethnicization among people who are still heavily racialized.

Origin difference was overwhelmingly racialized from the early 1800s to the early-mid 1900s. Every "ethnic group" that now exists in the United States was once racialized; every immigrant population and particularly every population subsumed into the United States through slavery or colonization. Most immigrant populations have become ethnicized with considerable success, while enslaved and colonized populations have had less success. Ethnicizing through political representation and through public demonstrations of group achievement, folkloric performances, and high-culture history have worked well for the "white ethnics" who found the route to social mobility opened after World War II by shifts in the economy. Hispanics, African Americans, and Native Americans have been less well-situated. Ethnicizing discourse alone can only unmark so much when economic openings are absent.

The most visible and influential authors of racializing discourses occupy power positions. They are in a position to say a great deal, and the people racialized are not in a position to say much in return. Ethnicizing discourses allow some voice to ethnics to speak for themselves and their "group" as long as they do so in ways that fit the interests of the nation-state—hence the emphasis on ethnic achievement and ethnic community. The problem is, however people may try to ethnicize (having few other options for respectability) their success depends largely upon their political/economic base. The growing business presence of Asian-Americans has made it possible for them to be cast by media and politicians in more ethnicizing, less racializing terms than they were a few decades ago. *Hispanic Magazine* emphasizes upward mobility and political activity among Latins, casting them as a social force to be reckoned with and culturally respected.

Racializing discourses equate language difference with disorder, with images of illiterate foreigners flooding the United States and refusing to speak English or hordes of the underclass speaking an accented English with "broken" grammar and "mixed" vocabulary. In ethnicizing discourses, linguistic differences are delegated to venues where difference is carefully contained in folkloric performance, religious expression, or ethnic press and broadcasting media. Difference is safe when it cannot impede the "natural" progress of social mobility in the United States, but language difference is spoken and written about as an insurmountable barrier to such progress. People may safely retain their own language so long as it does not show in their English, which must display no more than a slight accent and occasional quaint expression. Pragmatics—the social interpretation of meaning—does not enter the picture. Ignored are the facts that people face information barriers that go beyond word meaning or that certain accents put speakers at risk of being judged as stupid or unworthy of notice.

Mexicans, Puerto Ricans, and Other Others

U.S. racialized perceptions developed in conjunction with the institution of slavery, with aggressive engagement of Native Americans, and the expansionist policy of Manifest Destiny. Horsman (1981) traces the growth of U.S. self-identity as "Anglo-Saxon" from the late 1700s in newspapers, books, scientific treatises, religious tracts, and political speeches. Black slaves fit into the lowest level of the racial hierarchy, as unfitted by nature for any place in society other than slave labor. Indians presented a more complex picture, at least initially, when many Americans (influenced by Enlightenment principles) saw them as savage but as part of the same order of creation. After 1800 polygenist race discourses multiplied, justifying slavery and expansionist policies by positing separate creations for separate and inferior races. By 1850 the race-hierarchy model was firmly ensconced in public consciousness as "science." The United States was thus imagined to have a natural right to sweep aside the Indians and Mexicans who stood in the way of U.S. expansion. Racial discourses developed steam, encompassing "other white races" who would "be absorbed into the existing mass while non-white races would be rigorously excluded from equal participation as citizens" (Horsman 1981:189).

The racial opposition of American and Mexican was well under way by 1840:

> In confronting the Mexicans the Americans clearly formulated the idea of themselves as an Anglo-Saxon race. The use of *Anglo-Saxon* in a racial sense, somewhat rare in the political arguments of the 1830's, increased rapidly later in the decade and became commonplace by the mid 1840's. (p. 208)

As the United States became increasingly concerned with spreading Anglo-Saxon Christian civilization across the continent, Mexicans were cast as failures, "a mixed inferior race with considerable Indian and some black blood" (p. 210). The "Mexican character" was seen as idle, animalistic, vicious, shiftless, dumb, ineffective, cowardly, and mongrel increasingly lumped in with Indians and blacks (see also Steinberg 1989:21–24). Meanwhile, the United States was busily looking to its advantage with Mexico. Since the 1830's U.S. citizens had been moving into Texas, the New Mexico territory, and California. Eventually President Polk attempted to buy the territory but Mexico did not wish to sell. Territorial disputes broke out, U.S. settlers declared independence from Mexico, and war was declared in 1846. In 1848 Mexico ceded what is now California, Nevada, Utah, Arizona, and New Mexico for $15 million and relinquished all claims to Texas. The U.S.-Mexican boundary was set at the Rio Grande.

As U.S. racial perceptions of Mexicans evolved, they formed the basis for perceptions of Caribbean Latins. President Polk had also wanted to buy Cuba but the Spanish were not selling. President Fillmore in 1852 hesitated to pursue the purchase of Cuba only because it would bring too many Cubans into the United States. As Fillmore told Congress (*Congressional Globe,* 32nd Congress, 2nd session, appendix, p. 1):

> Were this Island comparatively destitute of inhabitants, or occupied by a kindred race, I should regard it, if voluntarily ceded by Spain, as a most desirable acquisition. But, under existing circumstances, I should look upon its incorporation into our Union as a very hazardous measure. It would bring into the confederacy a population of a different national stock, speaking a different language, and not likely to harmonize with the other members. (cited in Horsman 1981:283)

To the United States, the worth of Caribbean, Mexican, and Central American people lay in direct proportion to the raw materials and labor that they provided. Themselves natives of complex racial systems, Caribbean and Latin people found their encounters with the United States placed them squarely in the category "Other." Both the United States and Spain racialized, displaced, and often killed indigenous people, but where the United States did so without incorporating them into the economic or social system, Spain incorporated indigenous people into the bottom rung of their production system as peasants. Unlike the U.S. race model, the Spanish model afforded some degree of racial continuity from the

Spanish-born peninsular to the local-born *criollo* of Spanish family (the landowner and professional class) to the "mixed blood" *mestizo* of Spanish and Native American descent (farmers, possibly small business owners) to the *indigena* or *indio* (Native American peasant farmers). Thus, *raza* in Latin American usage has a connotation substantially different from that of *race* in the United States. Where the latter is a discrete, binary, naturalized classification, the former can mean a people, a lineage, a social group; it has finer shades and intermediate categories. Race is assessed as combinations of personal characteristics and social circumstances. Latin *raza* is about a complex identity in the New World. Race in the United States basically codes European versus non-European descent (Trouillot 1990). To U.S. eyes, most Latin Americans were (and are) racially Other, as disconnected from the Anglo-Saxon as are Indians.

In the same climate, the "new migrations" of southern and eastern Europe, while providing a labor reserve for work that native-born, white Americans could not or would not do, were seen as immoral, unhealthy, and unintelligent. Discriminatory policies were justified by "scientific" measurement. Objectifying and measuring difference in the United States has deep roots in nation-building: the first population census was mandated by the Constitutional Convention of 1787. Through much of the nineteenth century, measurements of population growth and diversity fueled pride in the success of the American experiment (Conk 1986:160). But as the republic's labor pool filled with people who were not northern European or not European at all, growth seemed less wonderfully progressive. A quarter of the U.S. work force was foreign-born by 1910; in the same year, the Dillingham Commission (a congressional investigation of immigration) reported that 58 percent of the mining and manufacturing work-force in twenty major industries surveyed were foreign born (Steinberg 1989:36). The National Origins Act, passed in 1924, sought to control dangerous foreign elements by allowing a maximum of 150,000 immigrants a year with 71 percent allocated to Great Britain, Ireland, and Germany. These proportions, based on immigrant demographics in the 1920 census, were thought to represent a reasonable U.S. racial balance (Conk 1986:164).

Limits on immigration from southern and eastern Europe were further justified by "hard data" supplied by the new science of intelligence testing and by sociological surveys. In 1921 Robert Yerkes administered intelligence tests to Army recruits. He mapped his results onto what he saw as a distribution of innate intelligence, placing the mental age of Anglo whites at 13.08, Europeans at 10–11 (Russians 11.34; Italians 11.01; Poles 10.74), and Negroes at 10.41. Yerkes's arguments were further developed by C. C. Brigham in his 1923 work *A Study of American Intelligence.* This "became a primary vehicle for translating the army results on group differences into social action" (Gould 1981:224).

In a survey of articles published in the *American Journal of Sociology* between 1895 and 1935, Phelan (1989) describes numerous sociological studies of racial habits, character traits, superiority, and inferiority. Of particular interest is a 1916 survey in which various sociologists were asked to rank ten groups (classified as white Americans, Germans, English, Hebrews, Scandinavians, Irish, French, Slavs, Southern Italians, and Negroes) by personality trait:

> White Americans were ranked first in intellectual ability, cooperation, leadership and efficiency, while Germans ranked first on self-control, moral integrity and perseverance, and Hebrews were first on aspiration. Southern Italians and Negroes were ranked ninth and tenth respectively on all traits except sympathy, on which Negroes were second (after the Irish) and Southern Italians were third. Of particular interest is the ironic conclusion of the study: "The object of this study is to urge upon sociologists the wider collection of data and its precise arrangement, so that expressions of personal opinion may yield to widely accepted statements of fact, and the general affirmation may give place to quanti- tative estimates." (Phelan 1989:381–390)

By the 1920s, academic racializing was being challenged by Franz Boas and his anthropology students at Columbia University, and by Robert Park, Louis Wirth, and their students and colleagues in sociology at the University of Chicago. Boas stressed the universality of culture and the absence of any inherent connec- tion among race, culture, and language. Park and Wirth proposed the existence of a race-relations cycle, whereby groups moving into the United States passed through five stages (contact, competition, conflict, accommodation, and assimilation), each group retaining its territorial locus until dispersed by assimilation. Boas and Park have been criticized for underestimating the importance and endurance of cultural difference in the social construction of race (see Szwed 1975 on Boas; Stanfield 1985 on Park). Nevertheless, the very fact that they saw race as a construct was a signal development. Park, with his stress on assimilation, was closer than Boas to the 1930s "good ethnic citizen" philosophy by which churches, unions, and politi- cal parties recruited immigrant membership. By World War II public education (beginning with citizenship classes) had come to be seen as the primary vehicle of assimilation. Assimilation meant the "good citizenship" enjoyed by the successful ethnic.[8]

By the 1940s, ethnicizing discourses had also emerged in popular portraits of ethnic working-class families striving to "make it." Ethnic literature and radio pro- grams presented the working class as the immigrant point of entry into U.S. soci- ety. The idea that the working class was also a point of departure into a life of social mobility was the advertising theme of the 1950s. Developers and manufacturers traded heavily on the image of the young man with the young family moving up in the world, from city to suburb, to a life of modern convenience and popular luxury, a move subsidized by servicemen's benefits and the establishment of credit. Lipsitz (1986) compares 1940s radio and 1950s television versions of programs about ethnic families—*The Goldbergs, Life With Luigi, I Remember Mama*. Where radio presents such details of working-class life as apartments in the Bronx, old fur- niture, or relatives and boarders living with the family, the television versions of the same programs presented houses in the suburbs inhabited by nuclear families buy- ing new furniture on the installment plan. On television, the working class was "interpreted through perspectives most relevant to a consumer middle class" (Lipsitz 1986:373)—a highly depoliticized vision.

There is a good deal of continuity between lay and academic ideas about ethnicity. Chock (1989) found recurrent moral themes in the "success stories" narrated by her Greek-American informants and the ethnic success (or failure) paradigms of Glazer and Moynihan's very influential *Beyond the Melting Pot* (see also Steinberg 1989:263–302 on "Ethnic Heroes and Racial Villains in American Social Science"). As popular discourses do, Glazer and Moynihan described ethnic groups in terms of attributes and interests. As they saw it, Italians, Jews, and Irish parlayed their interests into group success, but Negroes and Puerto Ricans lacked the right attributes. Juxtaposed with these racializing tendencies (judging a group's worth, or potential for worth, by its nature) is the ethnicized labeling system, allotting each group the same cultural space: "*The* Negroes, *The* Puerto Ricans, *The* Jews, *The* Italians, *The* Irish" (Chock 1989:166, her emphasis). Chock makes a similar point in her study of articles in the *Harvard Encyclopedia of American Ethnic Groups* (Chock 1995). Race is culturalized along the lines of the ethnic model. Class aspects of group history are elided. "Ethnic stories" dominate the discourse with their focus on the deeds of individuals and achievements of groups.

This domestic orientalism, as Ortner (1991) puts it, surfaces routinely in ethnic and immigration studies. In her study of U.S. migration processes, Chan (1990) argues that classifying migrations as "Asian" and "European" implies a fundamental difference between those who came from Europe and those who came from Asia. This sense of monolithic difference disappears when one examines the conditions at point of origin and point of arrival; Italians and Chinese have more in common along some axes of comparison than Italians and Irish. The same principle applies to uses of the term "Hispanic." There has been no one "Hispanic migration" so there can be no generic "Hispanic" immigrant (Nelson and Tienda 1985).

"Ethnic Success" and the Persistence of Racialization

Ethnicizing discourses are modeled after what is now the classic European immigrant success myth, in which all groups are assumed to start from the same point and move on to success or failure depending on each group's "value system." Research over the last couple of decades makes it abundantly clear that no one analytic model of ethnicity "explains" ethnic success (see Steinberg 1989:82–127 and Morawska 1990 for further discussion). The conditions from which people come and the social and economic capital they bring with them plays a central role in determining who becomes ethnicized and who remains racialized.

The groups most subject to racialization are those who have had minimal control over what is done with them and their labor. Slaves provide the classic case of completely coerced labor. For hundreds of years, the social identity of African-descended people was shaped by their existence as a commodity whose value depended on their role in a system of agricultural production in which they were nothing but labor. This profoundly shaped white assumptions about who and what black people were: to many whites, blacks outside slavery had no value at all (Fields 1990:115). Similarly, U.S. race perceptions of Asians were heavily shaped by the fact that a large proportion of Chinese, Japanese, Korean, Indian, and other Asian people came to the United States as contract labor. Chan (1990) notes that Asians who came from colonized places with no nation-state to protect them were most subject to labor abuse. All Asians were subject to prejudice in the form of exclusionary laws, and all were subject at some point to mob violence and murder, as many southern and eastern Europeans had also been.

The process of colonization establishes racializing conditions. The English perception of the Irish is a case in point. The English occupation of Ireland, culminating in the Penal Laws of the early 1700s, effectively prevented the Irish from owning land. The Irish were virtually nothing but tenant labor. By the late 1800s the English had come to see the Irish in fully racialized terms, using English perceptions of Africans as a model (Szwed 1975). Hechter (1975) examines the process of "internal colonialism," that is, the geographically and economically marginalized positions of the Irish and other Celtic people in the "cultural division of labor" during the course of British industrial development. He links this phenomenon to perceptions of Celtic identity, including English characterization of Irish as "white chimpanzees." In the United States, however, the Irish built an economic-political base (Miller 1990) through which they could ethnicize what had originally been a heavily racialized identity.

So long as a labor force remains cheap and highly controlled, it is likely to stay racialized. The European labor migrations originally supplied cheap, expendable labor. Lieberson (1980) offers massive evidence that the economic gap that developed between European immigrants and African Americans who moved to the north was not due to differences in "culture" or "group norms" but to shifts in hiring patterns. European migrants were in the right place in the labor market at the right time, with that advantage greatly enhanced by the race-shaped preferential hiring practices of employers. Residential, educational, and other forms of segregation soon widened the gap. Gordon, Edwards, and Reich (1982) argue that industrial practices of the late 1890s gave management increasing control over production techniques and consequent ethnic/race segregation by occupational specialization. This specialization gave later migrant groups fewer choices as to their place in the labor force. Nash (1989:67) argues that quite a few immigrant laborers themselves took part in the ethnic/race segmentation of the work force. Nationality and race were given priority over class identity. Davis (1986) describes a long-standing pattern of nativist/racist attitudes among immigrants (Irish toward blacks in the mid–1800s; Germans toward the "new immigrants" of the 1890s) superseding class identity. The more vulnerable people are to being racialized, the lower they find themselves on this scale of fragmentation. Thus, African American craft workers, who had had relative freedom of occupation before 1900, found themselves selectively structured into the labor force, generally into unskilled labor, after 1900. Employers were willing to hire friends and relatives of European immigrant workers, but African American men had to find their own jobs (Model 1990).The "divide and conquer" strategy reinforced nativism and xenophobia, particularly in unions.

Factors that made some groups less vulnerable to being racialized left other groups more vulnerable. Lieberson (1980:368) argues that legal restrictions on Asian and European immigrations may have deflected long-term racializing dynamics. Chinese and Japanese populations remained small and relatively stable. Along the same lines, Model argues that the 1924 National Origins Act effectively cut off migration from Europe. Employers lost the pool from which they had recruited the least skilled white labor for the least desirable jobs, leaving those jobs for the non-immigrant reserve labor force. It is ironic that racialized legislation may have assisted, in the long run, the fortunes of the children of those whom it excluded. Yet if, as Lieberson (1980) and Wilson (1987) argue, the size and rate of migration are key dynamics, then Puerto Ricans moving to the continental United States and African Americans moving from the South to northern cities were peculiarly vulnerable to racialization in large part because they were *not* subject to immigration laws. In these internal migrations, Puerto Rican and African American laborers experienced many of the same labor market conditions (Gordon, Edwards and Reich 1982:209). Both groups were also sharply affected by the Depression, which undercut labor market gains made by African Americans during World War I and the growing business fabric and labor market position of Puerto Ricans in New York (History Task Force 1979:146).

Originally recruited for the garment and cigar industries, Puerto Ricans were channeled into low-skilled jobs with limited access to large, unionized companies, becoming a floating reserve labor army (Bonilla and Campos 1981, 1985). As southern and eastern Europeans became heavily unionized in the 1930s, with possibilities for mobility within their companies and increasing job security (Morawska 1990), Puerto Ricans and African Americans found themselves excluded. The 1950s was a period of closure for Puerto Ricans in three crucial areas: politics, labor unions, and the church (Falcón 1984; Stevens-Arroyo 1980). These three institutions had helped white ethnics locate themselves in urban political structures. But white ethnics became key players in unions and politics at a point when these institutions were retrenching instead of expanding, and they were not interested in recruiting Puerto Rican or black members.

In the 1950s, many children of European migrants were able to move out of working-class neighborhoods or out of cities altogether and into suburbs.[9] At the time, Puerto Ricans were moving in sizable numbers to the Northeast; at just that time, major industrial firms began to move away from cities. The jobs that Puerto Ricans found in the New York area in the 1950s and 1960s were in smaller firms and in the service sector. As the economy became increasingly segmented, fewer and fewer Puerto Ricans found themselves in jobs with a future, in a position to diversify through the labor market, or able to put together enough capital to develop their own businesses. By the 1970s, Puerto Ricans and

African Americans found themselves in an unstable job market. They also found themselves residentially segregated in centers of large cities. Although similarities between Puerto Ricans and African Americans should not be overstated, their positions vis-à-vis employers, landlords, teachers, police, politicians, and so on are similar.

Ironically, after decades of being racialized, Hispanics are not officially considered a race. *Hispanic* became a census category in 1980, partly through the efforts of Hispanic activists. It replaced "Persons of Spanish Mother Tongue" (1950, 1960) and "Persons of Both Spanish Surname and Spanish Mother Tongue" (1970) (Rodríguez 1989:63). *Hispanic* is not included as a choice in the census question that asks for racial identity as "White, Black, Japanese, Chinese, Filipino, Korean, Vietnamese, American Indian, Asian Indian, Hawaiian, Guamanian, Samoan, Eskimo, Aleut, or Other—please specify." (The results of the 1990 census state "Persons of Hispanic origin may be of any race.") Rodríguez found that a plurality of New York Puerto Rican respondents to the 1980 census made it clear that as far as they were concerned, "Hispanic" did mean race: 48 percent answered "Other," specifying "Spanish," "Hispanic," "Puerto Rican," and so on, while 44 percent answered "white" and 4 percent "black" (1989:64). Puerto Ricans (and Latin Americans in general) do not equate race in simple ways with descent-based physiological classification. Race in Puerto Rico also involves individual appearance, class, and cultural elements; above all, being Puerto Rican supersedes being black or white. The opposite is true in the United States. Puerto Ricans in the United States draw on both systems depending on context and social pressure. Even when faced with the rigid U.S. racial dichotomy, Puerto Ricans tend to blend categorical elements into a more culturally nuanced reading (Rodríguez, Castro, García, and Torres 1991).

The Conflation of Race and Class

As Steinberg, Omi and Winant, and Williams argue, class is key to constructions of race and ethnicity. This point is nicely illuminated by Rodríguez's (1990) study of Puerto Rican New Yorkers who self-identified as "Other—Spanish" (or a variant thereof) in the 1980 census. A higher proportion of Puerto Ricans who self-identified as "Other—Spanish" were poorer and younger, with worse jobs and less schooling, than Puerto Ricans who self-identified as white or black. Yet those who self-identified as white appeared no more "assimilated" than those who self-identified as "Other—Spanish" according to such criteria as proficiency in and preference for English, birth in the continental United States, or the number of children they had. In other words, self-identifying as white or "Other—Spanish" was not about assimilation in a conventional sense. It was about Puerto Rican perceptions of their own class status.

A distinction must be made between, on the one hand, class as a set of positions within a society (defined in opposition to each other and generated by the distribution of wealth, means of production, and control over labor) and, on the other hand, *talk* about class as a mode of cultural identity. Class positions do not correspond neatly with the class labels that routinely emerge when Americans talk about themselves and each other as "middle class" or "lower class" or "working class" or "rich" or "poor." These labels refer to cultural constructs that saturate popular and public discourses. Americans routinely connect income (poor versus middle class), living environment (slum versus nice neighborhood) and moral character (lazy versus hard working) to imply a category of person. In official poverty discourses, class is assumed to be a stratification of income, jobs, and education, a stepladder up which people can and should progress. In such discourses, class is measured by what individuals are or have. This perspective is entrenched by the assumed neutrality of the numbers-based model that naturalizes the moral dimensions of social achievement. According to Katz (1989), quantifying class in this manner legitimates the policies of public institutions precisely because the emphasis is not on social conditions but on types of persons. Policy can then be couched in "a vocabulary of invidious distinction," (p. 5) a vocabulary that stresses the incommensurability and moral distance between poverty and middle-class life. Social problems are realized as categories of people sorted out by income, race/ethnicity, age, gender. In this way, *black* or *Hispanic* or *Puerto Rican* become metonyms for (naturally connected to) the idea of an *underclass*. In this metonymy, class/race difference becomes morally marked. Activities seen as typical of bad citizens (dropping out of school, becoming teenage mothers, taking drugs, committing crimes, going on welfare) are habitually associated with, for example, *Puerto Ricans,* and become "explanations" for their "failure." Terms that do not fit the moral picture disappear from the discourse (Sánchez Korrol 1983; Jennings 1984; Rodríguez 1989).

Language figures into this race/class conflation in several ways. Hegemonically, Spanish itself is regarded as a barrier to class mobility because it displaces English. Accents, "broken" English, and "mixing" become signs of illiteracy and laziness, which people are morally obliged to control through education. Not controlling language results in "bilingual confusion." Bilingual neighborhoods are equated with slums, an equation familiar to people who live in them. When, during my 1979 fieldwork, I referred to their block as a bilingual neighborhood, Jenny Molina asked if I meant a poor neighborhood, and Carlos Guzmán said, "You mean a slum, don't you? You think anybody who grows up in a slum is going to talk like that, right?" Language, like physical features or a person's name, is metacommunicative, contributing to an interpretive frame in which anything one says or does is assessed in terms of the category suggested, for example, "Spanish," "white," "black." One's words and actions are read as "typical of people like that" and one's worth judged accordingly.

Stereotypes are, as Lieberson (1985) points out, judgmental, and stereotypes that conflate race and class are doubly so. Such stereotypes contrast ethnicizing themes (individuals working hard to sacrifice and improve their own and their family's lives) and racializing themes (the disorder and danger of certain types of people). In Rieder's (1985) study of race relations in Canarsie (Brooklyn), Jews and Italians define what they see as a generic ghetto black: animal-like, out of control, unable to plan for the future, unpredictable, criminal. These behaviors are considered responsible for ghetto residents going on welfare to get something for nothing, and cheating honest taxpayers. The racialized ghetto residents renege on their obligation to bleed for their country, as B. Williams (1989) put it. Chiseling is a severe charge of social immorality in the United States and an effective one. The "welfare chiseler" is seen to exercise illegitimate freedoms that contravene the moral bases of class position in the United States. As Sennett and Cobb (1972) argue, people earn respect when they move into positions in which they are valued for their unique talents. Mobility leads to individual choices and control over one's own destiny.

The process can work in reverse. Working-class Puerto Ricans and African Americans also construct discourses where whiteness and money are conflated and judged in moral terms: whites may be seen as naturally cold, controlling, and greedy. One of the boys with whom I worked, Fernando (age 15), explained a version of this theme that he had heard from the Nation of Islam building manager down the street. "White people are always thinking about themselves, always got their mind on themselves, and black guys and Spanish guys always got their mind on other people." I asked what that meant to him; he said, "The white guy is always thinking how a thing is going to work out for him, that's why he has a lot of things. Maybe he thinks he could do anything, so he could."

The race/class conflation always implies a hierarchy and an imbalance of power: someone is "lower" and someone else "higher." When racialized individuals try to beat the conflation by changing others' perceptions of them, their efforts remind one of the myth of Sisyphus, eternally condemned to push the boulder up the mountain. One individual may convince a teacher or boss of his or her intelligence and good intentions but that individual remains an "exception" to the social fact lodged in too many American minds. Being "low class" and Puerto Rican or black are unmarked with respect to each other, habitually and typically associated. Like a default setting, this conflation is the normal point of reference unless it is specifically (never permanently) reset. What is so profoundly frustrating for someone African American or Puerto Rican is that whites will admit the existence of "exceptions" *in theory.* As one of Rieder's (1985) informants put it:

> I wouldn't mind if a colored family moved next door if they were upstanding and fine like me. Educated and intelligent blacks, why not? . . . But I don't want trash who will frighten me. (p. 83)

The exception usually stays theoretical, because, as another of Rieder's informants explained:

> The problem is that we see blacks as a mass. It is unfortunate. We can't tell the difference between a black pimp and a black mailman. When I look at a white man I can tell what social class he is, but if he is colored, I can't tell. (p. 85)

A third informant sharply focuses the difference between (racialized) African Americans who do not produce and (ethnicized) West Indians who do:[10]

> Face it, the Haitians and the Jamaicans and the other islanders down in Flatbush don't consider themselves black. These island people are producing people, they're up early sweeping their stoops and taking care of their homes. They're producing people like we are. But the black lower element don't contribute to society, they just take. In my view, you should get what you put into. You have to contribute. (p. 105)

Rieder's informants illustrate two key aspects of the class/race/ethnicity complex. First, race/ethnic perceptions proceed from the speaker's perspective—the speaker compares others to people "like us." Racializing draws a strong contrast between "our" race and "theirs" while ethnicizing mediates the contrast by showing an other who is not totally Other but "like us" in key ways. Second, people "like us" means people who "make the kind of *economic* contribution that we do." All producers should be able to keep rising in the social system. Non-producers should not. If producers can no longer rise despite their best efforts, they are being squeezed out by an unfair conspiracy between people in power and people who cheat the system. Producing Americans are supposed to be entitled to protection from disorder. Rieder's informants allow that there are "respectable" blacks who live predictable, orderly, nonthreatening middle-class/working-class lives. Then they say in effect, "but we don't know any and we have to protect ourselves from what we do know." As soon as order is on the line, the conflation reverts to the default setting.

At the heart of the race/class conflation lies the American notion of the "middle-class." This is not class in any analytic or oppositional sense. The "middle-class" is a generic U.S. identity, a construct that defines a normative social perspective including that of much social science (Rapp 1987). The generic middle-class American is the exemplar of mobility and personal achievement. If people are not mobile, their "lack of progress" may be attributed to personal or psychological or racial or gender traits. People fail; the class system does not (Ortner 1991). This generic middle-class American is for all practical purposes classless, able to make any kind of social contact (DeMott 1990). Class is heavily identified with lifestyle: Halle's (1984) working man on the (dirty, dangerous, boring, tightly structured, and closely supervised) job becomes middle-class as a consumer. When Americans become downwardly mobile through shifts in the economy, they are likely to blame themselves for not controlling their situation (Newman 1988).

Because the middle-class position is in theory open to everyone, it is the cultural starting point, the position that defines the ideal American. As long as one is a "producing person," one has the right to protection from disorder. The "imperial middle" (as DeMott defines the middle class) has long been the moral starting point for official and personal discourses about poverty, work ethic, family values, and so on. The degree to which the imperial middle is assumed to be white is not evident to most whites. It is very evident to African Americans and Puerto Ricans who are subject to the accusation of "acting white" when they do such class-mobile things as working for good grades in school (Fordham and Ogbu 1986) or buying a house in a "nice" neighborhood.

Racializing discourses are exclusionary and monologic in Bakhtin's sense, referring to raced people as objects instead of addressing them as interlocutors. The people so labeled have few chances to challenge the basis for such labels, especially when the racializers claim to be giving objective facts. Ethnicizing discourses, however, are inclusionary within limits. They may be spoken by or addressed to ethnicized people, for example, when political figures talk about their ethnic heritage and its contribution to America. Ethnicizing discourses are so deeply embedded in the national common sense that they are hard to avoid even when speakers want to concentrate on structural issues. In her account of House of Representatives hearings on illegal immigration, Chock (1991) shows how the president of the National Congress of Hispanic American Citizens tried to challenge legislators' racializing assumptions by talking about employers' complicity in hiring undocumented aliens. In doing so, he found himself talking about the undocumented workers in ethnicizing terms as "individuals" seeking "opportunities."

"Community" as Ethnicizing Discourse

The ways in which "community" is talked about illuminate key differences between racializing and ethnicizing discourses. As R. Williams comments in his discussion of country and city, "class realities usually show through" human relations. Human relations are perceived as community—as "neighbors first and social classes only second"—only on those rare occasions when people have "a breathing space, a fortunate distance from the immediate and visible controls" (1973:106–107). This point is lost when "community" is used in ways that suggest groups of people acting consensually because they share defining traits.

The idea that "community" means a group united by common concerns and marked by specific traits has strong appeal to American common sense. Academic references to "community" are rooted in the late nineteenth and early twentieth century European sociological ideal of the small face-to-face society. The ideal was further entrenched in academic literature by the urban-rural studies of the 1920s. Sociologists Robert Park and Louis Wirth saw the city as the locus of conflict, change, and anomie, the other end of the spectrum from the "little community" described by anthropologist Robert Redfield. Sociologists partly resolved this opposition by positing the neighborhood as a community. Neighborhoods were presented as self-contained urban groups, the locus of ethnic identity. This local focus was lost when groups assimilated. Such a model of community is basically apolitical, taking little account of specific histories or class location (Hannerz 1980). The model was meant to be technical but an underlying romanticism emerges in distinctions like Parks' "descript" and "nondescript" communities:

> The former were places of unity and charm; the latter lacked these qualities. The
> Lower North Side of Chicago . . . was clearly nondescript. It was more question-
> able whether it could really be termed a community, since the area shares little
> more than a common designation. (Hannerz 1980:44)

Studies of ethnicity outside and within the United States heavily emphasized the self-contained community and its primordial traits. This is strikingly evident in U.S. ethnicity studies that sought to explain ethnic success through culture-specific traits. Culture does not move en masse from the old country. Networks move, as do certain culture-specific areas of practice and thought. But new practices, ways of thinking, and identities immediately begin to form in response to practices, identities, conditions, and pressures of the new place (Tilly 1990). The emphasis on a community identity built of cultural traits denies the part played by economics. Ignored is the fact that very few migrant networks were in a position to have a self-supporting economic base until many decades later. Most people had to leave the neighborhood to go to work. And the "ethnic community" did not control public education, a primary agent of socialization in the United States. There were sometimes ethnic language schools (often in churches), which had symbolic importance but little effect on day-to-day life. As Steinberg argues, the idea of an "ethnic community" is about a group's moral position in a fluctuating world far more than it is about actual lives (1989:53–59).

The idea of community is strongly infused with an American notion of individualism. Varenne sees in U.S. social science a fascination with the individual that permeates theory. The individual, the locus of mobility, is "a self-motivated agent" which is "a fundamental category in American culture" (1984:281). Therefore, "most American anthropologists feel more comfortable with theories of culture that can be read individualistically" (p. 291). Relating this point to the central thesis of his study of life in a small midwestern town, Varenne states:

> I do not think that one can understand any aspect of American culture without
> understanding the logic of community building . . . [which] emphasizes the cen-
> tral, encompassing place of the individual, the person, the "people" in their aggre-
> gation, as the motor of community. (p. 294)

Academics and media talk about diversity and multiculturalism in ways that take for granted this concept of the individual. The larger society is "diverse" insofar as it is composed of a number of "different" communities, each made of individuals like each other. Communities thus differ from each other in the ethnic traits that make up their content, not in the ways that social relations are politically organized.[11] With the individual as the defining unit, the American notion of "community" presupposes the following: communities are based on consensus among like persons; communities control space; communities are based on a morality of achievement in ways that mask historical and political considerations.

"Communities" Are Based on Consensus Among Like Persons

Varenne (1986:224) argues:"Community" is relevant to persons who live together, who act together, and above all who develop a shared state of mind. These assumptions have been at the heart of the sociology of community ever since.

That is, Varenne adds, ever since John Dewey said that people form communities because they hold values in common. Consensus appears to be arrived at without explicit communication or negotiation. The community becomes some typified individual writ large: community membership is based on a typifying construct that everyone shares. The blank space in "the _____ community" may be equally filled by the terms *Italian, business, black, gay, deaf, Spanish-speaking, baseball, Jewish,* or *academic.* Each term refers to a defining quality of person, whether ethnic, religious, sexual, occupational/institutional, or physical condition. The typifying condition is also seen as a common interest, hence the term "interest group." The same idea informs the term "language community": a common language equals a common group interest. Such focus on shared traits highlights notions of replication and mystical consensus and masks the ways in which actual social exchanges are hierarchized, contested, and politically charged.

In the phrase "the _____ community" the blank cannot be filled by an overt race term. In the phrase "black community," for example, *black* is used as an ethnic, not a race term, on par with *Italian, Irish,* or *Polish.* When a community is defined by ethnicity, sexual identity, or physical condition, the term in the blank is almost always marked, since the unmarked group (white, straight, or physically unchallenged) is metonymous with (a natural part of) the whole. As Lieberson (1985) argues, *white* is metonymous with *American.*[12]

"Communities" Control Space

> In anthropology, as in ordinary life, we easily use the word *community* without thinking of the chain of cultural premises that lie behind questions linking person and locale. (Greenhouse 1986:35)

The shared-trait model of community assumes that community residents control local space. This assumption is problematic when people live in conditions that deprive them of power over space: people who own few local buildings and have minimal power as tenants are likely to live in deteriorated spaces. They are also likely to be seen as responsible for that deterioration, a racializing assumption.

People build up power over space by owning homes and businesses. In the United States, the archetype of controlled space is the neighborhood of homeowners. In the U.S. myth of ethnic progress, the working-class immigrant first rents a crowded tenement apartment, then moves to a more comfortable space as the family's income improves. Eventually, the immigrants or their children build a nest egg that makes it possible to buy a house, modest perhaps but their own space. In this parallel progression of working class to middle class (Sennett and Cobb 1972:32) and renter to homeowner (Perin 1977), permanent renters are looked upon with suspicion. By not engaging in the natural progression, Perin argues, they promote the dissolution of the social fabric (1977:40ff). Just as producing Americans assume the right to be protected from "underclass" disorder, suburban homeowners assume the right to avoid urban disorder (1977:89).

Ethnic neighborhood tourism promotes an image based on a compromise between homeowners' controlled private space and the permanent renters' disordered, uncontrolled space: the neat working-class street of rented flats and a few houses, with tiny but well-tended lawns and gardens, all proclaiming the message, "I know how to take care of a house now that I have one." Restaurants, groceries, bakeries, and import stores project a vision of domestic tranquility. They provide a carefully structured view of tastes, practices, and objects, just enough of an "inside" glimpse to say "We're pleasant and safe. Our stores and restaurants show we know how to 'better ourselves.'" Ironically, the vision of community generated by, say, ethnic control of businesses and churches may hide the fact that most of the ethnic residents have already bettered themselves and moved to the (even safer) suburbs. As LaRuffa (1988) shows in his account of an Italian-American Bronx neighborhood, Italians now make up a demographic minority of that neighborhood.

This model does not work for racialized people. In New York, Puerto Ricans and African Americans are typically seen as problem tenants. Their neighborhoods are not regarded as safe, and they do not have much capital to invest in local business. In 1982, of 227,303 Latino-owned businesses in the United States, 14,690 or 6.5 percent were Puerto Rican-owned. The average receipts per firm for Puerto Rican businesses totaled $45,200 compared to $60,700 average receipts per firm for all Latino-owned businesses. At the same time, there were 339,239 black-owned businesses, with an average receipts per firm of $36,681—an average even lower than that of Puerto Rican businesses (Survey of Minority Owned Business Enterprises, cited by the Institute for Puerto Rican Policy Inc. 1987). Puerto Rican local groups and businesses have worked hard to generate a sense of community, of "neighbors first" but their efforts are rarely noted by academic, political, or policymaking observers (Sánchez Korrol 1983).

The use of Spanish in a neighborhood's public spaces is more likely to be seen in racialized than in ethnicized terms. Residents themselves appreciate and find comfort in the familiar accents of Spanish or Spanish/English switching, but they also know that outsiders generally equate "bilingual neighborhood" with "slum." The language that creates a sense of community for its residents is unacceptable to outsiders unless its presentation is tightly framed. Local foreign-language newspapers once fulfilled this role. Janowitz (1967 [1952]) documents the way in which community presses of the 1940s and 1950s emphasized a consensus of local values and de-emphasized conflict. Supported by local business people, the presses covered the pursuit of valued, safe American-style activities in school, youth and church groups, and voluntary organizations. The coverage of voluntary organizations, activities, and festivals was instrumental in developing a sense of place. Presses helped equate shared ethnicity with shared space and shared language, and they created a safe sense of boundary. Local stories about Italians, Poles, or Irish doing

American things in church and school groups were important ethnicizing discourses in the 1940s and 1950s. The ethnic press made immigrant families look American where it counted. They also drew a sharp line between ethnicity and race. Presses were vehement about racial intrusion into local space, for example, by housing integration (Janowitz 1967 [1952]:87–88).

A vision of ethnic community can also be fostered by large corporations. *Hispanic Magazine* regularly features articles and advertisements by major U.S. firms promoting their concern for the future of the "Hispanic community." Similarly, Nash (1989) documents General Electric's institutionalization of its role in Pittsfield from 1903 to 1986. General Electric became part of the definition of Pittsfield as a community, often through its constructions of ethnic identity. The company that would not hire Italians before 1917 eventually provided Italian-American employees with boccie ball courts and grapes for wine making. The corporate embrace of ethnically defined activities turns those activities into ways to be American. "The celebration of ethnicity is a recognition of the effectiveness of the corporate hegemony in drawing the immigrants into the mainstream of American life." (Nash 1989:212)

"Community" Is Based on a Morality of Achievement

Ethnic success depends on the achievements of its members and the marketability of its goods. When ethnic goods sell successfully as authentic folk objects, performance, or food, the ethnic group becomes more visible and respectable.[13] Neighborhoods that market ethnicity to tourists, like New York's Chinatown or Little Italy, do so in ways that resonate with ethnic images disseminated by popular media and advertising. The key image is the ethnic family: "The pizza-baking mother, the warm happy family sitting long at the traditional feast, the shopkeeper flourishing his sausages" (di Leonardo 1984:233). U.S. ethnics "become a market for an already commoditized version of their culture" (Nash 1989:211). Family is essential to this ethnic imagery, especially as it is defined by women's activities. The image of the happy, unified ethnic family, argues di Leonardo, eases anxiety about belonging to a community that no longer exists locally. Ethnicity may be culturally construed as a property of locale, but most second generation Italian-Americans trace ethnicity through descent and family far more than through co-residence and daily practice (di Leonardo 1984:133ff).

Community discourses are about success and contribution, the antithesis of poverty discourses. The ethnic commoditizing that typifies a community is part of a morality of achievement. The image of hard-working co-ethnics pulling together to make it measures up to the criteria that define any good American: work ethic, patriarchal family values, education. All these values are the antithesis of the stereotyped welfare underclass mother-centered family. Since any ethnic individual who makes the right choices should be able to achieve the "American dream" of economic security and home ownership, any ethnic individual who does not cheats the group and endangers the community. A community's success is measured, like ethnic success in general, by income, education, occupation, business ownership, and so on. Stories of community history—newsletters, photos and texts on the walls of meeting halls, ethnic press news stories—are tailored to fit the model of community success. Stories of strikes, riots, decades of housing and work discrimination, and violence are underplayed unless they culminate in triumph and harmony.

The idea that an ethnic identity has moral value rests firmly on the sense of achievement that develops through such commoditization. Clear, firm signs of ethnic achievement resonate with a romanticized high-culture identity: the map of Italy and the Italian flag in the neighborhood bakery and coffee shop link the touristic consumption of Italian-American culture with an image of Italy as a national culture. Such images also help erase signs of a past of coerced labor. When ethnicity is objectified as a commodity, a performance, or items in a museum, the ethnic objects readily invoke an image of a culture as a set of traits. As Handler (1988) argues, it is authenticity that makes objects desirable. The authenticity generated by the context in which objects are displayed, performed, or used becomes a property of objects themselves. When food and clothing are sold, when dances are performed, and when art and photography are displayed, they are all imbued with some authenticity. Selling, displaying, and performing these things implies space and facilities, that is, proprietorship. But proprietorship requires resources that are minimally available to racialized people. Moreover, because authenticity must be linked to a high national culture, racialized people are at a disadvantage. They are seen as people from colonized places so they must seek their authenticity in a past before or beyond colonial status: pre-contact Indian practices, slave customs that signal the "survival" of an African past, Latin hints of African, Native American and/or Spanish high culture, the higher the better.

Ethnic objectification is central to the performance of public festivals and parades. These contexts were designed to display connections to both the United States and the nation of ethnic origin, its history and its heroes. Ethnic festivals and parades provide each ethnic group with an equivalent social space in which they can perform and display bits of culture while demonstrating their achievements and contributions to the United States. All ethnicities assume a fictive equality as each performance tells the group's story.[14] Italian, Polish, Puerto Rican, African American, Chinese, and Irish are publicly enacted on equal terms. Bodnar (1992:70ff) locates this presentation style in the multi-ethnic commemorative events of the 1920s and 1930s. Contemporary accounts are provided by Estades (1980) on the New York Puerto Rican Day Parade; Kasinitz and Freidenberg-Herbstein (1987) on the New York West Indian Carnival and Puerto Rican Day Parade; and Schneider (1990) on Philadelphia's Puerto Rican and Polaski Day Parades. As Herrell (1992) puts it, the costumes, chants, hats, flags, music

> index (point to, focus attention on) but do not define "being Irish" or "being African" in Chicago. Parades assert identity and position in Chicago. . . . A *pava* in Puerto Rico may be a hillbilly hat but in a Chicago parade, it indexes the Puerto Rican community. (p. 242)[15]

When performances of "community" are officially promoted and framed, power issues like class or discrimination are further sidestepped. The idea of community can provide minorities with a rallying cry, but it can also provide hegemonic institutions with the means to co-opt the troublesome. Varenne (1986:226) emphasizes this, pointing out that the ethos of community may be imposed on social groups whether they want it or not. Terms like "Hispanic community," "African American community," and "Puerto Rican community" are useful for those protecting the status quo. Such terms make it easier to separate safe spokespeople who stand for the group from disorderly and disturbing race noise.[16]

The Racialization of Language Difference

The ordinary bilingual speech that people engage in every day is always subject to racialization. Whenever English speakers complain about the "unfairness" of hearing Spanish spoken in public spaces or in the workplace, they racialize Spanish by treating it as matter out of place. The influence of Spanish on English is racialized whenever an accent, "bad" grammar, or "mixing" are equated with bad habits, laziness, and speech that is somehow not really language. The language that works for bilingual at home and around the neighborhood is disallowed by outsiders who take to themselves the power to judge language difference in moral terms. Nearly every Spanish-speaking bilingual I know, academic colleagues and my own students as well as the people in this study, has experienced complaints about using Spanish in a public place. The English of African American neighbors (from whom many Puerto Ricans learn their own English) is similarly racialized, as is Puerto Rican Spanish when it is typified as a degenerate patois of Indian and African influences (Flores, Attinasi and Pedraza 1981; Zentella 1981a). Although such judgments appear to be about a language or a dialect, they are really about institutional legitimacy. It is no accident that the Spanish and English of Puerto Ricans and the English of African Americans are often said to be bastardized. Language varieties that evolve in colonized circumstances are unprotected from judgment unless and until they are approved by, for example, an elite language academy representing a nation-state.

Languages other than English become ethnically safe when used in carefully scripted contexts: print and electronic media, emblematic language in festivals and parades, waiters with accents in ethnic restaurants. In these contexts, the language is part of a commodity familiar and comfortable to most Americans. Americans may not understand the language but they understand its pragmatics, how it is used. Monolingual Americans generally do not understand the pragmatics of Spanish in ordinary speech. More accurately, what they do not "get" when they hear Spanish on the street or in the workplace is the metacommunication, the message about the message. Any kind of communication could be taking place—gossip, jokes, snide remarks about the nervous American, maybe the overthrow of the government. Such ambiguity in an unlegitimated language is a lightning rod for racialized judgment. Language difference is rendered unthreatening when the frame in which it is used is familiar and obvious. The content may not be known but if the speech event structure is safe and familiar, the language itself is not much of a threat. Safe genres include artistic performances, news reports, service encounters. Safe participant roles include writer-reader, broadcaster-listener, performer-audience, waiter-customer. If a foreign language is used in print or broadcasting, it is assumed to be grammatically correct. If it is performed in a parade or festival, a folkloric dialect is acceptable. An accented waiter or a clerk in an import/export store can enhance the authenticity of the experience, and a small degree of non-standard grammar, even of mixing, enhances the image of the hard-working ethnic. No welfare chiseler here.[17]

Language in public education is a different proposition. In addition to their pedagogical goals, bilingual education programs seek to legitimate minority languages by presenting them in standardized packages—grammars and dictionaries, the products of print capitalism outlined by Anderson (1983). But U.S. public education is supposed to be the source of the English that should provide all immigrants with equal access to class mobility, a tenet central to the U.S. nation-state ideology. So proponents of bilingual education are cast as separatist or as special interest groups. Moreover, arguments for bilingual education have been phrased as arguments for the needs of a special group, that is, as part of a discourse of needs (Flores and Yudice 1990:63). A discourse of needs may make people's political presence felt but in many American eyes it enhances a vision of special interest groups bleeding the nation for their own ends. In this racialized vision, people only have the right to hold onto their language when it does not impede the progress of individuals and the needs of the state, precisely the criticism leveled against bilingual education by voices speaking for the nation-state (see Hayakawa 1992 [1985]; Huddleston 1992[1983], both writing as U.S. senators).

English in the United States was not always seen in quite such ideologically monolithic terms (Marshall 1986; Heath 1992 [1976]). The linguistic philosophy of the architects of the founding institutions was to leave local languages alone so as not to encourage a destabilizing separatism by giving people a political cause around which to rally. In fact, several founding fathers were unhappy with the idea of language pluralism but treated it as the lesser of two evils. Considerably more leeway was allowed to language as a pragmatic instrument and a matter of individual choice. Eventually, however, the same nativism of the 1920s that gave rise to immigration quotas by national origin and the racist scaling of IQ scores also led to the first Official English bill, introduced to Congress in 1923 (Baron 1992 [1987]).

Sixteen English Language Amendments (ELAs) were proposed (though none ratified) between 1981 and 1990. Some were English-Only mandates, banning any law requiring publicly funded uses of languages other than English except in emergency situations or in foreign-language classrooms (Crawford 1992:112). This means no bilingual education, no bilingual ballot, no bilingual drivers' licenses. The rationale was at the same time political and utilitarian. Former Senator Hayakawa (R-California) said in his ELA proposal, "learning English is the major task of each immigrant" to "participate in democracy." He added that bilingual education and bilingual ballots are "dishonest" and "send confusing signals" that English is unnecessary (cited in Marshall 1986:23). The ELAs and the English Only movement of the 1980s stressed the idea that an official English facilitated equality by providing a common communicative vehicle, as if the code itself automatically overrode all political history. As the distinction between "good" and "bad" aliens was increasingly sharply drawn, the Official English rationale was strengthened by the utilitarian morality of English in the "good alien" success story (Tarver 1989:239).

This view of linguistic equality intensifies what Zentella (1988) described as the zero-sum ideology informing the Official English movement: one language's gain is the other's loss. The public use of languages other than English is seen to impinge on the public authority of English, and the idea that U.S. law actually allows such trespassing is an idea that many Americans, including many ethnic Americans, find unsupportable. Ironically, justifications offered for bilingual education are not all that unhegemonic. Utility is stressed: bilingualism is a cognitive tool to open cultural doors, which, as a participant in a panel on bilingual education put it, makes "bilingualism and bicultural education . . . as American as apple pie" (Ridge 1980:142).

Supporters of ELA and proponents of bilingual education equally take for granted that language consists of a set of sounds, rules, and words, that these come in bounded packages ("Spanish" and "English") and that these packages automatically represent a culture (ethnic or national). This is a definingly middle-class perspective. Working-class bilinguals do not often have a chance to voice their perspective, but when they do the difference is instructive: they are more likely to see what is pragmatically innovative in speech and part of one's cultural identity and less likely to equate language and culture in monolithic terms. According to a survey by the Center for Puerto Rican Studies' Language Policy Task Force (Attinasi 1983:59–60), teachers in East Harlem were nearly four times as likely as parents to equate speaking Spanish with being Puerto Rican. Teachers saw parents and the home as the proper venue for learning Spanish, whereas parents preferred a cooperative effort by the whole local social fabric. Teachers were not particularly offended by code-switching (a finding that somewhat surprised the Task Force) but most teachers saw nothing linguistically novel about it, arguing that switching used the same Spanish and English as monolingual speech. Parents saw switching as culturally innovative. In other words, parents assessed language as part of their lived experience while teachers assessed language as it is codified in dictionaries and grammars.[18]

The philosophy underlying U.S. linguistic racialization is that the natural language of the United States is an English as naturally unmarked as the white, middle-class heart of the nation-state itself. As Silverstein (1987) argues, Americans perceive English as the language of rational and unbiased perception, the logical choice for progress. Impurities interfere with progress, so everyone should want to rid their English of impurity in accent, word, or grammar. Speaking a second language is legitimate only when it leaves no trace in one's English. One must strive to erase one's personal and structural history, becoming the ultimate ahistorical bilingual. This ideology is not limited to folk-theory. Weinreich (1953) proposed the "ideal bilingual" as the type from which all real-world cases deviate through "interference" of one language on the other, a theoretical stance that has had great influence on subsequent research agendas in bilingual studies.

In the United States, such purity and parity is supposedly available to anyone willing to work for it through education, enhancing occupation, and building income. The big three American class markers, education, occupation and income, are natural, accessible objects—much like standard English:

> The naturalization of Standard at present is such, that its possession becomes a measure of (good old American) freedom, freedom to achieve professionally, personally and, as expressed by a number of speech consultants, psychologically. Freeing people from unwanted and unsightly ("unsoundly"?) accents, bad expressions, etc. frees their true inner selves, as it were. Be all that you can be; join the army of Standard bearers! It's *both* natural *and* patriotic. Standard is our manifest destiny! (Silverstein 1987:12)

Conclusion

Given the pain of racialization, why is it not possible to accept ethnicization as a simple pragmatic solution, a useful strategy? The reason why not is that ethnicization does not negate racialization but perpetuates it. Ethnicizing and racializing are both about markedness in ways that reaffirm the terms that define the unmarked American. Marked Americans either succeed as good ethnics or fail as members of a raced underclass. In either case, the goal, never quite achievable, is to be unmarked. But unmarked Americans have the option of neither succeeding nor failing. The unmarked American can be an average Joe from a small town in the Midwest. Marked Americans cannot.

Language difference in the United States is deeply racializing. When people use languages other than English in public and in ways that are not tightly scripted or framed by an unequivocally middle-class presentation, they are seen as dangerously out of order. This point is the one that most studies of bilingualism tend to miss, and this is where the political economy of language begins: with the matrix of conditions that shape racialized perceptions of language difference. Linguistic racialization is deeply internalized by its agents—the teachers who say things like "those poor kids come to school speaking a hodge podge" (Walsh 1991:106)—and by its objects—the students who disclaim "but I just speak English, I don't know no Spanish" except when speaking to family (p. 101). Racialization emerges in the moral contrast between the Spanish-dominant Puerto Rican student who looks at a Latin face in a picture and sees someone "Puerto Rican just like me" or who "speaks Spanish and . . . is respectful" (p. 86) and the mainstreamed Puerto Rican student who looks at the same picture and sees someone who "looks like he's in a gang or something" or who "could talk English but mostly he talks Spanish. And he does bad things sometimes" (p. 85). The rest of this book is about how such a state of affairs came to pass that children could think about themselves in such terms, and what people who grew up with that experience have to say about it.

Notes

1. I draw heavily from Weber's ideas of race and ethnicity as related phenomenon of social action, social constructions of descent and physical being with a political and economic basis (1978:389) and from Barth's emphasis on the canalizing nature of the ethnic *boundary* (1969:15).

2. Steinberg (1989:5–43) also distinguishes between racialized minorities and ethnic groups, based on historical and economic relations, and the legal institutionalization and hierarchization of difference. Similarly, Omi and Winant (1986) see *racialization* in the United States as "a *fundamental* axis of social organization in the United States" (p. 13), the ongoing and historically specific construction of oppositional categories rooted in institutionalized appropriation and exclusion. The idea of ethnicity, however, is rooted in the specific migrations and subsequent social and economic experiences of Europeans. The experience of the latter cannot serve as a model for the former.

Wolf (1982:380) similarly locates the distinction between race and ethnic in the history of global capitalist enterprises and the ways in which racial and ethnic distinctions "serve to allocate different categories of workers to rungs on the scale of labor markets, relegating the stigmatized populations to the lower levels and insulating the higher." While the capitalist system did not invent ethnic and race distinctions, it imparted to those distinctions their current value.

The fact that the origins of racialization are firmly anchored in global economic processes does not mean that race is reducible to class in an analytic sense (although class and race as American cultural categories are routinely conflated). Racial categories do not disappear when class positions are equal; rather they determine perceptions of racial others as classed (as, for example, when a black doctor is seen as automatically "lower" in status). Racial oppositions serve as focal points for ideas about belonging to the nation. Fields (1990), Shklar (1991), and Stanfield (1985) see such ideas embedded in the founding fabric of U.S. society.

3. *Discourse*, after Foucault (1972), refers to the ongoing, historically situated uses of language in ways that formulate a field of knowledge in a given time and place, though with an authority that seems to transcend time and place.

4. My use of racializing substantially derives from Stanfield's (1985) discussion of race-making, which emphasizes the ongoing socio-political dimension of race in the process of nation-building.

5. Williams sees race and ethnicity contrast as markers in the game of nation-building. "The ideological relations among the terms nationality, minority, ethnic group, and race imply more than label switches; they are reassessments of the political implications of identity construction for the goals of the homogenizing process" (1991:268). Ethnic groups compete with other ethnic groups to position themselves as worthy contributors to the nation-state, a competition framed by the "state-backed race/class conflation that becomes the ideologically defined 'real producers' of the nation's patrimony" (1989:434). Williams's

1991 study of Guyana develops the principle of race/ethnic competition in ways pertinent to the U.S. situation. The expression of ethnic heterogeneity is sharply circumscribed by the homogenizing politics of the nation-state. For ethnic markers to signify both belonging and safe difference, all groups must enact them in the same semiotic frame. In the United States this includes the "natural" progression of class mobility and the discourses of community.

6. This is much the same as *doxa* in Bourdieu (1977a).

7. Lyons (1977) provides a useful general discussion of markedness.

8. As Bernardo Vega, who moved to New York from Puerto Rico in 1916, recounts, Puerto Ricans were largely shut out of citizenship-as-progress discourses (Iglesias 1984:27): before 1917, they had no clear citizenship in any polity; after 1917 they were U.S. citizens. Before 1917 they had no point from which and after 1917 no point toward which to progress.

9. These moves were facilitated by the provisions of the 1946 G.I. Bill. Moreover, "ethnic success" operates far less homogeneously within groups than is often supposed. Class differentials among ethnics account for some "successes"; "failures" become invisible in the reflected glow (Steinberg 1989 [1981]:77–166; 261–302).

10. See also Foner (1987:206).

11. Chock (1994) and Varenne (1977:206–207) both raise this point. Moreover, as di Leonardo (1984:133) notes, both popular and academic discourses about community are based on assumptions that are ideologically slippery, serving different ends at different times.

12. Herrell (1994) describes how the metonymy of the straight American as model U.S. citizen is being challenged by gay, lesbian, and bisexual veterans' groups.

13. See Appadurai (1986) for supporting discussion of commoditization.

14. These ethnic performances package differences so as to allow each ethnic community to be "imagined" in the same way, much as the grammar-vocabulary-folklore texts of nineteenth-century Europe packaged different languages so as to allow each nationalism to be imagined as communities in equivalent ways (Anderson 1983).

15. Herrell (1992) develops this point in a comparative discussion of ethnic parades and Chicago's Gay and Lesbian Pride Day Parade in which he finds the same format for the construction of identity. In both cases, the *idea* of community is indexed in ways that reify a sense of locale. But locale is not prior.

16. Herbstein (1983) argues that discourses about Puerto Rican ethnicity are largely framed in an ideology of nationalism, emerging in political discourses fostered in the 1960s by people running local anti-poverty programs. Discourses of social needs made Puerto Ricans visible as a politically active urban group, but those speaking the discourse did not look or operate like the classic American ethnic community—they talked about being Puerto Rican in terms of political resistance; they did not commoditize Puerto Rican ethnicity. Herbstein calls the idea of Puerto Rican community "largely an artificial creation of the wider society" (p. 48).

17. Thanks to Carol Greenhouse for this suggestion.

18. Attinasi (1983:61–63) also points out similarly monolithic linguistic assumptions among the Puerto Rican elites interviewed for *Bilingualism in the Barrio* (Fishman et al. 1971). Attinasi and the Language Policy Task Force argue that the tendency to take bilingual teachers and elites as "cultural experts," ignoring the views of the working class, reinforces the classism ingrained in the educational institutions that reproduce a society. Along similar lines, Walsh (1991:114ff) describes her own attempts to treat students as experts on their own language experience in the face of the school's silencing judgments and practices.

Chapter 2

Visions of Disorder:

How Puerto Ricans Became Racialized

The ways in which Puerto Ricans have been racialized are embedded in U.S. action toward Puerto Ricans both in Puerto Rico and in the continental United States. There are no simple cause-and-effect sequences but there are persistent dynamics. U.S. perceptions of Puerto Ricans as formless and dangerous emerge from decades of cumulative discourse among policy makers, media, and academicians.

The United States sought to make Puerto Rico profitable by turning Puerto Ricans into a reserve labor supply. At the same time, the United States sought to turn Puerto Rico into a model bilingual democracy, where Puerto Ricans would stay in school and became fluent in English. In short, U.S. policies toward Puerto Rico were simultaneously racializing (seeing Puerto Rico as a disordered mass) and potentially ethnicizing (seeing Puerto Ricans as ordered citizens after the U.S. model). Ethnicized Puerto Ricans have generally learned English in private or parochial schools and lived middle-class lives in Puerto Rico. Racialized Puerto Ricans have generally learned English while making up the labor reserve recruited into service and secondary sector jobs in the northeastern United States. Simply to classify their neighborhoods as "bilingual speech communities" is to ignore the way class figures into the development of two different bilingualisms.

The United States in Puerto Rico

Restructuring Puerto Rico

To the inhabitants of Puerto Rico: In the prosecution of the war against the Kingdom of Spain by the people of the United States, in the cause of liberty, justice and humanity, its military forces have come to occupy the island of Porto Rico. . . . [We] come bearing the banner of freedom, inspired by a noble purpose. . . .

41

[We have] come to bring protection, not only to yourselves but to your property, to promote your prosperity, and to bestow upon you the immunities and blessings of the liberal institutions of our government. . . . (statement by General Nelson Miles, U.S. military governor, July 1898. Quoted in Osuna 1949:259 and Carr 1984:31)

From the day General Miles issued his proclamation, U.S. investors and policy makers redefined and reorganized Puerto Rico with two principle goals in mind: to make it profitable for U.S. business interests and to remake educational, political, and other internal structures in the image of a mini-democracy, albeit one in which the capacity for independent political action was strictly contained. Labor, education, language, and health policies were instituted to fix what was "wrong" with Puerto Rico, to take control of human matter out of place and relocate, contain, and reshape it. Puerto Ricans had always been subject to the U.S. racialized vision of Latin America. Once Puerto Rico itself became a colony, a kind of double vision set in, whereby Puerto Rico was seen as a potential model colony. Whereas labor and medical policies were meant to relocate and contain (encouraging migration to reduce "overpopulation" or sterilizing over a third of Puerto Rican women), education and language policies were meant to reshape. If Puerto Rico's impoverished, ignorant, tradition-bound *jíbaros* (peasants) could be transformed through education, English literacy, and class mobility, Puerto Rico could become a "showcase of democracy" in the Caribbean.

The United States was not the first colonizer to restructure a local economy or to impose its own language and institutions on the colonized. What is strikingly American is the combination of moral and utilitarian rationales that justified education and health policies and that served to mask or legitimate economic intervention and political ambiguity. Throughout this century, the predominant object of Puerto Rican public policy, reinforced by social science research, has been to figure out what is wrong with Puerto Rico and Puerto Ricans and what needs to be done to bring them up to American expectations. U.S. attention remained so focused on what was "wrong" with Puerto Rico that administrators and policy makers rarely acknowledged what actually existed, or how much economic damage had been done by incorporating Puerto Rico into the U.S. political economy after centuries of neglect by the Spanish. Education and language policies became an integral part of that political economy and eventually came to stand for it.

Spain's original interest in Puerto Rico lay in its mines. Once those were exhausted, Puerto Rico remained a largely subsistence economy. Its agricultural products were exported to the nations from which it imported consumer and manufactured goods, particularly the United States. Spain participated little in this trade, primarily imposing tariffs that brought money to Spain but did little for Puerto Rico's economic growth. Indeed, Spain did very little to encourage production in Puerto Rico; the sugar economy and its attendant business associations did not develop extensively until the 1870s. The pattern of labor fragmentation, of surplus in some parts of the labor market and shortage in others, had begun to develop by the mid-nineteenth century, as coffee production drew day laborers away from cane-growing areas. By the 1870s Puerto Rican laborers were emigrating to Santo Domingo, Cuba, Venezuela, Guatemala, and New York, despite the Spanish government's attempts to dissuade them. In short, Spanish economic policies (or lack thereof) had already helped facilitate U.S. intervention in the Puerto Rican economy (History Task Force 1979:69–86).

U.S. involvement with Puerto Rico falls into a larger context of U.S. relations with Spain's former colonies, beginning with the 1848 acquisition of Texas, California, and the New Mexico territory. By the late 1800s, the United States had sizeable plantation investments in Cuba and Central America. By the late 1890s, war between the United States and Spain was aggressively encouraged by the Hearst newspapers, many members of Congress, and, of course, investors with extensive interests in Cuba. Pro-war interests presented their position as support for Cuban independence, but their objectives were to forestall an actual war of independence and to replace Spanish control with U.S. control (Dietz 1986:79ff). The Spanish-American War was precipitated, pursued, and concluded between April and August 1898. When it ended, Cuba was nominally independent but actually under U.S. tutelage by the terms of the Platte Amendment. The United States had also acquired Puerto Rico and the Phillipines. Once acquired, Puerto Rico was clearly an economic and military asset.

U.S. investment in Puerto Rico's sugar economy began almost at once. The Foraker Act, which succeeded the initial military rule of 1898–1900, created a governing structure of maximum benefit to U.S. investors. Under its terms, Puerto Rico was governed directly by Congress, which had complete control over Puerto Rican trade and tariffs (Dietz 1986:89ff; Bonilla and Campos 1981). A 1930 Brookings Institute report rationalized the view of most U.S. authorities and investigators that the Foraker Act was meant to compensate Puerto Rican political shortcomings:

> The Foraker Act was designed to assure the people of Puerto Rico full opportunity to express their will in all public matters through regularly elected representatives but to prevent their political inexperience from provoking crises or engaging them in unwise public projects. (cited in Dietz 1986:92)

The Foraker Act was succeeded in 1917 by the Jones Act, which assigned U.S. citizenship to Puerto Ricans and created a legislative structure tightly controlled by the congressionally appointed governor. The Jones Act left intact the trade and tariff provisions of the Foraker Act.

At first, Puerto Rican sugar producers welcomed U.S. investment, which seemed to promise increased access to U.S. markets. They soon found their interests undercut as U.S. investors bought out the smaller *haciendas* and restructured the older system into fewer and larger *centrales*. Coffee had been an important small farm crop in the nineteenth century, but the United States dropped the coffee tariff, and coffee production waned. The production of tobacco, another important small farm crop, was continued through the 1920s. The tobacco tariff was retained, but as cigarette displaced cigar production (which predominated in Puerto Rico), tobacco farming also waned. Subsistence farmers found themselves pressured to sell out. People who had supported themselves and their families through small farms joined the wage-labor market that grew throughout the 1920s and 1930s, seeking work in the coastal areas in sugar production and in tobacco factories.

The population centers began to shift accordingly, especially toward the San Juan area (History Task Force 1979). By the 1930s, U.S. investment in the sugar industry had effectively incorporated Puerto Rico into the U.S. economy. The production process was controlled by U.S. money and management. Even the cane itself was sent raw to the United States for processing and marketed there. Puerto Rico contributed only the labor to farm the cane (Dietz 1986:104ff). Puerto Ricans found themselves in an increasingly desperate situation over which they had minimal control.

The integration of the Puerto Rican economy into U.S. production processes also led to the integration of the Puerto Rican labor market into the U.S. class system and, in turn, to the formation of Puerto Rican neighborhoods in U.S. cities, especially in New York. Although pre-World War II migration from Puerto Rico to the continental United States was relatively limited, the dynamics that shaped the extensive migrations of the late 1940s and early 1950s were in place by 1940. From the beginning, the Puerto Rican work force provided U.S. investors with a convenient mobile labor source: in 1900–1901, U.S. sugar companies in Hawaii contracted and imported Puerto Rican workers; Puerto Rican laborers were also contracted for U.S. work camps to fill the World War I labor shortage. These experiments failed: many laborers died enroute; many contractors complained about the laborers who did survive the journey. By 1940, the economic restructuring had resulted in sizeable internal labor migrations away from what had been inland coffee-producing areas toward coastal sugar cane and urban tobacco production. As fewer non-sugar jobs became available and as there were too many men for the jobs available in sugar production (especially during the Depression), increasing numbers of men found themselves outside the work force altogether. At the same time, women supplied the labor for the Puerto Rican needlework industry and, to an increasing extent, for tobacco manufacturing (History Task Force 1979:93–112).

A People out of Control

The vision Americans developed of Puerto Ricans was anything but that of an ordered community. Sánchez Korrol (1983:18–19) argues that almost as soon as Puerto Rico became a U.S. territory, U.S. policy makers talked about its "overpopulation." In doing so, they focused on Puerto Rico as an undifferentiated and uncontrolled mass, which further essentialized their notions of an assumed Puerto Rican character. Overpopulation was seen as a grave obstacle to Puerto Rican industrial development, and migration was proposed as a solution as early as 1901. Images of excess population regularly informed government policy planning and surfaced in addresses and memoranda by the governor and the Secretary of War. By the 1930s, overpopulation had become an axiom of social science research by

Lawrence Chenault and Oscar Handlin, whose work, Sánchez Korrol (1983:17) argues,

> Maintained that the island was plagued by an excess population, partly resulting from health and medical improvements made under United States policies, whose basic needs could not be met by the island's limited resources.

Biological control was also encouraged. Citing Vásquez-Calzada's (1978) discovery that 35.5 percent of the women between the ages of 15 and 45 in Puerto Rico had been sterilized by 1968, López (1987) argues that such practices are part of a U.S. ideology of population control. Doctors treating women in Puerto Rico and Puerto Rican women in New York found sterilization an efficient way to deal with patients they considered too ignorant to practice effective birth control.[1]

Two economic solutions to overpopulation were developed in the 1940s: industrialization and labor migration. The industrialization program, Operation Bootstrap, was originally intended to encourage Puerto Rican investment in local industry and to create jobs. But there was little local investment capital available. In 1947 the Industrial Incentives Act was passed, granting a ten-year exemption from local taxes. The Fomento program, which oversaw the building of factories in Puerto Rico, attracted heavy U.S. investment. Fomento offered investors exemption from U.S. income tax and guaranteed that wages could be kept low—both powerful inducements. But as had been the case with sugar investment, U.S. corporate capital was generally limited to "enclave firms" with few local economic links. Puerto Rico was treated as one step in a production process that took place primarily on the mainland (Dietz 1986:249ff). By the 1970s, Puerto Rican wages began to approach parity with those in the continental United States, at which point many Fomento companies found more profitable sites in Mexico, Brazil, Taiwan, Korea, and Hong Kong (Bonilla and Campos 1981:137). By the mid-1980s, the Puerto Rican economy had shifted largely from industrial to service jobs with the government as the major employer (Bonilla and Campos 1985).

After World War II, labor migration was encouraged by the Puerto Rican government. U.S. firms recruited Puerto Rican labor for unskilled manufacturing, service, and agricultural work, both within and outside the Northeast (Maldonado 1979). Migration to northeastern cities expanded as people moved to join family and friends. Immigrants often found themselves employed below their skill level. A small proportion of this work force had moved into white-collar (clerical and sales) jobs by 1960, at which point the Puerto Rican unemployment level in the continental United States approximated that in Puerto Rico. But the vast majority found themselves channeled toward industry or service-sector work. As the U.S. and Puerto Rican economies converged, migration patterns eventually added up to "the massive displacement of members of a single class" (History Task Force 1979:145). People did not decide to leave Puerto Rico because an array of options beckoned them to New York. Rather, they were recruited for or channeled toward specific jobs in specific industries at specific levels, and these defined the class of worker and the class structure of the migration process.

Throughout this time, Puerto Rico's political status remained ambiguous. Under Spanish rule, the Spanish Antilles, including Cuba and Puerto Rico, had no representation and had begun agitating for autonomy. By 1897 it became increasingly obvious that the United States was likely to intervene on behalf of Cuban separatists, and Spain ceded autonomy to the Spanish Antilles in an attempt to defuse the separatist movement and retain control of Cuba. The charter of autonomy had been in effect for four months before Spain ceded Puerto Rico to the United States in the Treaty of Paris in 1898 (Carr 1984:19–20). The rhetoric of speeches like that which opened this chapter led many Puerto Ricans to expect they would have a similar autonomy. But autonomy was not seen as an option by President McKinley, nor by Elihu Root, who, as Secretary of War, was responsible for new possessions. Under the Foraker Act, Puerto Rico was an "unincorporated territory" ruled directly by Congress (Carr 1984:35–36), neither foreign country nor part of the United States.

The ambiguity was compounded when the 1917 Jones Act gave Puerto Rico a legislature over which the U.S.-appointed governor had veto power, an administration largely chosen by the President, and a form of U.S. citizenship that permitted Puerto Ricans no vote in federal elections and no voting representation in Congress but made Puerto Ricans eligible for military draft. During the next three decades, it became clear that Congress would favor neither statehood nor independence. The Commonwealth status adopted in 1952 under Luis Muñoz Marin, the first elected governor, gave a name to Puerto Rico's political status but still left unresolved the nature of its political representation. Carl Friedrich, one of the original architects of commonwealth status, later criticized the fact that it gave Puerto Ricans no voice in the passage of federal laws that shaped every aspect of their lives (Carr 1984:82).

The Colonial Double Vision

Being Puerto Rican is structured by ambiguities. Puerto Ricans can only take part in U.S. elections by leaving Puerto Rico and voting as residents of a state, in which case they are not voting on Puerto Rican issues. An 1927 editorial from the New York Puerto Rican newspaper *Gráfico* commented that having U.S. citizenship deprived Puerto Ricans of the protection of a consulate (Sánchez Korrol 1983:73). As citizens, they are free to migrate but hiring practices have effectively locked them into a limited segment of the labor market. Whether they stay in Puerto Rico or migrate makes little difference to their class situation. They are routinely regarded as an excess population requiring policies of control, both economic and medical.

Social science research, like economic and political policy, started from assumptions about order and disorder, examining Puerto Rican progress away from tradition through education and social mobility. Steward and his associates (1956) examined the multilinear evolution of labor patterns in various Puerto Rican subcultures. Tumin and Feldman (1961) measured Puerto Rican social mobility through education as movement from tradition to modernity, concluding that order would be achieved through the reform and modernization of Puerto Rico as a whole. In these works, the authors saw some potential for order in Puerto Rico. Lewis's *La Vida* (1966), which massively influenced popular perceptions of Puerto Ricans, focused on disorder. He presented his portrait of the Puerto Rican family in New York and San Juan as a classic case of the culture of poverty that exhibited the same social pathology that typifies underclass literature of the 1970s–1980s.

U.S. economic and political policy and social science research is saturated with assumptions about what Trouillot (1991) describes as the "savage slot." From the sixteenth century onward, Europeans typified the savages of the new lands as the "absence and negation" of the order into which their own lives were inscribed. Trouillot argues that anthropology as a discipline inherited this slot; I would say that it generally informs academic research and social policy grounded in colonial relations. The savage/order dichotomy certainly informed U.S. perception of Puerto Ricans and shaped resultant social, economic, political, and educational policies. If the "savages" followed the rules laid out by these policies, they could, in theory, achieve U.S. style democracy. Because Puerto Rico came to the United States as a self-contained unit, it might, if properly guided, become nation-like. Puerto Ricans who stepped outside that order-making process remained savage, especially as a mass of Spanish-speaking immigrants in U.S. cities. Spanish was seen as a powerful linguistic undertow in the "traditional culture" of Puerto Rico.

English Language Policy in Puerto Rico

English was brought to Puerto Rico as a pedagogically, politically and ideologically liberating medium.[2] As Martin Brumbaugh, the first U.S. Commissioner of Education, put it:

> The spirit of American institutions and the ideals of the American people, strange as they do seem to some in Porto Rico, must be the only spirit and the only ideals incorporated in the school system of Porto Rico. (Carr 1984:282)

The first Puerto Rican school laws were adapted from existing Massachusetts school laws (Osuna 1949:138). English was assigned as a special subject in grades 1 through 8 and the medium of instruction for grades 9 through 12, to prevent younger children's Spanish from "degenerating" from over-exposure to English. The immediate concern was with elementary education: 77.3 percent of the population was illiterate and 92 percent of children age 5 to 17 did not attend school (Osuna 1949:341–343). The policy of shifting public education to English was meant to prevent the elites from monopolizing English and to defuse the prestige of the elites' Castillian Spanish over everyone else's "patois," as it was called (Epstein 1970:56). English was to be the vehicle of this social realignment, "the chief source, practically the only source, of democratic ideas in Puerto Rico" (Osuna 1949:363). U.S. educators thought that Spanish lacked a vocabulary of democracy and that distributing

English through the public school would place it in the public, universally accessible domain.

At first, Puerto Ricans were enthusiastic about the teaching of English, but enthusiasm began to die when in 1903 the U.S. Commissioner of Education decided children had insufficient English practice and instituted English as the language of instruction at all grade levels (Osuna 1949:343). By 1905 all subjects except Spanish and all grades were taught in English with mainland texts. This policy soon drew reaction from Puerto Rican teachers and administrators who sought legislative relief from the resultant pedagogical mess, requesting passage of a bill to eliminate the English-only policy in the lower grades. A *New York World* editorial of March 15, 1907, took these protesters to task, pointing out that the governor would not let the Puerto Rican legislature pass so ill-considered a bill and that Puerto Ricans were impractical and unrealistic by seeking to "close the door" on opportunities for their children.

The idea that English was democratic and practical meant that Puerto Ricans who argued with U.S. policy found themselves having to defend their right to protest and assert political loyalty to the United States. On the eve of the legislative vote to reinstate Spanish as the language of instruction, Luis Muñoz Rivera (leading pre-1898 autonomist, journalist, politician, and father of Luis Muñoz Marín, Puerto Rico's first elected governor) wrote an editorial for the newspaper *La Democracia* (March 2, 1915, p. 1) describing the law's intent as *"para el mejoramiento de la instrucción publica en el lenguaje castellano, y la perfecta enseñanza del inglés en Puerto Rico"* (for the improvement of public education in the Spanish language, and the perfect teaching of English in Puerto Rico). An editorial on March 3, 1915, defended José de Diego, who introduced the bill, against charges of anti-Americanism, saying that de Diego advocated immediate self-government and ultimate independence in accordance with the principles of U.S. democracy and that de Diego was not attacking the teaching *of* English but teaching *in* English. (The law was passed by a vote of 20–12.) A March 16, 1915, editorial pointed out that New Mexico, which had just become a state, also had thousands of children who only spoke Spanish. Yet several U.S. educators, including the State Commissioner of Education, argued that their education should be in their home language. A prominent member of the Bureau of Education in Washington even argued that the language itself was not the point of education; the point was to help children become better citizens. Why did the same principle not apply to Puerto Rico?

The carefully worded appeals of Muñoz Rivera and his colleagues faced an opposition convinced that its linguistic makeover policy was not only practical but morally correct. The overwhelming evidence found by both U.S. and Puerto Rican educators that the language policy was unrealistic and unproductive counted for little. Finally, Herbert Hoover appointed the first Puerto Rican Commissioner of Education, José Padín, who established Spanish as the language of instruction for grades 1 through 8, with English as a special subject. This policy lasted for seven years. In 1937, the chair of the Senate Committee on Insular

Affairs, investigating the Ponce Massacre (in which police fire killed 20 Nationalist marchers and injured 200), associated the general climate of political unrest with a lack of knowledge of English. Padín was forced to resign and a new all-English policy was re-instituted (Zentella 1981a:220–221). When José Gallardo took office as Commissioner of Education in 1937, Franklin Roosevelt informed him of his mission in no uncertain terms:

> What is necessary . . . is that the American citizens of Puerto Rico should profit from their unique geographical situation and the unique historical circumstance which brought to them the blessings of American citizenship by becoming bilingual. (cited in Osuna 1949:377)
>
> It is an indispensable part of American policy that the coming generation of American citizens in Puerto Rico grow up with a complete facility in the English tongue (to understand) American ideals and principles. (cited in Carr 1984:284)

But Gallardo reinstated Spanish, a move which forced *his* resignation. Finally in 1948, Mariano Villaronga (the first Puerto Rican Commissioner of Education under Muñoz Marín) instituted Spanish as the language of instruction in grades 1 through 12, in defiance of President Truman's order. This policy became law in 1952. Since 1949, all grades have been taught in Puerto Rico with English as a Second Language required from primary grades through senior high school.

Education and English in Puerto Rico and the United States: Parallels

These policies have not created a democratizing education. The Puerto Rican school system is distinctly two-tiered. Public school students are born mostly to the working class, and a large proportion are born into migration cycles. Private school students come from the professional and managerial class, which is under little pressure to migrate. Private schools teach English effectively, and nearly all their students graduate. Some children of the managerial class are sent by their families to private schools in the United States, and many go to college in the United States. This is the class from which Puerto Rico's intelligentsia and political elite are drawn, including many supporters of Puerto Rican political independence. A command of middle-class speech styles in English and Spanish is important social capital and, whatever one's politics, one cannot be a player without it (see also Carr 1984:288ff; Walsh 1991:24ff).

Bonilla and Campos (1981:162–163) note that in 1976, about the time I started fieldwork, 12 percent of students attended private schools. Forty percent of these students were subsequently admitted to the University of Puerto Rico. Bonilla and Compos (1981) further note that the 1977 expenditure per pupil in public schools was $694, compared with the U.S. average of $1,740. The dropout rate was 54 percent. Moreover:

The problems of education for the Puerto Rican on the Island and in the United States are not simply similar or parallel but deeply interconnected. The operation of a dual and underfinanced educational system in Puerto Rico produces a mass of undereducated Puerto Rican youth on the Island. Pushed from their schools, these young people are forced to choose between a life of dependency, idleness or underemployment, and emigration to the States, where a similar experience awaits them and their children. (p. 164)

Insofar as the word "bilingual" focuses on language forms, its connotation obscures the political dynamics integral to language acquisition. "Bilingual" might refer to a Puerto Rican factory worker who learned English on 110th Street or to a Puerto Rican government administrator in Hato Rey who learned English in a private school. These people would have had opposite political experiences of English. The factory worker who must "defend" himself or herself to an American or white boss has an experience of English far more analogous to the monolingual Puerto Rican faced with English in the classroom or any other official venue.

Because they grow from the same political-economic bases, working-class experiences of English in Puerto Rico and in New York are dynamically parallel. The parallel lies not in form but in the politics of the opposition. In form, the differences are clear. Puerto Rico is largely monolingual. Puerto Ricans in continental U.S. cities are largely bilingual. Spanish in Puerto Rico incorporates English borrowing, but it is undeniably Spanish. The Spanish of Puerto Ricans in the continental United States may stand by itself when rules of respect so require or may mix comfortably, playfully, and routinely with the English of family, friends, and neighbors. In Puerto Rico, people who are not truly comfortable in English express a range of reactions when they encounter it: sometimes fear and resentment, sometimes resignation. Puerto Ricans migrating back from the continental United States, where they have grown used to code-switching, find that their inadvertent use of English elicits sharp hostility. In her study of adolescent returning migrants, Zentella (1990) found that their language habits and social identities were regarded as contaminated.

In U.S. cities, Puerto Ricans may not react at all to English around the house or neighborhood unless someone uses it disrespectfully, in which case he or she will probably get told as much. English spoken by working-class non-Latin (usually African American) friends and neighbors evokes little more reaction than the English in the mouth of a working-class Latin. If someone is offensive, they can be told off or ignored. English spoken by white, middle-class teachers, bosses, landlords, doctors, or social workers parallels "official" English in Puerto Rico in that it must be complied with properly and cannot be ignored.

The parallel lies in a political polarity, when English typifies the position of social, economic, and cultural control, and Spanish typifies the opposite. The difference between the dangerous, English-controlled Americans and the safe English used by Puerto Ricans is functional and political and cannot be reduced to grammatical or phonological description. English is not always functionally or politically American. English becomes functionally American when it is used in contexts and relationships that bar the use of Spanish. English becomes politically American when any use or index of Spanish (such as an accent) puts the speaker at risk. There are contexts in which a functionally American English is not a major issue; there are even situations where Puerto Ricans "accidentally" use a little Spanish with African American friends and neighbors. Such occurrences suggest that the real parallel is not English or Spanish as codes. The real parallel is in the speech event structure, especially setting and participants.

Puerto Ricans in the United States: Living an Invisible Life

Puerto Ricans have lived in U.S. cities since at least the 1890s. By 1920 Puerto Rican neighborhoods had begun to develop where people found jobs in East Harlem, the Lower East Side, and the Green Point section of Brooklyn. Sánchez Korrol (1983) documents the growth of a Puerto Rican social fabric in New York since the early twentieth century. People worked in garment, cigar making, laundry and other forms of light industry, and in hotel, restaurant, and domestic service. The *Memoirs of Bernardo Vega* (Iglesias 1984) gives a detailed, personal account of life, work and politics in this world. By the late 1920s, the growth of Puerto Rican businesses, professional services, and print media had knit a strong local identity. Yet studies of Puerto Ricans from the 1950s and 1960s treat the migration as a largely post-World War II population influx which moved into a social blank slate and failed to meet North American standards for social life. For example, in writing about local organizations and hometown social clubs, Moynihan and Glazer saw the "relative weakness of neighborhood organizations and community leadership (as) characteristic of Puerto Ricans in New York" (Sánchez Korrol 1983:132), and Chenault saw these organizations as immature, and their members as uncommitted or dissatisfied (pp. 133–134).

The Morality of Being Minority:
Public Representation in Politics, Policy, and the Media

Racializing discourses make defining connections among a group's location, circumstances, ascribed traits, and language. For decades research, media, and public entertainment have either ignored Puerto Ricans or portrayed them as a social problem, regarding initiative, solidarity, or a coherent social fabric as unlikely or extraordinary. U.S. citizens and potential citizens are measured against the moral ideal of taking onto themselves the responsibility to "get on in life." The more racialized a group is, the more any individual's misdeeds or even "lack of progress" is seen to reflect on or stem from traits defining the group. Jennings (1988:480) argues:

> Some researchers and governmental leaders will claim . . . that the reasons Puerto Ricans suffer from adverse social conditions has more to do with the level of education, inability to speak English, or as stated earlier, simply having inappropriate attitudes for the realization of mobility in America.

Jennings also points out that conservative, liberal, and radical public policy thinkers assessing Puerto Rican social status all ignore the problem of the community power base. Liberals and conservatives ignore the crucial question of whether voting should affect the power structure or fit the status quo. Radicals subsume Puerto Rican concerns into those of the working class, ignoring racial and ethnic fragmentation of the work force, especially since World War II. Liberals take the opposite approach, treating the Puerto Rican experience as primarily a race/ethnic phenomenon. All political positions assume that it is in the interests of Puerto Ricans and other minoritized people to work as individuals within existing structures. All political positions downplay that which makes Puerto Ricans a historically specific group in the United States—the same factors that underlie race and ethnic identity and that might effectively result in group political action. All political positions prefer the model of the individually registered voter to the idea it is feasible and desirable for Puerto Ricans to organize politically *as Puerto Ricans*.

The New York political establishment has never gone out of its way to find room for the Puerto Rican voter. The Democratic Party political machine Tammany Hall worked to attract (and co-opt) Italian, Irish, or Jewish support but largely discounted the worth of African American and Puerto Rican votes. In the 1930s Democrats began to notice that Puerto Rican voters tended to vote Democrat, but no Democrat represented Puerto Rican interests with the thoroughness of Harlem Congressmen Vito Marcantonio or Fiorello LaGuardia, both Republican-Fusion reformists (Falcón 1984). By the 1950s, argues Baver (1984), New York Democrats had become a party of white ethnics, a machine with no place for a non-white constituency. When Puerto Rican issues arose, New York Democrats talked to Puerto Rican politicians from Puerto Rico, who represented familiar and orderly party structures, not to Puerto Ricans in New York who remained to the Democrats a disorderly mass. Instead, Puerto Rican power in New York was organized in the 1960s and 1970s around neighborhood-based organizations and programs, especially anti-poverty agencies, as Rivera (1984) charts in some detail. Such ethnic-based activism can threaten established interests: Fuentes (1984) documents Lower East Side school board elections of 1973–1975 in which the all-white slate supported by the United Federation of Teachers accused the opposing Puerto Rican/black/Chinese/white neighborhood-based slate of "separatism."

Social policy since 1968 has been heavily influenced by arguments that hold excluded people responsible for their own exclusion, although such arguments have been around in one form or another for at least a century. Analysts like Edward Banfield (author of *The Unheavenly City)* and Charles Murray (author of *Losing Ground* and coauthor of *The Bell Curve*), who treat race and class as moral or intellectual attributes of individuals rather than as structural properties of social groups, served as advisors in the Nixon and Reagan administrations. Polarized thinking about race and class began to dominate U.S. politics and public policy not long after the peak of federal support for civil rights. Although the Nixon administration strengthened Social Security benefits, it undercut efforts to use federal housing subsidies to desegregate, and federal control was ceded to state and local officials (Myles 1988; Orfield 1987). Social Security benefits are not marked for race or class as public housing benefits are. Cuts to public housing and Medicaid by the Reagan administration severely affected African Americans and Hispanics in general, and Puerto Ricans in particular (Slessarev 1988). Cuts in funding for Hispanic education made by the Reagan administration were rationalized as a way to prevent separatism, "immersing" students in English to bring them into the middle class (Orfield 1986).

Liberal solutions may be equally problematic. Stanfield (1985:168) argues that anti-poverty programs privilege the notion of individual achievement over changes in the system of class relations. Wilson (1987:146ff) argues that race-specific economic policies downplay the need for class-oriented solutions. Working-class minorities are hurt by structural problems that eventually hurt the entire working class. Puerto Ricans, like African Americans, are hurt first because they are structurally the most vulnerable.

The "Common Sense" of Racial Hegemony

In his ethnography of Puerto Ricans in San Juan and New York, Lewis (1966) theorized that a culture of poverty developed where people were systematically dislocated in a capitalist economy. This dislocation resulted in the development of adaptive mechanisms including welfare and crime that were passed on generation to generation. Onto this structural analysis, Lewis grafted a psychological paradigm:

> A high incidence of maternal deprivation, orality, weak ego structure, confusion of sexual identification, a lack of impulse control, a strong present-time orientation with little ability to defer gratification and to plan for the future, a sense of resignation and fatalism, a wide-spread belief in male superiority, and a high tolerance for psychological pathology of all sorts. (p. xlvii)

Lewis stated that he did not equate a culture of poverty with race or ethnicity. Yet his depiction of his *La Vida* informants made these traits appear unequivocally Puerto Rican, and this picture of Puerto Ricans has dominated media since.

The media have used the term "underclass" in similar ways. Wilson (1987), one of the term's originators, defined it as the effect of economic displacement on human lives and behavior. He has emphasized that the term refers to a social *process*, but he has no control over who appropriates the term or to what ends or in what context. Once such a volatile term is published, the venues in which it is published bring it new connotations, as has happened with the equation of "underclass" and, variously, "black," "Hispanic," and "Puerto Rican." In the U.S. public consciousness, the worst too often comes to stand for the whole. Thus, the equation of Puerto Rican and underclass is based on New York Puerto Ricans, who, Rodríguez (1992) argues, are much worse off than Puerto Ricans elsewhere in the United States. Naming groups is a political act: those with power assign names (Darder 1992).

Once a group is named, that name enters public consciousness as cultural common sense. Gramsci (1971:420) asserts that "In common sense it is the 'realistic' material elements which are predominant, the immediate product of crude sensation." Common sense grows from the conception of the world that derives from one's social group (p. 324). To those in that group, common sense is definite, however ambiguous, contradictory, and multiform it may become upon analysis. When common sense is shaped by the politics of group relations, it is deeply hegemonic, saturating thought, action, and representation in the way that R. Williams (1977) argues. Abstract ideas such as "culture of poverty" or "underclass" do not stay abstract for long but take an essentialized, almost tangibly human form, entering U.S. public consciousness as natural, obvious, and needing no explanation (see Geertz 1984). The welfare queen, the dope dealer, the street kid who racks up arrest after arrest, the thirteen-year-old mother, all become natural, obvious results of group-defining traits.

Hispanic and African American working-class people remain *de facto* segregated by urban development policies, private developers, and rental and real estate brokers. This segregation reinforces public perceptions that racialized people are aggregate populations which must be contained and controlled.[3] In her examination of Congressional hearings on the Immigration Reform and Control Act of 1986, Chock (1994) finds speakers using "population" as if referring to a biological population undifferentiated by gender, race, or class. Animals, microbes, and illegal aliens all appear to form non-societies whose members must be controlled. This is consonant with images of Puerto Ricans as unevolved and as diseased. Falcón (1984:23) cites the *Boston Globe* and the *New York Times* in the early 1900s describing Puerto Ricans as aborigines incapable of governing themselves. Vega (Iglesias 1984:230) cites these examples from a series of 1947 *New York World-Telegram* stories about the postwar migration:

> The Puerto Ricans are destroying the economy and suffocating the culture of their adopted community.
>
> [Puerto Ricans] are the cause of the incredibly bad housing situation.
>
> The most serious thing about the poor health of those [Puerto Ricans] who have just arrived is that the large majority of them work in the city's restaurants, hotels and clubs, where they handle food, plates, and other kitchen utensils, and in commercial laundries where they handle clothing.
>
> Being so uncivilized, a trait common to people from the tropics, many of them buy furniture on credit and don't even have the decency to keep up with their payments.
>
> The police have followed groups of them arriving at the airport in Teterboro, New Jersey, and heading straight for the welfare offices in East Harlem.

Labor and Life Structures

Puerto Ricans, Mexicans, and Cubans

Table 2.1 compares income and labor force participation among Puerto Ricans, Mexicans, Cubans, non-Hispanic white, and non-Hispanic black Americans from

Table 2.1   U.S. Hispanic income and labor force participation rates

	Puerto Rican	Mexican	Cuban	Non-Hispanic White	Non-Hispanic Black
1960 income					
per capita	$2,596	$2,540	$3,983	$4,771	—
mean household	10,386	11,172	12,750	15,267	—
labor force rate of participation:					
male	84.7%	85.7%	87.1%	88.5%	80.6%
female	40.3%	31.5%	51.5%	39.5%	47.2%
1970 income					
per capita	3,698	3,599	5,183	6,538	—
change from 1960	42.4%	41.7%	30.1%	37.0%	—
mean household	13,680	14,757	1,762	19,615	—
change from 1960	31.7%	32.1%	38.2%	28.5%	—
labor force rate of participation:					
male	77.8%	81.9%	86%	85.4%	75.2%
female	32.9%	39.6%	52.8%	46.6%	51.1%
1980 income					
per capita	3,828	4,216	5,744	7,635	—
change from 1970	3.5%	17.1%	10.8%	16.8%	—
mean household	12,633	16,021	18,957	20,615	—
change from 1970	−7.6%	8.6%	7.6%	5.1%	—
labor force rate of participation:					
male	73.8%	83.5%	85.0%	84.6%	73.3%
female	41.7%	52.0%	64.2%	57.9%	61.1%

Note: Income figures in 1979 dollars.

Source: Bean and Tienda 1987: income figures p. 198; labor figures p. 290.

1960 to 1980. Of these three major Latin migrations of the time, Puerto Ricans emerge as worst off.

While there were Cuban labor immigrants in the United States since 1900, Cuba was never a primary target of labor recruitment nor did the U.S. economy pull Cubans into the kind of migration cycles that Puerto Ricans and Mexicans experienced. The Cubans who came to the United States after Castro's revolution had educational and class advantages and were welcomed as victims of the latest onslaught of encroaching world communism. They established a thriving enclave economy which allowed many Cubans to bypass restrictive unskilled factory or service jobs. In Miami, a strikingly Cuban fabric of business and institution developed (Wilson and Portes 1980; Portes 1990; Nelson and Tienda 1985). As Table 2.1 shows, Cuban men and women have been employed at consistently higher rates than Mexican or Puerto Rican, and the gap among them has grown since 1960. Their per capita and mean household incomes have grown proportionately.

Unlike Cubans, Puerto Ricans and Mexicans were both actively recruited into unskilled manufacturing, service, and agricultural work. In 1960 their economic fortunes were relatively parallel except that a higher proportion of Puerto

Rican women worked. This has since changed. By 1970 a lower proportion of Puerto Rican women worked and the proportion of Puerto Rican men working was 4 percent less than Mexican instead of 1 percent less, as it had been in 1960. By 1980, where Mexican mean household income had steadily risen for 20 years, Puerto Rican mean household income had dropped by 7.6 percent. More Puerto Rican women, but fewer Puerto Rican men, were working. By contrast the labor participation rates for Mexican men had stayed relatively consistent and the rate for women had risen.

Ironically, since 1960, Puerto Ricans had the same or more median years of schooling than Mexicans: 10 for Puerto Ricans and 9.1 for Mexicans in 1980 (Bean and Tienda 1987:234). Moreover, the Puerto Rican labor force had a slightly higher percentage of professional and managerial workers (13.6 percent) than did the Mexican labor force (12.4 percent) in 1980 (Bean and Tienda 1987:92). This modest edge in education and training has not overcome the effect of increasing structural discrepancies. From 1960 to 1980 the number of families headed by a husband and wife decreased for both Puerto Ricans and Mexicans, but much more sharply for Puerto Ricans (p. 190). Puerto Rican female-headed households also have the highest proportion among all U.S. Hispanics of separated or divorced women and of very young children (p. 194). They also have the lowest incomes (p. 201).

The growing discrepancy between Mexican and Puerto Rican income and labor force participation can be partially explained by the fact that the heavy concentration of Puerto Rican labor in the northeast has been strongly affected by the restructuring of blue-collar industry, as plants have moved to the suburbs, southern states, or out of the United States altogether (Rodríguez 1989). Puerto Rican women in the labor force are particularly affected by local labor market conditions: as factory jobs disappear and markets in clerical and communications work expand, job requirements are restructured in ways that put Puerto Rican women in the least competitive position (Ríos 1985; Meléndez and Barry Figueroa 1992). Moreover, where Puerto Ricans in the Northeast have been hurt by restrictive union policies (Rodríguez 1979; González and Gray 1984), there is increasing evidence of Mexican-American integration into local urban economies and into union-protected agricultural jobs, as well as growth in Mexican-American self-employment (Nelson and Tienda 1985).

Bonilla and Campos (1981, 1985) argue that the constraints experienced by the Puerto Rican labor market in the continental United States, as in Puerto Rico, are embedded in the political-economic basis of Puerto Rican-U.S. relations. The mechanisms that structured Puerto Ricans into a floating reserve labor force also channeled them into the most vulnerable areas of the economy, the industrial northeast. Factory jobs open to Puerto Ricans were most likely to be minimally skilled assembly line work, wrapping, packing, grading, sorting. Service jobs included kitchen help, cleaning and janitorial work, orderlies and health aides, and for women in particular, clerks, secretaries, cashiers, bank tellers, teachers' aides (Bonilla and Campos 1981:159–160). This has been exacerbated by the decline in northeastern manufacturing jobs, reflecting a polarization of the employment structure itself, with an increased number of high-income professional jobs, an increased number of low-wage service and manufacturing jobs, and a decreased amount of middle-income blue-collar and white-collar work (Sassen-Koob 1985). These structural changes have polarized the Puerto Rican labor force into skilled and nonskilled workers, the latter exiting the labor force as fewer and fewer jobs exist (Falcón and Hirschman 1992).

This picture is made more complicated by the fact that New York Puerto Ricans find themselves in competition with more recent migrants, especially Caribbean migrants, for the decreasing number of blue-collar jobs and the increasing number of jobs in the "downgraded manufacturing sector" (Sassen-Koob 1985:302), that is, jobs with little prospect for advancement, with minimal benefits and wages and that are often seasonal—typically, sweatshop jobs. Many of these jobs are going to other Caribbean and Central American immigrants who, unlike Puerto Ricans, may be threatened with deportation and may have had little experience with unions or job standards (Rodríguez 1989:97). The establishment of enclave businesses and kin- and friend-based recruiting has led to Dominican and Central American displacement of Puerto Ricans in the garment industry. One employer who noted the effects after the fact commented: "I woke up one day and realized that my Puerto Rican workers, who used to make up two-thirds of the plant, had all moved out of the shop" (Waldinger 1985:338). Finally, in the last twenty years, New York has experienced a significant shift in investment toward luxury residences, upscale office buildings, and designer-style marketing and manufacturing. The specialized needs that these generate are largely met by workers in the service sector and what Sassen-Koob sees as the growing informal economy that draws its workforce primarily from the new immigrations (Sassen-Koob 1989).

Where and How People Live

In 1980, 7,071,639 people lived in the five boroughs of New York: 1,406,024 (19.9 percent) were Hispanic; 860,552 (12 percent) were Puerto Rican. In 1990, 7,311,966 people lived in the five boroughs of New York: 1,783,511 (24.4 percent) were Hispanic; 896,763 (12.3 percent) were Puerto Rican. (All census figures from U.S. Bureau of the Census 1983, 1993, unless otherwise noted.) The Puerto Rican population has grown largest in the poorest boroughs. In Manhattan, Puerto Ricans made up 13.3 percent of the population in 1960, 12 percent in 1970 and 1980 and 10.4 percent in 1990; Puerto Ricans in the Bronx made up 13.1 percent of the population in 1960, 21.5 percent in 1970, 27 percent in 1980 and 29.2 percent in 1990. (1960–1980 figures from City of New York Planning Department 1979, 1983; 1990 figures from Bureau of the Census.) Rodríguez (1989:107) reports that of the total decrease in U.S. housing units between 1970 and 1980, 80% were accounted for by units destroyed or demolished in Brooklyn and the Bronx. In the 1980 census (corresponding to my 1978–79 research), 35 percent of Manhattan Hispanic families were below poverty level, as opposed to 29.4 percent of black families or 9.4 percent of white. In the

Bronx, 40.3 percent of Hispanic families lived below poverty level, as opposed to 29.5 percent of black or 14.4 percent of white families. In the 1990 census (corresponding to my 1988 research), 33.9 percent of Manhattan Hispanic families were below poverty level (as opposed to 29.5 percent of black families or 7.7 percent of white). In the Bronx 38.7 percent of Hispanic families lived below poverty level as opposed to 25.7 percent of black or 15.5 percent of white families.

Puerto Ricans are a highly segregated population in New York. They have least contact with whites and most contact with African Americans and with other Spanish-speaking groups. This is not the pattern for other Spanish-speaking populations. Generally, a group's degree of contact with the general population varies inversely with its size in proportion to the whole: the larger the proportion, the less likely the degree of contact. Yet Mexicans in Los Angeles are more likely than New York Puerto Ricans to have contact with whites and less likely to have contact with either African Americans or other Spanish-speakers; this pattern of contact occurs despite the fact that Mexicans make up about 22 percent of Los Angeles while Puerto Ricans make up about 10 percent of New York (Massey 1981). Massey and Bitterman (1985) explain this as a function of Puerto Ricans and African Americans having a common racial heritage. Santiago (1992) argues that "shared ancestry" does not explain shared segregation patterns (other Caribbean people who "share ancestry" do not share space in New York), and the explanation is much more likely to lie in similar constraints on both. Moreover, Puerto Ricans may seem less segregated than African Americans because Puerto Rican neighborhoods are scattered throughout New York while African American neighborhoods are more localized. In this case, Puerto Ricans experience a pattern of "detailed residential segregation" (Falcón 1988:185) that isolates them just as effectively.

The quality of life in a segregated New York Puerto Rican neighborhood can be illustrated through a demographic examination of the area in which the 1978–1979 study was done (Tables 2.2–2.10, all based on 1980 census). Table 2.2 gives the 1980 census figures for four adjacent Lower East Side census tracts (CT). (A census tract—the minimal unit in which census figures are given—is made up of several adjoining city blocks; the figures do not add up to 100 percent because I have omitted figures for Asian/Pacific Islander, Amerindian, and Other.) The

Table 2.2   Lower East Side census tracts according to 1980 census

CT:	26.01	26.02	32	38	Manhattan
Total Population	2721	1876	8369	8665	1,428,285
White★	11%	28%	73%	70%	50%
Black★	13%	13%	5%	4%	20%
Hispanic	72%	58%	16%	13%	24%
Puerto Rican	66%	52%	12%	8%	12%

Note: ★non-Hispanic black and white

1978–1979 work was done in the area encompassed by CTs 26.01, 26.02, and 32. I include CT 38 for comparative purposes. The area that these CTs constitute ranges from Ninth Street south to Third and from Avenue D west to Third Avenue. CTs 26.01 and 26.02 make up the eastern third of this area, 32 the middle third, and 38 the western third. The population from east to west is increasingly white, with fewer African American and Hispanic, especially Puerto Rican, residents. Table 2.3, based on the 1980 census, lists the proportion of households on Aid to Families with Dependent Children (AFDC) in each of these tracts. This proportion decreases from east to west. The figures in Table 2.4 suggest that not everyone who is eligible for AFDC may in fact be receiving it (see Sharff 1987; Susser and Kreniske 1987, for a more detailed discussion). In the tracts that are poorest and most black or Hispanic, no one is well-off, but Hispanics are the worst off. This is so in 26.01; the figures for 26.02 are incomplete, so we cannot compare. As the white population increases in a given tract and as the tract's population becomes better off, African American residents also become better off; however, Hispanic families tend to remain below poverty level. As the white population decreases and the general degree of poverty increases, the proportion of Puerto Ricans in the Hispanic population increases. It appears that African Americans in the better-off census tracts are less socially isolated from white residents than are Hispanics, especially Puerto Ricans.

These conditions keep race/class conflation firmly in place. Puerto Rican and African American residents have little choice about where they live. Puerto Ricans and African Americans in poor neighborhoods are assumed to be on welfare whether they are or not and usually face considerable housing discrimination. If they are living below poverty level (and they might well be without being on welfare), they face even greater discrimination because they have even fewer resources. Most "nice" buildings are simply too expensive—and too white. These buildings are rarely available

Table 2.3 Households receiving AFDC

CT	Hispanic	Black	White
26.01	67.8%	36.9%	37.0%
26.02	51.0%	NL	NL
32	34.4%	12.3%	11.7%
38	23.0%	14.3%	10.0%

Note: NL = Not Listed

Table 2.4 Families below poverty line

CT	Hispanic	Black	White
26.01	69.1%	61.8%	56.7%
26.02	76.1%	NL	NL
32	47.8%	35.0%	14.5%
38	35.7%	14.8%	8.8%

Note: NL = Not Listed

to AFDC recipients. The most common and most effective discriminatory policy is to not rent to families with young children, an easy policy to maintain in an area with many one-bedroom or efficiency apartments.[4]

This policy kept every family I worked with from moving into "nice buildings" since most received AFDC and in a few cases Supplemental Security Income (SSI), a disability supplement. They lived in buildings in which landlords set the rent to the maximum that welfare would pay. In such cases, AFDC payments toward rent are effectively channeled to the landlords (Sharff 1987). All were officially female-headed households, though most women did in fact live with male companions. As Table 2.5 shows, most Puerto Rican and black families in this area (like most white families in CT 26.01) had children under 18. As Table 2.6 shows, a sizeable proportion of these were (officially) female-headed households. The 1980 census figures indicate that female-headed household income is about half that of the undifferentiated family mean. It is almost impossible to prove that housing discrimination is directly motivated by anti-black and anti-Hispanic prejudice. I once recommended a building to a Puerto Rican friend who earned well above the local mean. She reported back to me that the manager told her there were no vacancies. The manager told me, "Don't send around any more Puerto Ricans."

The poorer the population in a census tract, the younger they are (Table 2.7) and the more women there are (Table 2.8). Wilson (1987:142) notes a statistical correlation between median age, welfare, poverty, female-headed households, and rate of employment in inner-city neighborhoods. The same correlation appears if Table 2.7 is compared with Tables 2.3, 2.4, 2.6, and Table 2.10. The female-male ratio in these four tracts is higher for Hispanics in the poorer and most heavily Puerto Rican tracts, 26.01 and 26.02, where it is close to the general Puerto Rican ratio of 54 percent to 46 percent noted by Rodríguez (1989:28–31). The years

Table 2.5   Families with children under 18

CT	Hispanic	Black	White
26.01	65.7%	61.8%	65.2%
26.02	78.6%	NL	NL
32	65.7%	55.2%	28.0%
38	58.1%	81.4%	30.5%

Note: NL = Not Listed

Table 2.6   Female-headed families with children under 18

CT	Hispanic	Black	White
26.01	79.3%	71.1%	79.6%
26.02	84.6%	NL	NL
32	79.2%	69.4%	46.5%
38	70.2%	85.7%	36.1%

Note: NL = Not Listed

Table 2.7 Median ages in years (1980 census figures rounded off to nearest tenth)

CT	Hispanic	Black	White
26.01	21.7	27.2	27.2
26.02	21.9	NL	NL
32	26.6	32	43.7
38	29.5	32.6	32.2

Note: NL = Not Listed

Table 2.8 Females in 15–44 age bracket (1980 census figures rounded off to nearest tenth)

CT	Hispanic	General population
26.01	54.3%	50.6%
26.02	53.6%	48.0%
32	48.8%	44.2%
38	43.2%	44.0%

15–44, when men in these tracts are least visible, are crucial to men's social visibility. This is when men establish careers and families, buy homes, and generally establish a social persona that is judged in terms of failure or success. When men are less visible, as they are in the poorest neighborhoods, everyone is more vulnerable to being racialized.

In some cases, men are present but not counted. In 26.01 and 26.02, the tracts with the highest percentage of families on AFDC, men are almost certainly not counted if they are not officially supposed to be there. This is likely to be the case whether or not the interviewer has anything to do with AFDC. For example, in May 1979 I interviewed six local women for a housing survey not connected with my own work or that of the study project. I had known them all for at least a year, and they realized that I knew their living arrangements. When I asked the question, "How many adults over eighteen live here?" each respondent said, "One." Five of the six were living with male companions; the sixth had an adult son living in the house. Their replies were addressed to the survey, not to me.

Men are also not officially visible if the activities by which they support themselves and their families cannot be reported. Sharff, director of the study project with which I worked, gives a detailed account of the economic life of this area based on household surveys, interviews, and participant observation, 1975–1979 (Sharff 1986, 1987). She argues (1987:19–20) that chronic unemployment leads people to public assistance, and then (public assistance supplying a hopelessly inadequate income) to seek additional and unreportable sources of income ranging from the marginally licit to strictly illegal. The very forces that set up these conditions establish the parameters into which local people must fit their responses to their situation. Sharff (pp. 27–30) describes sixty-one "regular" jobs held by local people; six were in an income range extending to $200 or more at its highest; five more in a range that at best extended to $140 or $150 a week. The other fifty jobs paid at best $120 a week. Most paid a good deal less. The jobs described show the limited work options available to residents of a downgraded manufacturing area. Several were sporadic, part time, or work done at home. Those who did have factory jobs were rarely able to work steadily and could face a lengthy and difficult commute.

A good proportion of these workers lived in households receiving AFDC. Their economic activities constitute a major share of what Sharff calls the underground economy, that is, work that is not or cannot be officially reported. Without their earnings, the families' incomes could not have covered their most basic expenses for food, rent, utilities, and clothing. Sharff also lists several "irregular" (illegal) occupations that brought in further income: *bolita* (numbers), stealing and fencing stolen goods, and drugs. At this level, this income is minimal and acquired at considerable risk, especially to the teenage boys most readily recruited to this irregular economy. It is easy to see these activities as entirely initiated by local people. But the real drug profits are made by organizers outside the local area, and, Sharff notes, many customers are also well-off outsiders. In many ways, these neighborhoods are conduits that funnel money from outside sources to outside recipients, whether from well-off drug consumers to drug profiteers or from tax coffers via welfare to slumlords. Sharff argues that the options of the people who live in these neighborhoods are limited and co-opted by the larger economic interests and labor structures that bound their lives. In response, people diversify their possible access to resources in as many ways as possible, particularly through family roles played by children, and there were many children in Sharff's study: of 133 people, 80 were nineteen or younger. Some—especially those who perform well in school—become "straight" workers, some become advocates for the family, and some, sadly, enter the irregular economy.

The irregular economy is linked to a second, grimmer reason for the male-female ratio. Citing a study by Oscar Alers (1978) showing homicide to account for almost 20 percent of Puerto Rican deaths, mostly male, Sharff documents eleven violent deaths in the project's three years: ten men and one woman, age nineteen to thirty-two.

Tables 2.9 and 2.10 complete the picture of the progressive shift in poverty-related factors as one moves from east to west. Census tracts 26.01 and 26.02 show a high proportion of Hispanics in general and Puerto Ricans in particular; each has few African American and fewer white residents. A demographic picture of life in a poor, Puerto Rican neighborhood emerges: a young, less educated population, more female than male, a high proportion of families with children under eighteen, a high proportion of female-headed households, a high proportion of families below poverty level, a high proportion of families on AFDC. There is also a relatively low rate of employment reported in the census although for reasons dis-

Table 2.9   Hispanic population completing school

CT	Left school by 8th grade	Left school by 11th grade	High school diploma	Some college
26.01	52.4%	82.3%	17.7%	4.3%
26.02	52.6%	81.8%	18.2%	2.8%
32	34.7%	54.0%	46.0%	26.5%
38	44.8%	61.0%	39.0%	21.2%

Table 2.10   Hispanic population over age 16 working

CT	Percent working
26.01	23.6%
26.02	33.2%
32	42.5%
38	51.2%

cussed above, more people may be working "off the books." Census tracts 32 and 38 have smaller Hispanic populations and smaller proportions of Puerto Ricans within those populations. They are predominantly white. They have more single men and women, a higher rate of employment reported, more high school and college graduates. In these two tracts, Hispanic population characteristics change: they are older and better off, better educated, with a higher reported rate of employment; there are more men and fewer children. This presents an interesting twist on Massey's idea that Puerto Ricans are isolated in larger white populations. In true pocket segregation, as in tracts 26.01 and 26.02, this is indeed the case. In tracts 32 and 38, where they are a small fraction of the population, Hispanics, including Puerto Ricans, may very well reside in a pattern of class mobility, engaged in activities that appear respectable to the American public eye; in short, relatively "assimilated." Unlike the families Sharff describes, these residents have the social capital to afford a greater degree of interactive contact with whites.

Scenes from Everyday Life

These census figures take us as close as numbers can to the world known by the eight families who took part in the 1978–1979 study. Five of these—Rosa Rivera and her sons; Adelina Mendoza and her children; Luz Guzmán, her husband Carlos González and their children, Luisa Muñiz and her family; and Lena Johnson and her children—took part only in the 1978–1979 study and appear here under pseudonyms. I also worked with Eugenia (Jenny) Molina (who resumed her maiden name, Pacheco, by 1988) and her children including Luis; the Mojica family including Marilyn and José; and Millie Wright and her children including Cathy, all of whom took part in the 1988 and 1991 studies and appear here under their own names. The Johnsons were African American, everyone else Puerto Rican.

Everyone lived within a few blocks of each other and eventually they all came to know each other, in part through their involvement in the study project where I worked.

N Street between Avenues X and Y was the central "block" in this study, and most families lived on or near its eastern half. The residents of the west half of the block were older, and more were white than black or Hispanic. There were fewer children. The buildings were almost fully occupied and in fair condition. On the east half, buildings were in poor condition with many vacancies.[5] The east half resembled census tracts 26.01 and 26.02; the west half resembled tract 32.

The west half contained a Catholic church with its school, schoolyard, and parish offices. The students were Polish, Ukranian, Puerto Rican, African American, and Asian. Across from the church were twelve small apartment buildings. These contained eight to ten three-room apartments, most rented to single people or couples without children. Many residents were older, white people, and some were younger African American or white adults. Judging from a survey of mailbox names, about 70 percent were Eastern European.[6] The African American residents included several Nation of Islam members who managed five of the buildings. The east half of the block contained eleven buildings, four on the south side and seven on the north. Most of these buildings were larger than those on the west half and contained larger units, many with four to five rooms.

There were many more families with young children on the east half. Of 202 residential units, 183 were occupied. One building of 30 units was abandoned, though tenants had gone on living there for some time after the landlord had abandoned it.[7] Of the occupied apartments, 106 were Hispanic, 37 black, 36 white, and 4 Asian.

The buildings on N Street were tenements, four-, five- and six-story walk-ups, built late in the nineteenth century. In some of the older units, the bathtubs were in the kitchen. In many buildings, especially on the east half, doorbells did not work and front doors did not lock. Windows were often broken and rarely had full screens or storm windows. The plumbing was recalcitrant, the walls were cracked, the windows were loose, and the doors did not quite close. Most buildings had rats and mice, and everyone had cockroaches. As Carlos González put it, "They don't tell you these places come with pets."

The eight families shared network connections of varying intensity. Lena Johnson and Luz Guzmán were good friends, as were their daughters. Lena was also on friendly terms with Luisa Muñiz, as were their daughters. All three girls were friendly with Millie Wright's daughters, and Millie and Lena were on friendly terms. However, the ties among these families were looser than those between the Rivera and Molina families. Rosa Rivera and Jenny Molina were friends, Rosa's husband and one of Jenny's sons were co-workers, Rosa's cousin was Jenny's son-in-law, and there were close friendships among their children. Rosa and Lena were on friendly terms, but Lena stood well outside the Rosa-Jenny network. The Mojica children were closest to Rosa Rivera's and Luz Guzmán's children. The Mendoza family was least connected.

Women were more likely to be the continuing household head than men, which made women pivotal in network formation. They became acquainted through mutual friends and relations and often through their children. Luisa Muñiz, Lena Johnson, Luz Guzmán, and Millie Wright became acquainted because their daughters were playmates. Many of the connections between the Rivera and Molina families formed through Rosa and Jenny. The building entrance was a key point of contact for women, a place to meet while keeping an eye on kids, taking a break from housework, chatting, watching out for strangers, and sizing up residents. All this kept them visible to each other and informed about the local scene.

Men were more likely to meet at clubs, garages, or work, perhaps through wives or girlfriends, sisters, or mothers. Boys began forming cliques outside the house at a young age. In adolescence, boys' groups became fairly tightly structured, with emphasis on "being together," that is, dressing alike and adopting public display routines of gestures and props. Girls were more likely to stay in the house and to form small, fluid girl groups of two or three, playing much closer to home than boys.

In this context, Puerto Ricans and African Americans do not make up entirely separate groups. They differ in how they define themselves and are defined in many of the things they do and in language. But in part through their shared history of class exclusion, they share a great deal of what they do, how they talk, and how they define themselves. They constantly interact. They make friends and sometimes enemies. They date and marry each other. They mix in adolescent cliques. Puerto Rican boys pick up slang, pronunciation, and grammatical phrasing from African American boys, who pick up Spanish phrases from Puerto Rican friends (Wolfram 1973, 1974; Flores, Attinasi, and Pedraza 1981). Boys' friendships may last to adulthood. Women often form individual friendships, though they tend to shy away from full-scale incorporation into each other's networks.

Puerto Ricans and African Americans are not seen as racially the same, but they have had similar experiences of racialization. They are often ambivalent about each other in everyday life, yet points of sympathy constantly emerge. Where working class Puerto Ricans and African Americans on the Lower East Side have a clear and fixed sense of exclusion from the world of the middle-class white, how they define each other is less fixed. Whether a Puerto Rican calls an African American "Mary next door" or "*esa morena*" (that black woman), or whether an African American calls a Puerto Rican "the Fernandez kid" or "that Spanish kid" may depend on, for example, whether Mary's daughter and the Fernandez kid have just had a fight.

There is no fixed boundary between Puerto Rican and African American social life in this neighborhood. People live in the same buildings, put up with the same conditions, complain about the same landlords, and know the same neighbors. They use the same stores and take the same trains and buses. Their children attend school together and play together. They share a common habitus in Bourdieu's (1977a) sense:

The structures constitutive of a particular kind of environment (e.g., the material conditions of existence characteristic of a class condition) produce habitus (p. 72)
    . . . a universalizing mediation which causes an individual agent's practices, without either explicit reason or signifying intent, to be nonetheless "sensible" and "reasonable." (p. 79)

Routine ways of thinking, acting, and talking readily become "sensible" and "reasonable" to people sharing the same forms of exclusion from the middle-class, white world. If habitus is defined as dispositions that organize perception and practical sense, Puerto Rican and African American residents share habitus insofar as their social actions and understandings fit together. They need not be identical, only congruent. The degree of congruence depends on one's place in local structures, which in turn depends on gender, family role, generation, and age. The world of teenage boys is probably most congruent, women's lives probably least congruent. But all had more in common with each other than with the middle-class, white world and it could be seen in talk in everyday routines (Urciuoli 1991).

Because there are no fixed boundaries or group homogeneity, there is no simple distinction between a Puerto Rican and African American speech community. Puerto Rican and black mean what they mean as identities because both are nested in exclusion from the white, middle-class world (see discussion in Herzfeld 1987:154ff). In their shared exclusion, a strong sympathy of attitude has developed. In a series of 1988 interviews, people explained the opposition between white and Puerto Rican or black:

Jenny Pacheco: The white wants to be rich and always wants to be on top. So because we are Spanish and we are black, well, they have us in the dirt, as if we're beneath them. And we cannot improve our lives the way they can, not in any way.[8]

Luis Molina: I'm more comfortable with blacks than with whites because blacks live in the same environment as us, they relate to us better than whites.

Nilsa Buon: It's sort of bizarre when I hear other Hispanics say how much they dislike blacks. I'm like, my enemies are not blacks, my enemies are whites. If anything, they're the ones who try to put me down, who are constantly criticizing me and judging me. I don't have blacks aggravating my life.

José and Marilyn Mojica (BU refers to me):

   BU: Is it easier to deal with blacks or whites?
   MM: Blacks, because a lot of white people put themselves too high, like they have it all.
   JM: Black people do that too.
   MM: Now, but before white people treated Spanish and black people bad.
   BU: Who do you find easier to get along with in general?
   JM: More—is equal to me. . . . They're equal. If they're friendly to me, I be friendly to them. But if you're saying, if I come up, probably a black person.

Marilyn and José thought African Americans were better off on the whole than Puerto Ricans. Jenny saw African Americans as more visible than Hispanics in public agency positions and in banks and post offices. Luis saw them in similar terms:

> Housing gets distributed to black people rather than Hispanics. For example, we applied for housing across the street, we were interviewed and we had no chance to get in. Maybe because we're Hispanic and not black. Blacks seem to get more attention, fall in a better category than Hispanics, get more breaks. Across the street the majority of people living there are black, in a renovated building with cheaper rent.

Nevertheless, despite some feelings of resentment or expressions of irritation, anger or disapproval toward African Americans, no one found whites easier to live near or get along with.

Becoming an Other on Your Own Block

This is a world in which people move frequently. Rodríguez (1989:107) reports 1980 census figures indicating that more than half of all New York Puerto Rican residents had moved within the previous five years. This is certainly the case for the families in this study. During my 1978–1979 research, the Mojica family moved around the corner into the building on N Street where our study project office was located. The Mendoza family moved out of an apartment a block from us to public housing projects further south in Manhattan. The Wright family moved to the block from out of town. The Molina family moved to the Bronx. By the mid 1980s, the Johnson family had moved to Brooklyn and the Muñiz family moved to East Harlem; I have since lost track of them.

Luz Guzmán and Carlos González and their children moved from N Street to public housing some blocks north. Rosa Rivera and some of her children moved to Puerto Rico and then returned to the New York area, living first in New Jersey and returning to the Lower East Side in 1991. The Mojica family remained on the Lower East Side, found themselves displaced from their building and spent several months in a homeless hotel. Marilyn's mother eventually found an apartment in public housing on the Lower East Side near Chinatown. Marilyn and her husband found a tenement apartment on the Lower East Side a few blocks from N Street, but in 1991 they moved to public housing in the Bronx. Millie Wright and her daughters moved to the Bronx in 1980, moving again a few years later to the apartment where Millie lived until 1993. Jenny is still in the Bronx as is Luis and his family.

People move because they find cheaper, better or larger accommodations, or because there was a fire, or they had been broken into, or the building had become too insecure, or the landlord never heated the apartment, or there was too much drug traffic. If these incidents accumulate and accelerate, people look to move away from their old area. Many of these areas have seen massive withdrawal of investment capital by landlords and businesses, resulting in neighborhoods that look and feel like a war zone.

Unlike the South Bronx, disinvestment on the Lower East Side (beginning in the 1970s) was followed by reinvestment and gentrification (late 1970s and early 1980s). Smith, Duncan, and Reid (1989) chart the turning points from disinvestment (usually through non-payment of building taxes) to reinvestment (by repaying at least some back taxes on buildings whose value seemed about to increase) in this area. They posit a "shifting gentrification frontier" which operated for about a decade. It began in the mid–1970s along Second Avenue, where the quickest profits could be made (buying and reselling buildings, raising rents) with the least risk. It reached the eastern stretch of Delancey Street and thereabouts by the early to mid-1980s. I first noticed a change in this area in 1981. By 1986 it was obvious, especially in new businesses designed to appeal to the "urban pioneer." Glittery New Wave resale shops and boutiques appeared in Avenue A storefronts that had housed dry cleaners, drug stores, or appliance repair firms five years earlier, though the buildings themselves showed little extensive refurbishing.

The areas most resistant to the reinvestment process were the poorest and most Hispanic (Smith, Duncan, and Reid 1989:249), the areas where this study is set. The last grand push was Operation Pressure Point in 1985, a massive police crackdown on drug dealers. These are the areas which most strongly provoked the uses of frontier imagery, which Smith (1992) explores in media and advertising aimed at "urban pioneer" life on the Lower East Side in the 1980s. The imagery constructs a new reality: as gentrification displaces working class lives, "the frontier ideology rationalizes social differentiation and exclusion as natural and inevitable." It does so by "defining the poor and working class as 'uncivil'" (p. 75). In an obliging illustration of Smith's point, the *New York Times Magazine* ran the following article during my 1979 research:

> I am sitting in a patrol car with two uniformed policeman at 3:00 A.M. on East 7th Street, one of the worst blocks in the city. The Ninth Precinct runs from 14th down to Houston Street, from Broadway to the East River, and has a good mix of ethnic groups. It's the home of the F.A.L.N. Puerto Rican terrorist group, the Black Liberation Army, communities of Dominicans, Ukrainians, Lithuanians, Poles and Jews, and the New York Headquarters of the Hell's Angels. There are brave little pockets of renovated brownstones here and there, but mostly the Ninth Precinct is an ugly and terrifying place. It is a place of stinking tenements with no heat, whose occupants wear overcoats indoors and keep the gas jets on the stove going night and day in vain efforts to keep warm. It is a place of burned-out buildings, of burned-out abandoned cars, of drunken derelicts and muggers. Packs of wild dogs prowl the empty street at night. (Greenberg 1979:31–35)

Seven letters were printed in response. Two applauded the author for "telling it like it is," one pointed out that crime exists everywhere, one (from a state senator) took the author to task for seeing ethnic diversity as a minus instead of a plus, and three (including one from the president of the local Small Business Association and one from the director of a renovation organization) took the author to task for not focusing on the resurgence of business life and renovation.

Smith also argues that one of the accomplishments of the Lower East Side art industry was to create a depoliticized sense of wildness and individualism that masked the reproduction of the dominant social order (and facilitated development). A *New York Times* article that appeared during my 1988 research describes a local artists' cooperative:

> On a rather foreboding block of the Lower East Side, amid art dealers and drug dealers, rats and real estate speculators, dancers are dancing, actors are acting. (Yarrow 1988)

The article goes on to describe an arts organization "in which artists and tenants not only collaborate on projects but also bring a whiff of culture to one of Manhattan's most devastated neighborhoods."

Although the article implies an art-to-the-people mission, few of the people living on this block in 1988 were there in 1978, as two of its former residents pointed out to me. In 1988 Marilyn Mojica and her family were still living on the Lower East Side, in a tiny one-bedroom apartment. She, her brother José, and I took a walk down the street described in the article two months before it was published. They had lived there ten years earlier. As we passed their old building, they said it was "almost all white now," and pointed out its burglar gates and storm windows as evidence: "It must be white people putting them up, and the door never locked for us and it locks now." As we walked along the street, they said again that the Lower East Side seemed to be "all for white people now." Where were all the blacks and Puerto Ricans supposed to go? Marilyn said; they couldn't afford to live there any more and they were being pushed out. Her perception was right on target. In the words of a developer interviewed by Smith (1992:90): "They'll all be forced out. They'll be pushed east to the river and given life preservers."

The Move to the Bronx

In the 1988 and 1991 interviews, people often spoke of feeling pushed into the Bronx. Yet when they moved away from the Lower East Side in 1978–1979, the move seemed a good idea. The drug traffic on the Lower East Side was becoming much worse by 1979, thanks to non-local investments of non-legal capital. The Bronx offered larger and less expensive apartments. But the neighborhoods to which people moved in the Bronx were already feeling the slide of disinvestment. The "nice" (too often "white") buildings were either unaffordable or run by people who would not rent to Puerto Ricans. From 1970 to 1990 the population of the census tracts from Yankee Stadium to Fordham Road became steadily less white as the line of hypersegregation—residential segregation radically polarized by race (Massey and Denton 1985)—moved north. This means that as people in this study tried to find safer and less deteriorated neighborhoods, the line of residential segregation (which became a line of hypersegregation and disinvestment in the southern Bronx) followed them. The message was, if you're Puerto Rican, you do not deserve a safe, affordable place to live.

The Bronx is considerably less negotiable than the Lower East Side. Buildings are smaller on the Lower East Side, and people moved easily from the front of the building to their apartments. Women could watch children, slip out to the store, stand out front and chat. People could call from the apartment to the street or watch for a visitor. Getting to know one's neighbors was easier. In the Bronx, buildings are larger and public space less readily accessible from the apartment. The larger buildings in the Bronx, designed for spaciousness and privacy in the 1930s, now create social barriers. Neighbors are less socially visible. One hesitates to pursue an acquaintance or let people into one's apartment when one cannot see who they associate with or what they do all day. Shopping is more of a chore. The Lower East Side is extensively served by public transportation; getting around the Bronx by bus and train requires many changes and a fair amount of walking. On the Lower East Side, one can hail a taxi; in the Bronx, one calls for car service. All this adds up to social isolation. At the same time, people are now alienated from the now white Lower East Side, as Luis Molina and his wife Rosalina (Rosie) sadly reflect:

RM: The Lower East Side used to be fun.
LM: You couldn't be afraid of the neighborhood, now you walk down there and you're scared.
RM: I went to buy a jacket for little Luis [their son] on Orchard Street and it looked so different. It made me sad.
LM: And I got stopped just driving around by this cop, just pointing things out to Rosie.

Rosie commented on how expensive and ugly she found the art for sale in the Lower East Side boutiques and said, as Marilyn did above, "They push everybody out." She added, "I used to know a lot of people downtown. But here I don't like to make friends."

For Millie Wright, getting to know people on the Lower East Side was easy. In the Bronx, she has known few of her neighbors. As for the hangers-out in front of her building, the best thing was to be polite, friendly, and not too chummy. She would have happily moved back downtown but it has become terribly expensive, and no one she knew still lived there. Millie said:

Well, I was raised downtown, between Houston and 14th Street. I didn't maybe know people in N Street and all that but by seeing them I knew who was who. And I knew if somebody, if this was a person that you just saw on the street and that's it, you wouldn't let them in your house, because you see how they are and you more or less know what's going on. And of course it'd be a little easier down there (to let) someone come to your house than it would be up here. If you didn't know there would always be someone there who'd know, look out for that one or look out for the other one. Because I knew more people down there than I do up here, and I don't trust that much.

Marilyn Mojica and her family were evicted from their old building on N Street and spent many months in a transient hotel. Her mother and brother were assigned public housing on the Lower East Side, but her own application for the same place was turned down. Finally, she and her family found a small place on the Lower East Side. She was assigned to public housing in East Harlem but did not care for the building, nor did she want to live so far from her family. But her building continued to deteriorate and some of her husband's family needed a place to stay, which only she could provide. So in early 1991, when she received a new public housing assignment in the Bronx, she decided to accept it. Public housing allows the applicant three calls; if all are turned down, the applicant goes to the bottom of the list and starts again. Marilyn had already turned down one assignment and felt she had better not turn down another. Once one accepts a housing assignment, one can reapply after a year, which gives the applicant three more chances. She planned to reapply in 1992. She was still there in 1995.

When I visited her in the Bronx in 1991, she said the new place was fine as long as she stayed inside but there was no place for her children to play outside. As we talked, we looked out the window to the street seven floors below. She pointed out a playground where she never saw children: it was too far for mothers to monitor safely. Her two girls often played in the hall but she said there were some strange types in the building and one had to watch out. She said she could not get downtown to her mother's often because the train took an hour and a half. Her mother and brother did not often come visit her in the Bronx.

In this chapter, we have seen the race and class structures that shape New York Puerto Rican neighborhoods. In the next chapters, we see how people experience, perceive, and classify English and Spanish in those structures.

Notes

1. A less drastic biological solution is described by Falcón (1984:21), who cites a *New York Times* article (4 April 1901 p. 5) reporting that agents recruiting Puerto Rican labor "have orders to enlist no Spaniards, and no blacks of unmixed blood are to be taken, the idea being to have the men marry Hawaiian women and thus lose their identity with Puerto Rico." The idea here was not so much to reduce the population as to disconnect it.

2. Discussion of U.S. education and language policy in Puerto Rico is provided by Osuna 1949; Epstein 1970; Negrón de Montilla 1975; Zentella 1981; Walsh 1991.

3. Perin documents the developers' philosophy of "like living with like": one developer said that people who buy $40,000 homes are "a different class people" from those who buy $60,000 homes (1977:85).

4. Sharff (personal communication September 1994) points out that while some housing in the area was physically upgraded to price families out of the market, other housing, though not upgraded, was rented at particularly high rents to drug dealers.

5. The Hispanic Study Project surveyed the correlation of ethnic surnames and housing conditions. Of the Spanish surnames surveyed, two-thirds lived in poor or deteriorated buildings and one-third in fair buildings while "white Jews and Slavics" lived in excellent, good, and fair buildings (Interfaith Adopt-A-Building 1978:7).

6. There were 101 residential units, of which 100 were occupied. As far as I could tell, 68 were occupied by white residents (predominantly Eastern European, judging by the names on the mailboxes), 16 Puerto Rican or other Latin, 5 African American, 5 Asian, and 6 unknown.

7. A building is abandoned when the landlord has stopped providing services—heat, repairs, and so on—and paying property taxes. After three years of tax arrears, ownership is ceded to the city, which may then sell the building at auction. Abandoned buildings are usually targets of vandalism and frequently of arson. In 1978–1979, large portions (often half or more) of blocks in this section of the Lower East Side were either city-owned or in tax arrears, which seriously undercut the local tax base (Interfaith Adopt-A-Building Inc., 1978).

8. This is translated from Spanish; the original follows.

El blanco quiere ser rico, siempre quiere estar arriba. Entonces porque nostros somos hispanos y somos negros, pues ellos nos tienen a nostros como si nosotros fuéramos de abajo. Y no podemos jamás en la vida igualarnos hacia ellos en ninguna posición.

Chapter 3

The Political Topography of Bilingualism

Walking into Boundaries

Late in the afternoon of January 12, 1978, I walked up N Street for the first time, looking for the study project office. I had gotten off the subway two stops early and had walked most of West N and much of East N before I found the address I wanted. It was chilly and damp and starting to get dark. Near the end of the block, I saw a boy in his mid-teens watching me approach. He held a portable radio on his shoulder tuned to a disco station. I thought he looked the epitome of a Puerto Rican street kid and wondered what I had gotten myself into. When I was a few yards away, he asked if I were looking for the study project office. I said I was. "Right in there," he said, and pointed to an open door.

Months later, I asked Luis Molina how he knew what I was looking for. "What else would a white person be looking for in this neighborhood?" he said, and asked if being approached by "this Puerto Rican kid" had made me nervous? I said yeah, a little, and what had he thought when he saw me? "What's this white woman want here?" At the moment of meeting, each of us epitomized to the other the opposing category. Although we soon became acquainted (and have now known each other for many years), this fact has remained, small and usually unspoken but always there, in all my relations with people I knew here.

In "Fieldwork in Common Places," Pratt (1986) describes significant moments of meeting in ethnographic literature. In literary reconstructions of such moments, authors crystallize key perceptions of the ethnographer/subject opposition, perceptions rooted in the politics of fieldwork. The political is precisely what I wish to foreground in Luis's and my accounts of our meeting. The opposition, in all its manifestations, between *Puerto Rican* and *white* or *American* has rung through and shaped all relations with everyone in this account. Things could hardly be otherwise,

73

since the opposition generally shapes bilingual New York Puerto Rican life, as this chapter, based on eighteen months of research in 1978–1979, demonstrates.

Making Linguistic Sense out of the White Woman

When I began working on N Street, I thought that relations would take some time to develop. This turned out to be true. I also thought that my having recently come from Puerto Rico with freshly tuned-up Spanish would provide an entrée. This turned out not to be true. As I met people, they humored, tolerated, or ignored my Spanish while making up their minds about my intentions. For example, Luz Guzmán and Carlos González usually ignored my attempts to initiate Spanish but Carlos might tease me in Spanish, especially at dances and parties. If I were with Nilsa, Luz, and Luisa, they would code-switch to each other and talk to me in English. If I were with Nilsa and Jenny, Jenny would speak to me in Spanish and Nilsa would sometimes summarize in English or check to see if I understood, which I often didn't in rapid conversation.

To teenagers and children, my use of Spanish did not fit my "white" persona. They reacted in different ways. For example, starting a few days after we met, Luis would sometimes insert a Spanish comment, question, or interjection in our conversation, sometimes asking what I thought of a person or situation. I asked if he were testing me, and he said he was, to see how good my Spanish was. He would also tease me about the American accent in my Spanish and imitate an American speaking Spanish. On the other hand, his younger brother Jesús expressed polite surprise at my Spanish but never spoke it with me. Adelina Mendoza's teenage son Reynaldo would move away from me if I spoke Spanish; I suspect he found it intrusive. Marilyn laughed one day at a remark I made in Spanish, telling me I "said the words right and all" but my pronunciation sounded "funny"—not in English, just in Spanish. Rosa Rivera's son Rafael said that I mixed up both English and Spanish in my accent so that part of a word sounded English and part Spanish. Luz's daughter Terri said of a comment I'd made in Spanish, "Say it in English. I didn't understand a word you said."

With time, adults found ways to become comfortable with my Spanish. Jenny made a point of correcting my errors and exhorting me to practice. On one occasion, we had been kidding around about dieting; when I switched from Spanish to English in mid-answer, she said, "*Habla español, tu puedes, tu sabes hablar y tienes que practicar*" (Speak Spanish, you can, you know how to speak and you have to practice). By the time I left New York in September 1979, she, Carlos, and Rosa pronounced my Spanish much improved, Carlos chalking it up to my Italian blood, which he once told me was "practically Latin." The last couple of months before I left, I realized that Rosa had been greeting me in Spanish, or asking me things like "*¿A donde vas?*" (Where are you going?). When I asked if she realized she was doing it, she said no. But she taught me Spanish "snaps" (teasing insults, as they were then called) to call out to non-Latin ballplayers at games in Yankee stadium. Others never quite became comfortable with my Spanish. Adelina Mendoza said she "kept forgetting" I knew Spanish although she did occasionally speak it to me. Once, while watching slides I had taken in Puerto Rico, she commented in Spanish on the scenery and how she'd love to be able to afford a trip. My occasional use of Spanish sometimes generated another boundary. When Lena Johnson, often excluded by the women's Spanish, heard me give Jenny a telephone message from her daughter in Spanish, she snapped, "What was that, Bonnie? I don't understand all this Spanish."

Toward the end of my stay, José (Marilyn's brother) and Terri would occasionally switch words or phrases with me—*porqué* (because); *d'eso* (that whatever-it-is, one of those); "there's this apartment in there *que tiene como cinco cuartos*" (that has like five rooms)." Still, like other children and teens, they could not reconcile my persona with Spanish and to the very end they found it "weird." When he was thirteen (in 1979), José said of my accent: "The sound, it comes out more different from real people's Spanish." His sister also found the accent odd and thought my words sounded unfinished. José also said he was unaware he was speaking Spanish to me: "It just came out."

In some ways, people's perceptions of me shifted with time. My part in this process consisted of waiting while finding ways to connect. The study project that I had joined in January 1978 had built itself local credit on which I could draw. I tutored after school and taught arts and crafts in the summer and on Saturdays. I also made strategic errors. After I had been on N Street a few months and had begun telling people about my project, I thought I should let people see me take notes (I was mapping social interaction along N Street) and I ended up looking like a social worker nosing around unasked. Some people tuned me out, a few probably for good, others for a few weeks. Eventually the incident was allowed to pass.

In time, I got to know families through the children I tutored. I was rarely asked to interpret, but I was often asked to make sense of bureaucratic regulations or to prepare forms. I did the study of boys' language between September and December 1978, writing it up in spring of 1979. During this time I got to know Fernando, the oldest member of the boys' clique. He had been in legal trouble and none of his family would go to court with him so I did, four times. I did this out of concern and affection for Fernando and gratitude for his help with the boys' language project, but it paid unexpected dividends when Rosa Rivera told me she had worried about Fernando and was relieved that I was willing to watch out for him.

It is willfully naive to expect that these people would see me as anything other than white, but with time my whiteness was less constantly intrusive. Many of the people I met those first months reminded me of some of my own aunts and cousins; perhaps that made it easier for me to act in ways that made local sense. Still much of what I did never made sense to people, and what I did must have seemed very white. If people created places for me to speak Spanish and told me I didn't always "act white," they in effect acknowledged one moment in our relationship when points of opposition dissolved. But there were many more moments when points of opposition crystallized. Given the politics framing our relations, it could not have been otherwise.

The central problem was how to represent what I was there to study. I told people I had come to study their use of English and Spanish and the circumstances shaping that use. To me this was a neutral object of study. To most of them it was not: if nothing were wrong with the way they spoke, why study it? The demurrals raised during my first fieldwork helped me formulate the object of study in my second and, finally, in this book. When working-class Puerto Rican experience with the middle-class white world is framed by stigmatization, it is disingenuous, even arrogant for any analyst to expect them to cede the terms of their own experience to those of academic authority. When Luz told Carlos, who was reluctant to be interviewed, that "it isn't like she's trying to find out all about our lives and everything, she just wants to do research about the way we talk," Luz was being kind about my intentions but Carlos's apprehensions were accurately founded. I could not do research about how they talked without finding out about their lives. For the project participants, supplying natural speech data in a project like this is risky. As analyst, I may promise to use this data in neutral ways, but I cannot prevent readers from focusing on just those aspects that seem most marked. Moreover (as Carlos also pointed out), the analyst arrives, defines terms, gathers data, and leaves. The analyzed stay where they are.

Spheres of Relationships and Communities of Speakers: The Politics of Linguistic Experience

Code refers to a language or dialect; here, broadly, English and Spanish are codes. Codes are not automatically loaded with cultural meaning: people develop their sense of what codes mean in specific relations and contexts. People may assume one code to be normative in a particular context. They may use another code as contrast to shift what happens in that context. They may also have different notions of what the same code means in different relationships. Analytically, then, the social politics of relationships comes before interpretations of code.

Whether or not people regard English and Spanish as rigidly separate depends on the dynamics of the situation. Sometimes the social functions of language—the ways people use language, for example, scolding, teasing, gossiping—can be done in either code or in both, code-switched. There is no clear sense of code boundary. At other times, one code may specifically heighten the function by making the scolding more pointed, the play funnier, the gossip more biting. In these cases, a sense of distinction between English and Spanish becomes important. This sense of language boundary can flicker in and out of existence in a single conversation, depending on such subtle dynamics as someone leaving or joining the conversation. This plasticity of boundary disappears when the same bilinguals act as tenants, employees, students, patients, or clients, when they must talk to landlords, bosses, teachers, doctors, or bureaucrats. In these relationships, authority structures are reinforced by race/class polarities and English displaces Spanish. Spanish itself and any index of Spanish can be marked and risky in these contexts.

Since code boundaries fade or emerge depending on the politics of relationships, it is helpful to classify situations by equality structure rather than by code. Everyone deals with authority at some point, seeing a doctor, facing a boss, or taking an exam. But when patient and doctor, or boss and employee are both white and middle-class, authority itself is the only important point of contrast. To use a topographical metaphor, the "slope" between the people involved is minimal. The slope increases as authority, class, and race differences polarize, and the slope maximizes when gender polarizes as well. A white, male corporate executive talks to his doctor across a shallow slope and need not shout to be heard. A black or Puerto Rican woman on AFDC talks to her doctor up a very considerable slope, and she is the one who must work to be heard. Not only are gatekeepers in social service agencies more responsive to clients who are most like them, as Erickson (1975) has shown, they are more responsive to clients to whom they must listen. The less seriously people are taken, the more they are regarded as a disordered mass. The familiar, comfortable mixed Spanish-English world of New York Puerto Ricans is seen by social workers, doctors, or teachers as a paradigm of sociolinguistic disorder. Puerto Rican clients, patients, or students are responsible for keeping their English orderly and their Spanish out of earshot.

I propose the idea of *spheres of interaction* as a starting point for code analysis. Spheres are sets of relations polarized by axes of social inequality. One's inner sphere is made of relations with people most equal to one; one's outer sphere is made of relations with people who have structural advantages over one. There is no precise line between inner and outer; the key distinction is the polarity of equality. For people whose lives and options are not greatly constrained by race and class difference, the polarity is minimal. The more race and class disadvantage limits people's options, the greater the polarity.

Linguistic differences are mapped onto this polarity. Working-class Puerto Ricans have an *inner sphere* of relations among family, friends, and neighbors with whom English is no problem. Their *outer sphere* is defined by relations with bosses, landlords, teachers, doctors, social workers, and others with the advantage of authority, class, and stereotypically (though not always actually) race; with these people, English can be a problem. Between these poles are more or less neutral relations with Anglophone storeowners, co-workers, and other relatively distant people who have no direct authority over one; these do not concern us here.

The idea of spheres shifts focus from codes per se to what speakers do with codes. In his work on the ecology of language, Haugen (1972:329) stresses the importance of not assuming that codes naturally exist as clearly defined entities. This is the foundation of his study of Norwegian-Americans in the midwest (Haugen 1969), which documents the varieties of English that co-evolved with Norwegian in all the places where Norwegians dealt with Americans or American social concepts: farms, markets, work, school, and so on. Similarly, Puerto Rican immigrants and their families have developed uses and forms of English that work with Spanish in their everyday, urban U.S. life. This English can be borrowed from or switched with Spanish; it can be used to tease, scold, gossip, and generally carry out everyday functions of language. It has expanded and reorganized functional resources available in Spanish.

The Language Policy Task Force at the Center for Puerto Rican Studies (1980), Pedraza (1987) and Zentella (1982, 1997) have studied the bilingual networks of East Harlem at length. In these networks, Spanish is the baseline language but there is little predictable code compartmentalization, in which Spanish always fills one social function and English another. These researchers stress the importance of analyzing Spanish and English in specific contexts without presupposing their existence in the separate domains described by Fishman, Cooper, and Ma (1971). Romaine (1989:281ff) questions whether there is any point to classifying a code-switched speech event by one code or the other and even questions the assumption that codes themselves are stored in separate cognitive compartments.

The linguistic world of the New York Puerto Rican working class is woven into that of their African American neighbors. The boundaries are not fixed. Points of language contrast emerge, as when Puerto Ricans cut to Spanish in front of black neighbors, but such contrast can also fade. Other boundaries may fade as well, as when shared class identity ("poor people like us," as Rosa Rivera once put it) subsumes being Puerto Rican or black. Given these considerations, the idea of a bilingual speech community is misleading if it implies a discrete group sharing two discrete codes and sets of rules of use. The idea of a speech community is useful when it refers to relations in which people co-negotiate meaning and identity; Hymes's (1974) and Gumperz's (1968) formulations of speech communities both highlight the importance of social relations. Milroy's (1980) idea of an interactive network conserving in-group forms and meanings (see Gal 1979:12) is also central to this sense of speech community, but as Dorian (1982) suggests, the group's boundaries or "working margins" depend in large part on how the group defines itself.

As Zentella (1997) shows in detail, linguistic activity in New York Puerto Rican neighborhoods encompasses a wide range of Spanish and English formal variation, and the pragmatics of switching are complex. These patterns of language use evolve in network relations and are never fully predictable. The working margins of such a community include people whose Spanish fluency is limited but who deploy it in socially effective ways. One does not need to speak Spanish to be considered Puerto Rican, but one does need a Puerto Rican family. Nor is English a simple index of American assimilation: people can be interpenetratingly "Puerto Rican" and "American" at the same time (Flores, Attinasi, and Pedraza 1981). Spanish is always desirable but not always possible.

Pragmatically, the bottom line means respecting and accommodating the preferences of Spanish-dominant, usually older, speakers and knowing when to express regret for one's inability to accommodate fluently in Spanish. I knew several boys whose Spanish was minimal but who knew when and to whom to make this expression of regret. Adults see it as their responsibility to teach younger people what they need to know and allow for the possibility that younger people might grow into a fuller knowledge of Spanish (see also Attinasi 1983). Unfortunately, as Zentella points out, there are few institutional channels that can effect that growth. Children who do not know enough Spanish to show respect, to code-switch fluently, or to talk to a recent arrival are regarded as "less than fully active" (Language Policy Task Force 1982:165). Moreover, as I argued in the previous chapter, Puerto Rican and African American neighbors do share networks, speech events, and a common identity grounded in a common habitus distanced from middle-class whites.

The Puerto Rican speech community is in effect an inner sphere linguistic habitus without neat boundaries. Its linguistic actions enact relations in particular contexts. In terms of speech event structure (Hymes 1974, after Jakobson 1960), its settings are routine and comfortable. Participants are equal in race and class. Where they are unequal (in gender, age, generation, family role) the inequalities can sometimes be negotiated or mitigated. Goals and topics are familiar and consensual, not forced by official requirements. People respect each other's code choices. Words, sounds, and grammar are not labeled "broken" or "mistaken." English and Spanish are formally and pragmatically familiar and people routinely code-switch, alternating English and Spanish words, clauses, or sentences.[1]

Frequent sentence-internal switching may affect the formal structure of the language varieties involved. Citing his own work on U.S. Norwegians and work by Gumperz and Wilson (1971) in India, Haugen (1972:335) proposes this as a principle of language ecology:

> In stable bilingual communities there is a further accommodation between symbiotic languages, such that they cease to reflect distinct cultural worlds: their sentences approach a word-for-word translatability, which is rare among really autonomous languages.

A similar argument can be made for Spanish and English in New York. Poplack's formulation of the Equivalence Constraint (1979) shows that New York Puerto Rican intrasentential switching preserves intact grammatical structures of both English and Spanish. This is most likely to happen at a sentence or clause boundary but fluent switchers do it at phrase boundaries with great élan. Here, Luz Guzmán switches at a conjoined sentence boundary in answer to a request from a neighbor's child for an egg from the carton in her grocery bag:

> *Dame los cincuenta y nueve chavos* [Give me the fifty-nine cents] and you could do whatever you want with all of them.

José, describing an apartment building down the street, switches at a relative clause boundary:

> There's this apartment in there *que tiene como cinco cuartos* [that has like five rooms].

Carmen from our project office switches at a prepositional phrase boundary:

> *Empezó ese revolú* [This uproar started] down in the basement.

Here Carmen switches within a noun phrase (though the status of hamburger—whether switch or borrowing—is indeterminate):

Me mandó un [he sent me a] hamburger with cheese on it.

In each case, people switch at points where the structures of each language are syntactically parallel. What they do not say, for example, is "Started *ese revolú*" (where the switch would violate English subject-verb order) or "He sent *me un. . . "* which would violate Spanish verb and personal object pronoun *(me)* order.

Poplack herself argues against the existence of formal convergence (in Spanish at least, see Pousada and Poplack 1979)[2] but her statistical verification of an Equivalence Constraint suggests that over generations of frequently switched discourse, people come to favor patterns and meanings common to both languages and to make less use of those that are not. Klein (1980) confirms this in her study of New York Puerto Rican bilinguals who lean toward a present progressive form common to both English and Spanish to refer to the moment of speaking with less use of the Spanish simple present. This does not look like formal interference (or convergence) if the pattern is grammatical in either language, but bilinguals gradually work out formal use and a semantic shift that fits their situation (Romaine 1989:162ff). In some cases, this may lead to the formal convergence that Gumperz and Wilson describe; in other cases, it may not. Whatever the outcome, such formal continuities challenge the idea of monolithic code distinctions.

Pragmatically, the analysis of code-switching involves knowing how speakers perceive each other, how marked either code is at a given moment, and how the speech situation is structured (see Gumperz 1982; Heller 1988; Scotton 1988 for discussion). It cannot be done without extensive knowledge of people's relations in context, as Zentella's (1997) East Harlem study demonstrates. Using Goffman's (1981:124–159) notion of "footing"—shifts in the construction of self/other relations—and drawing on a database of 103 hours of code-switched conversation among children, she shows the range of discourse functions marked by code-switches. Shifts of footing marked by code-switching may not differ in kind from shifts of footing in monolingual speech. The contrast itself, rather than the particular code, may do the pragmatic work (Valdés 1981). A code-switch may mark a *we/they* distinction as Gumperz (1982) argues, but this must be decided on the basis of context-specific social function, not code alone (Singh 1983).

As Gal (1979) has shown, functions identified with one code or the other can shift as people's roles and social world change. Contrasting New York Puerto Rican patterns with those found among Francophone speakers in Ottowa-Hull, Canada (a far more overtly ideologized linguistic atmosphere), Poplack (1988) argues that the frequent intrasentential switching of New York Puerto Ricans has minimal rhetorical importance. Zentella's close analysis of New York code-switching suggests this assessment is too broad but Poplack raises an important point: there has been significant functional convergence between inner-sphere English and Spanish. In fact, inner-sphere English and Spanish do not map neatly onto relations of power and solidarity (after Brown and Gilman 1960) whereas in outer-sphere relations, Spanish is far more likely to map onto solidarity relations and English onto power relations.

The problem lies in the confusion of linguistic ideology and linguistic practice. When people ideologize language, they talk about it as a concrete object. In doing so, the essence they distill masks everyday ambiguities. Language as a compendious and discrete thing becomes what Sapir called a condensation symbol, that is, involving "meanings which cannot be derived directly from the contexts of experience" and which "expresses a condensation of energy" (1949:564). This condensation is grounded in the politics of the outer sphere, but inner-sphere life is never quite free of its penetration. There may always be moments in which a solidarity/power contrast is indeed mapped onto inner-sphere code-switching but, as Zentella found, it is difficult to find predictable patterns connecting strategies linked to code with symbolic values traditionally associated with Spanish and English. Values belong to Spanish and English as discrete and incommensurate condensation symbols. Code-switching belongs to practice in which, as Alvarez (1988:171) explains:

> The relationships established in any social context need to be discovered, rather than merely assumed on the basis of fixed, external social categories.

Life in the Inner Sphere

Creating a Common Culture in Inner-Sphere Language

Inner-sphere genres such as gossip and teasing establish a sense of cultural focus. Gossip in particular recreates a moral point of reference. When people gossip, they refer to and judge actions that are culturally problematic and reinforce each other's sense of right and wrong. When bilingual women do this in Spanish, they recreate the connection between Spanish itself and their own moral and cultural center: "This is how we should be," particularly "we mothers." People who do not speak Spanish may well be excluded from such discussions, but bilingual women see that as a "natural" mistake, not as deliberate exclusion. At the same time, such moments bring forth sharp linguistic and cultural boundaries. The following scene is an illustration.

Lena Johnson (who is African American) had told Rosa and two other neighbors, all Puerto Rican, about a fight between her daughter Candy and another girl. Lena won considerable sympathy at first as the other three women disparaged the other girl's behavior and compared that of their own daughters. Functionally (Hymes 1974), their conversation was *referential* in that they described a series of events. It was *phatic* in that they gave each other feedback, letting each other know they were tuned in. It was *directive* in that they were persuading each other how to act in such a situation. Above all, it was *expressive* in that they asserted their knowledge and authority as mothers. Indeed, the three

Puerto Rican women became increasingly expressive as they described how to raise children properly ("What I tell my child is—").

For the first few minutes, as Lena retold the story of the fight and how angry it made her, they responded and commented in English. As Lena continued talking about how silly both girls had been, the other women focused increasingly on what the other girl's mother should have done, explicitly formulating and discussing rules for proper child rearing—in Spanish. Soon Lena felt blindsided by "all that Spanish" (as she so often put it) apparently coming out of nowhere.

What blindsided Lena was a shift in the functional organization when the three Puerto Rican women expressed and formulated a specific style of cultural behavior and affirmed its moral rightness. This seems natural to the participants. As Rosa put it:

> Like Lena, she get mad the other day, they told me. But she have to understand that we're Spanish people, right? We forget easily that she can't talk Spanish. But it's not that we talk about her, anything like that, no.

"We're Spanish people" means that their functional solidarity, expressed in Spanish, generates a strong sense of cultural focus. This excuses "forgetting" and speaking Spanish in front of someone who does not know it, an act otherwise regarded as rude. Lena only sees the rudeness, because the idea of such an "accident" does not seem possible to her. As she said later:

> They never "just forget." They pretend on purpose that they forget, like when they pretend on purpose that they don't know English. I know they know it.

This ideology of "forgetting" is markedly female. Men, at least young men, do not "forget" but they do speak of sharing Spanish with black friends. Luisa's husband Hector reminisces:

> If you lived someplace where practically everybody was Spanish and if a black guy would hang out with us enough, he would start talking Spanish. He would know a lot of the words and even understand everything, you know? Being that he already felt comfortable and he knew that we weren't talking about him.

Teenage boys' groups are frequently mixed Puerto Rican and black. The groups overwhelmingly spoke English, but there were instances of emblematic Spanish slang and swear words that seemed to be understood by all the boys. For example, Rafy Rivera and his friends Leo, Jesús, and Daniel (all Puerto Rican, ages twelve to fourteen) engaged in this bit of dialogue while cleaning the yard one autumn afternoon:

> Jesús: Ring around the socks.
> Rafy: Look at that.
> Leo: Look at that leg from here, c'mere.
> Dan: *Cabrón,* it stinks.[3]

Several hours of recorded conversation turn up a tiny handful of such instances, usually initiated by Dan. Later on, Gus, an African American member of the group, picks up Dan's lead:

Rafy: Yo, man—
Dan: *Cigarillo pa' mi.* [Cigarette for me.]
Rafy: Yo, Gus, man, I wanna say—
Gus: *¿Cabrón, qué pasa?* [Bro, what's up?]

This highly formulaic bit of emblematic Spanish initiated no more switching but it let the others know that Gus was equally tuned to the common channel; that is, it was phatic. I noticed similar usages in the older boys' group, where the black member used similar phrases *(qué pasa, qué tal)* and epithets. Gus said he had taken Spanish in school and his brother knew even more; a Puerto Rican friend confirmed the value of this accomplishment. Such occasional emblematic uses are performance, enacting a way to be "young guys together." As a couple of the boys put it, "We be thinking alike." By contrast, by "forgetting" that someone present does not know Spanish (which men and boys insist they never do), women enact an equal-but-relatively-separate identity.

Puerto Rican and African American relations are far from perfect, and sometimes when boys or young men use Spanish, it creates a sharp sense of boundary. So it is ideologically important for boys or young men to agree that the Spanish is shared, something they all know. In this way, the use of Spanish can highlight "us neighborhood guys together" over Puerto Rican versus black. By contrast, when women "forget" and speak Spanish, they highlight what it means to be a Puerto Rican woman.

In both the boys' group talk and the women's gossip, what one talks about depends on who one is vis-à-vis the group. This in turn affects one's presentation style. In both genres, the speaker *(I)* relates to the addressee *(you)* with a sense of person tightly tailored to the group, forming a focused sense of *us*. When young guys are acting most "together" or women defining themselves as most "Spanish," *I* and *you* match up point-of-view for point-of-view. The result is a clearly aligned sense of *our* identity.

Such moments in artful, playful, and gossipy speech are deictically tight: like a knot, they pull together strands that define who and what one is, creating a *here* and *now* that makes sense to people like *us,* forming a point from which understanding and judgment radiate—in effect a moral center. This, Haviland (1977) argues, is the function of gossip, defined as it is by its concern with moral arbitration, criticizing, and justifying the actions of others. Artful, playful, and gossipy speech are highly performative, acts of discourse that affect or create social reality, embracing first and foremost a sense of *us*. This need not emerge as a specific sense of "Puerto Rican" versus "American" and can embrace elements of both.

In the inner sphere, people are most metacommunicatively in tune with each other, using linguistic signals to establish a shared frame of interpretation (see Hymes 1974; Bauman 1977; and Goffman 1974 after Bateson 1972). This is where people joke, tease, and play on an equal basis. This is the site of Fernandez's quality space (1986) and Friedrich's poetic imagination (1986). In outer-sphere relations, as Chapter 5 shows, people get teased but not in play among equals. This is meta-communicative bullying by someone able to impose an interpretive frame. Where inner-sphere teasing recreates a common cultural identity, outer-sphere teasing re-inforces racialized stereotypes.

Playing Around in the Inner Sphere

The following transcript of a 1979 Saturday afternoon in Jenny's apartment gives a fair sample of inner-sphere language. Jenny was cooking in the kitchen. Her daughter Iris was bathing, dressing, and feeding Iris' baby Yolanda. Luis, his brother Leo, their friend Camy, and I were talking and watching television in the living room, where I had set up the tape recorder. At this point I had known them for a year and a half and was often in the house. My presence may have made for more English than usual but the switching dynamics seemed the same as usual.

Below are selections from two intersecting speech events. In speech event #1, Luis, Leo, Camy, and I watch and comment sarcastically on the television show *Space 1999*. We are occasionally joined by the child of a visiting friend of Jenny's (the voice marked "Child"). The second takes place in the middle of the first: Jenny comes into the living room and scolds Leo and Luis. Each speaker's turn is numbered to facilitate the analyses that follows.[4]

Television emits weird science-fiction sounds.

1.   Luis: That's not supposed to look like that room.
2.   Camy: They're in a different room, they're in a blue room—that's the way he looks.
3.   Luis: Yeah he looks—
4.   Camy: See, they're in a blue room— you see, *eso es allá*. [It's over there]. (Pause) Look at his hotpants! (Laughter)
5.   Luis: Shortpants!
6.   Camy: He got some terrific hotpants!
7. Bonnie: Oh he's gorgeous.
8.   Camy: Huh?
9. Bonnie: What are you watching? What is this?
10.   Luis: "Space 1999."
11. Bonnie: Oh. I've never seen this.
12.   Leo: *¡Uy, qué feo!* [How ugly!]
13. Bonnie: *¿Verdad?* [Right?]
14.   Luis: That was that little boy.
15.   Leo: I know.
16. Bonnie: That's what the little boy became?
17.   Luis: Uh huh.
18.   Camy: That was the little boy wasn't it?
19.   Luis: Yeah.
20.   Camy: I told you he was gonna be a traitor.
21.   Leo: *¿Quién es ése?* [Who is that?] Who's that?

22.   **Luis:** [[*El xxxxxx.*]]
23.   **Camy:** It's all in the eyes, you know?
24.   **Leo:** What he's doing?
25.   **Luis:** He's forcing—
26.   **Camy:** He's got some kind of power—
27.   **Luis:** —he's forcing him to do something that—
28.   **Camy:** —that they don't wanna do.
29.   **Child:** What they gonna do?

Television dialog: "Hold your fire."

30.   **Leo:** *¿Qué le pasa?* [What's happening to him?]
31.   **Luis:** They're sending something.
32.   **Leo:** *¡Oh no, mi—uy! Qué es eso?* [Uh-oh, my—what's that?]
33.   **Luis:** *Una muchacha—* [A girl—]
34.   **Leo:** *¿Cuál? ¿La que el tenía?* [Which one? The one who was with him?]

Pause as everyone watches the screen.

35.   **Leo:** Luis, *mira,* [look] they're giving her some power I think. *La están matando.* [They're killing her.]
36.   **Luis:** He's killing her—
37.   **Camy:** (Overlapping Luis) *Él tiene un ojo mas chiquito que el otro.* [One of his eyes is smaller than the other.]
38.   **Luis:** —he's making a baby that's what he's doing—
39.   **Camy:** (Repeats sarcastically) He's making a baby.

We all laugh.

40.   **Leo:** *¡Qué loco!* [He's nuts!]
41. **Bonnie:** Luis, you always got your mind on the same thing.
42.   **Luis:** He's making love through his mind—
43.   **Leo:** Now he's giving her that—how you call that?
44.   **Luis:** It's sperm cells.
45.   **Leo:** —power to her so she could become one of them.
46.   **Luis:** He's giving her sperm.
47.   **Child:** He's killing her.
48.   **Camy:** He's getting her high, that's what it is.
49.   **Luis:** He's getting her horny, that's what's he's doing. (Giggles) He's turning her on. You see, ah, watch her get up—
50.   **Camy:** Oh, look at this. I mean, now she got makeup on, she's all sexy and all.
51. **Bonnie:** Mmm.
52.   **Luis:** Told you she looks sexy now, she gots her pajamas on.
53. **Bonnie:** Oh, she was putting somebody else's mind in there.
54.   **Camy:** Yeah and—
55. **Bonnie:** I bet he was—
56.   **Leo:** —*poniéndole, este,* [giving her, um—] power to her.
57. **Bonnie:** Right.
58.   **Leo:** That's what he was trying to do.
59.   **Camy:** *Por eso la mujer se hizo pasar—* [That's why the woman pretended to be—]
60.   **Luis:** He's gonna disappear, watch.

61.   Camy: I don't see anything.
62.   Luis: I told you they'd disappear. (Pause)
63.   Luis: Ah, you see, they shut off the light. (Luis picks up Yolanda, teasing her in Spanish.) Come here, *ton ton—ven acá piloncito, ven acá piloncito.* [Come here, cutie pie.]

A television commercial comes up. A minute or two passes while Iris tells Luis to stop teasing the baby. Then Jenny enters, addressing Iris and launching into speech event #2 for 40 turns after which event #1 resumes.

How a speech event plays out depends in part on its participant structure: the relationships among the participants and how their interaction is culturally organized (Philips 1983). Also important is their metacommunicative awareness, their perception of the signals by which people know how to "take" the event at hand (seriously, playfully, ironically). In play, people take a routine "strip of action" and fashion a nonliteral version of it, a secondary text which selectively distorts elements of the primary text (Basso 1979; Goffman 1974).

Camy, Leo, and Luis mix playful and straight (non-playful) comments on the show's action. Straight comments include literal descriptions (4: See, they're in a blue room, you see, *eso es allá*), explanations (35: *Mira,* they're giving her some power I think. *La están matando)* and evaluations (12: *¡Uy, qué feo!).* Interspersed with these are playful descriptions and explanations that reinterpret, often in sexualized ways, on-screen objects (4: Look at his hotpants) or activities (38: He's making a baby, that's what he's doing; 48: He's getting her high). Play is largely metacommunicated by facial expression and vocal inflection ("tone of voice") and by the exaggerated nature of the reference; how much is metacommunicated by code is less clear.

The participant structure consists of three adolescents on equal footing. They differ from each other in how much they talk and how much English or Spanish they use. In all of speech event #1 (part of which is omitted here), Camy takes 40 turns, Luis takes 32 and Leo 24. Luis's turns are 84.4 percent English, 12.5 percent Spanish, and 3.1 percent code-switched. Camy's turns are 57.5 percent English, 30 percent Spanish, and 12.5 percent code-switched. Leo's turns are 41.7 percent English, 37.5 percent Spanish, and 20.8 percent code-switched.

They also differ from each other in how much they play and in the functions of their straight comments. Straight comments ask for information, describe, agree, explain or interpret, exclaim or interject.[5] Luis never asks for information. He describes (21.9 percent of his total functions), agrees (9.4 percent), explains or interprets (34.4 percent), and interjects (3.1 percent). Out of his comments, 31 percent are playful. Leo asks for information (16.1 percent), describes (19.4 percent), agrees (12.9 percent), explains or interprets (32.3 percent), and exclaims or interjects (19.4 percent) but makes no playful comments. Camy asks for information (4.3 percent), describes (15.2 percent), agrees (4.3 percent), explains or interprets (41.3 percent), and exclaims or interjects (4.3 percent). Out of her comments, 30.4 percent are playful.

Camy and Luis take the most turns and are functionally similar: each does a lot of describing, explaining, and playing. Neither asks for much information nor agrees much nor interjects much. By doing much of the explaining, asking few questions and doing little agreeing, they focus much more on their own perspective ("expressive" in Hymes's functional terminology) than does Leo, who does most of the describing, asking for information, agreeing, and interjecting. Camy and Luis also dominate the speech event by competing with each other in playful performance while Leo acts as the straight man.

Luis and Camy contrast in how they use Spanish in their performances. Luis uses Spanish once in each straight function: describing (one of seven times that he describes), agreeing (one of three), explaining (one of eleven) or interjecting (one of one). He uses no Spanish in his playful comments. Camy uses Spanish much more frequently: in asking for information (one of two times that she asks), describing (four of seven), explaining or interpreting (five of nineteen), exclaiming or interjecting (one of two). Four of fourteen playful comments are in Spanish. Leo uses the most Spanish, much of it in code-switches. The only function he does in English alone is agreeing (four times); otherwise he uses Spanish while asking for information (four of five times), describing (four of six), explaining or interpreting (three of ten), exclaiming or interjecting (five of six).

What emerges are three different personal patterns that work together. Camy talks the most. Leo uses the most Spanish. Camy and Luis have the same functional patterns, but Camy does much more of it in Spanish than Luis does. Luis's preference for English may be gender-linked (though that does not explain Leo); Camy's preference for Spanish almost certainly is.[6] What results is a functionally convergent speech event in which it matters little which function is in which code because each participant's preferred pattern works.

Spanish may be triggered by the addressee's persona. For example, Camy and Luis switch into Spanish to address the baby. Iris walked in during the second half of event #1, after Camy and Luis had been playing in English, and asked about one of the characters. For the next ten turns, Leo and Camy described and explained to Iris in Spanish what had happened. Camy then switched to English in the middle of an explanation. A few turns later, Camy, Luis, and Leo resumed a largely Spanish interchange:

128. **Camy:** *¡Uy!* (In disgust) *¡Qué hombre feo!* [What an ugly guy!]
129. **Luis:** *¿Víste qué feo?* [You saw how ugly he is?]
130. **Camy:** *Se puso feísimo, feísimo. Se puso mas viejo de la cuenta mas viejo que lo viejo.* (Laughs) [He turned really ugly, ugly! He became really, really old, as old as Methuselah.]
131. **Leo:** I know. *La única que yo no he visto es la que se cambia mucho, Mara.* [The only one I haven't seen is the one who changes a lot, Mara.]
132. **Camy:** *Ésa es ella, ésa fué la que cambió.* [That's her, she's the one that changed.]

Shortly thereafter I asked a question about a detail I had missed, and Luis and Camy developed a similar exchange in English.

Description, explanation and exclamation may involve formulas that flow more easily in Spanish, as in Camy and Luis's use of *qué feo* above and Leo's elsewhere.

Exclamations like *qué feo, qué loco,* or *míralo ahí,* and WH-questions (who, what, where, and so on) like *qué es eso* can be and often are said in English, but they are more presupposed (easier, more routine) in Spanish. However, the idioms that Camy uses in her Spanish play (130: *mas viejo que lo viejo* [older than old]) or *te tienen el tres y dos* "they got you bouncing around," used elsewhere) have no real English equivalent. Such usages reinforce a Spanish baseline.

In both speech events (#1 and #2), people play out distinct cultural dramatis personae. Code takes on different importance in each of these. In event #1, Spanish and English work in pragmatic syncretism, as Luis, Camy, and Leo play out their performance in ways that are both Puerto Rican and American. In event #2, through her scolding and teasing in Spanish, Jenny plays out a culture-specific "mother" persona, authoritative, smart, and ironic. Leo and Luis play out their roles as sons, not docile but not too rebellious. Their uses of Spanish and English highlight dimensions of these personae in ways that do not come into play in event #1 because the playfulness of the second event reinforces a sense of how to be Puerto Rican in ways that the playfulness of the first event does not. Goofing on television shows is embedded in the U.S. popular culture in which Leo, Luis, and Camy grew up. Teasing *mami* and being teased and scolded by her involves culture-specific Puerto Rican knowledge: knowing when one's mother is serious and when she is playing and just how far one can go in teasing her without being disrespectful.

Speech event #2 begins as Jenny enters the room where we are watching television.

64.   **Jenny:**   *¡Iris!*
65.   **Camy:**   *Ella te llamo allí.* [She called you over there.]
66.   **Iris:**   *¿Qué?* [What?]
67.   **Jenny:**   *El verano se acabó, el verano se acabó—* [The summer is over—]

Voices of Luis, Leo, Jenny, and Iris are heard in combination.

68.   **Jenny:**   *—esos pantalones te quedaban* high water. *Están pensando en el invierno o sea que sigan cortando los pantalones que cuando venga el invierno gritan porque no tienen pantalones.* [Those pants used to be "high-water" on you. You all are thinking about winter, so keep cutting your pants, when winter comes you'll all scream because you don't have any pants.]
69.   **Luis:**   *Mami, el verano no se ha acabado.* [Mom, summer hasn't finished yet.]
70.   **Jenny:**   *Bueno, está, está vera—el invierno* [well, it's summ—winter], right Bonnie? It's winter? (Leo and Luis laugh) Yes!
71. **Bonnie:**   It's getting there, I think, it's awful cold.
72.   **Luis:**   Uh-uh. You know what? We always—you know that it always—in August we get two weeks of, you know, Canadian air.
73. **Bonnie:**   Is that what it is?
74.   **Luis:**   That's what it is.
75. **Bonnie:**   Oh.
76.   **Luis:**   We're gonna get that for at least two or one and a half weeks.
77. **Bonnie:**   No, we already—

78:    **Luis:**   No, because every—

Jenny cuts in, unintelligibly overlapping Luis and me.

79.   **Leo:**   No, ah, ah, 'cause summer's not going to finish this year. They're not—
porque siempre hay mas que two months or one month *de* summer; *este* summer *va a seguir, va a haber* winter, (raising voice) *va a haber* winter—*va a ser
mitad y mitad.* [Because there's always more than two months or one
month of summer, this summer's going to continue, it'll be winter, it'll be
winter— it'll be half and half.]

80.   **Jenny:**   ¡*Va a haber* winter, *la mitad de* August—*ya empezó hoy!* [It'll be winter half
of August, it started today!]

81.   **Luis:**   It's not gonna—

82.   **Leo:**   You don't understand, *mami, mira, va a haber* summer. [Mom, look, it's going
to be summer.]

83.   **Jenny:**   *Empezó, estamos en otoño.* [It started, we're in autumn.]

84.   **Luis:**   No, no! (Raising his voice) *No estamos en otoño, otoño no empieza hasta sep-
tiembre mami!* [We're not in autumn, autumn doesn't start until September,
Mom!] Doesn't it start—doesn't it start in September or October?

85. **Bonnie:**   Autumn?

86.   **Luis:**   Let me see—

87. **Bonnie:**   September 23.

88.   **Luis:**   What? Right, September 23.

89. **Bonnie:**   September 23 officially but it feels like it started for real today.

90.   **Jenny:**   Right?!

91.   **Luis:**   It didn't start—!

92. **Bonnie:**   But it feels like it!

93.   **Jenny:**   *No importa que es la fecha, porque ellos pueden decir, ellos pueden decir ahora
mismo*— [It doesn't matter what date, because they can say, they can say
right now—]

94.   **Luis:**   *Mami,* but look! That [[xxx]] every year, *todos los años es lo mismo* [every year
is the same thing]: we get two weeks of cold air, my Go—forget it, you are
one hundred percent right. (Silence. Leo laughs.) Well? Any comment?

95.   **Jenny:**   *[[xx xx]] esa boca.* [—that mouth]

96.   **Luis:**   I guess [[xx xx xx]] your mouth shut. See, I know—

97.   **Jenny:**   (Raising her voice but laughing a little) *Para mí, empezó el invierno hoy
porque yo tengo frío.* [For me, winter already started, because I'm cold.]

98.   **Luis:**   Good for you then. Why didn't you say so?

99.   **Leo:**   *Mami eso es para tí* [Mom, that's how you feel] 'cause you feel cold.

100.   **Luis:**   So why didn't you say something? Now you can take your coat and go
downstairs and watch yourself you don't slip.

101.   **Leo:**   *No, que se ponga el que tenía los* children—(laughs) [No, let her put on the
one the children had on—]

102.   **Luis:**   *El* teddybear?

103.   **Leo:**   *El* teddybear—(laughs) *Mami, es tu* teddybear. [Mom, it's your teddybear].

104.   **Jenny:**   *Llévaselo allá a Iris, [[porque le doy]]. Vente, Yolanda.* [Bring it over there to Iris,
[[because I'll hit you]]. Come here, Yolanda.]

Commercial ends.

We resume speech event #1, watching and commenting on the television show until it ends.

Unlike event #1, the cultural script on which event #2 is based—how mothers raise children and how children should behave—has an important moral dimension: respect for a hard-working mother and her limited resources. Neither Leo nor Luis defend themselves from the charge of cutting up their pants. The play starts after Jenny's initial scolding (68) with her exaggerated reference to weather (70) and her willingness to tolerate some back-chat from Leo and Luis (69–103). She has finished scolding for the rest of event #2 though she returns to it later in the afternoon. Throughout the teasing, which grows out of the scolding, she retains her maternal authority. Each participant necessarily speaks from a position relative to hers.

Jenny establishes an interaction membrane (in Goffman's sense 1961:65) by tying a Spanish "authority knot" into her talk with Iris (also a mother) to start off the scold (64–67). This sets up performance of her mother persona. Luis answers in Spanish, setting himself up as counter authority (69). Jenny pulls in my testimony to back up her authority with a strategic little switch, "Right, Bonnie?" Here Jenny is negotiating my persona a bit. There were many occasions on which she spoke Spanish to me, as if I were one of her children. When she looks for authority support, she addresses me as an Anglophone adult.

Jenny sets up the play as stating a logical proposition which is what Luis targets when he invokes a scientific explanation of the weather (72). But Jenny (unlike Luis) is in charge of the rules which she cheerily changes as she goes along. The lines between Jenny and Luis are more sharply drawn than those between Leo and Jenny, though Leo also attempts an explanation, switching even more than in event #1 at constituent phrase boundaries (79). Jenny parodies Leo's switching (80); she herself switches at sentence boundaries. Leo gamely tries to convince her that summer isn't really over (82), but he does not appeal to an outside authority as Luis does, and she teasingly reasserts her own authority (83). Luis again (84) draws on a public scientific authority (the calendar), appealing to Jenny in Spanish and to me in English. I unhelpfully temporize, offering a statement that supports both arguments. Ultimately, Luis's arguing is useless since, as Jenny announces in 93–97 *("para mí")*, it is indeed what *she* says, never mind the date or when "they" say a season begins or ends. At this point, though she is teasing (evident in the remarks she lets Luis get away with in 96 and 98), she is first and foremost *mami*. This is a highly recreative piece of cultural discourse. Jenny's deployment of both English and Spanish gives her latitude for acting out how to be a mother that English alone certainly could not provide and that even Spanish alone might not.

Since play creates a reality that is not literally there, participants must make a concerted effort to sustain that reality, that is, to "get" the joke, with no literal reality check. Participants must each "take" the metacommunicative signals in the same ways or the participant structure falls apart, as Basso's (1979) analysis of Apache joking demonstrates. When people do "get" this pseudo-reality, their cultural self-definition and their relationships are reinforced. When play works, it is highly performative.

Forming a Metalinguistic Sense of Spanish

People's metalinguistic sense—how they define and analyze the elements of a language—is worked out over the course of their lives. A metalinguistic sense involves both private and public perceptions and experiences of language. New York Puerto Ricans have few opportunities to experience Spanish as a public language and, as children, they may find the dictionary version of Spanish jarringly dissonant from their experience. Some aspects of children's Spanish metalinguistic awareness can be seen in the following episodes.

In the first, Luz Guzmán's daughter Terri (age twelve) and José Mojica (age thirteen) are baking cookies in my apartment one July afternoon in 1979. While we wait for the oven to heat, Terri and José kill time looking up dirty words in my Spanish-English dictionary. They then switch to looking for Spanish equivalents of familiar English words. José asks how to say "peach" in Spanish:

Terri: *Piche.*
Bonnie: Wait up, lemme think. (Pause) I don't know.
José: They say *piche.*
Bonnie: Yeah, but that's not Spanish really.
Terri: But I heard of it, *piche.*
Bonnie: OK, bet.
José: But I don't know how they call it.
Bonnie: I don't know, lemme look it up.
José: (Laughing) *Plome*— they call "plum" *plome.*
Bonnie: "Plum" is *cereza*—no, that's "cherry." Wait up.
José: *Piche*—they call "peach" *piche.*
Bonnie: (Looking in dictionary) All right, "peach"— *pérsico?*
José: *Pérsico?* I didn't—
Bonnie: *Melocotón.* That's what it is, *melocotón.*

Terri and José laugh.

Bonnie: Really!
José: No wonder they call it *piche.*
Bonnie: In Puerto Rico, they call it *melocotón.*
José: Not me.
Terri: How about "plum"?
Bonnie: (Looking in dictionary) Lemme see.
José: (Laughing) *Plome.*
Bonnie: No, not *plome.*
José: If it's a weird name, it's *plome* to us.
Bonnie: *Cire*— *ciruela.*
José: *Sí, duele*— *y que se vaya.* (Laughs) *¡Ciruela!* [Yes it hurts—and let it pass].
Terri: *¿Y duele* for what? (She laughs too.) [And it hurts . . .]
José: *Está bueno.* [O.K.]
Bonnie: You asked.
Terri: How about "soda"?
José: *Soda.*

Bonnie: *Refresco.*
José: They don't say *refresco* around here. They never say *ese* [that] *refresco* around here.
Terri: They say *soda.*
José: *Soda.*
Bonnie: I know. Hey, c'mon, the oven's heating up.
José: How do you say "oven" in Spanish?
Bonnie: *Horno.*
Terri: (To José) You don't know that? If you don't know that, I don't know who you is.

The crucial terms are (as José puts it) what "they say" or (as Terri puts it) what "I heard of." José and Terri have developed enough metalinguistic awareness to know that *piche, plome* and *soda* are much more like English than Spanish words, that is, they have some sense that these are borrowings, but at the same time, these borrowings are absolutely real to them. So when confronted with *melocotón,* José responds "not me" and "no wonder they call it *piche. "* There is nothing about this form that sounds at all familiar. His reaction to *plome* versus *ciruela* makes this even more explicit: "If it's something weird it's *plome* to us." He and Terri then pun on the pronunciation of *ciruela (sí duele,* yes it hurts), in effect wrapping a cloak of playful familiarity around the strange form.

By nesting strangeness in familiar form and play, they create a moment of relative non-arbitrariness, in Friedrich's (1979[1978]) sense that arbitrariness is total only in structures with no actors. The human imagination works from the context-specific. Children grow into metalinguistic awareness in highly structured and contextualized ways (see Heath 1983; Romaine 1984:159ff). Looking up words in dictionaries is a standard way to develop metalinguistic awareness in contexts like school where languages are assumed to be discrete and monolithic. But Terri and José are not in school talking to a teacher. They are in my apartment cooking and playing, and my metalinguistic assertions and *Vox Concise Spanish and English Dictionary* do not carry much weight. To them, what makes a word "really" Spanish depends on whether they have experienced it in a familiar context or relationship. The dictionary alone cannot effect this. So they use verbal play to weave familiarity around the dictionary's strange signs and to sort out what is meaningfully Spanish to them from what is not.

Children have far less access to codified Spanish than to codified English. Their sense of "what is Spanish" arises mostly from what maps onto familiar relations and practices. This is probably why children found my speaking Spanish so odd. In many ways, metalinguistic classification is social classification. Children found my Spanish "weird" because it did not fit their classification of social relations; to them, Spanish is bounded by the familiar and the familial. To them, a "real" Spanish accent is the sound of a familiar reality, belonging to the internalized "home" language of their primary socialization (Berger and Luckmann 1967:135ff). Thus, to José, my accent was hopelessly (as he put it) "different from real people's Spanish." José's reaction to finding Spanish in a speaker where it should not be (me) is, in a way, the opposite of Terri's surprise that José does not know that "oven" is *horno* in Spanish. She does not find Spanish where it should be. She is surprised to find their everyday linguistic experiences not quite parallel: "If you don't know *that*, I don't know who you is." This sense of displacement, of not quite knowing who one is or where one fits in, often emerges when children talk about their linguistic knowledge. In the next episode, which took place later that afternoon, Rosa Rivera's son Freddy (age nine) and his buddy Mike (age ten, and Terri's brother) come by to see if the cookies are done:

Terri:　You got to talk Spanish into the tape we got.
Freddy:　I can't talk Spanish.
Terri:　*Habla español.* [Speak Spanish]
Freddy:　*Que no pue*—I can't *talk* Spanish.
Terri:　*Ah pues, si tu no puedes hablar español*—that's why the tape recorder. [Oh, well, if you can't speak Spanish—]
Freddy:　Yeah? I'll go—I'll go—I'll go uh-uh-uh-uh. That's gonna come out, that's gonna come out. Uh-uh-uh-uh.

In what sense does Freddy "not know Spanish"? He can make requests and code-switch with his mother, as he demonstrated one evening in the middle of an interview in their apartment. He asked Rosa if he could stay over at Mike's:

Freddy:　*¿Si yo puedo* spend the night *abajo?* [If I could spend the night downstairs?]
Rosa:　*No estás*— [You're not—]
Freddy:　*¿Qué?* [What?]
Rosa :　(To me) Do you see what he do? "*¿Si yo puedo* spend the night *abajo?*" He just did it, he didn't say it in English and he didn't say it in Spanish. He mixes every-thing.
Freddy:　[[xx xx xx]] the refrigerator?
Rosa:　Shut up or I scream.
Freddy:　*¡Mami!*
Rosa:　Hmmmm?
Freddy:　*¿Adonde están ropas?* [Where are my clothes?]
Rosa:　(Teasing) *¿Adonde están ropas?*
Freddy:　*¿Ropas?*
Rosa:　I give it to you tomorrow. Just put on shorts and go downstairs. I'm busy now.

　　In functional terms, Freddy's Spanish competence grows from familiar household routines (the kind Terri, above, assumed she and José shared), where he routinely code-switches. He knows the forms and how to put them together. What he has not learned is to classify this as "Spanish." This gives him stage fright when Terri tells him to act on his metalinguistic sense and "talk Spanish into the tape." *What* metalinguistic sense? Freddy asks in effect. As a nine-year-old boy, he has no clear-cut set of practices and relations in which his language behavior is clearly defined as Spanish, whereas for girls like Terri there are. It may be that to Freddy and other boys his age, Spanish is not a "thing" that they "have" in the way that girls do. How much he may grow into it is an open question. Language Policy Task Force work (1982:165–166) suggests that although boys grow up in overwhelmingly English-speaking networks, they may by their late teens learn adult roles and relations that reactivate their Spanish. This may enhance their metalinguistic sense. This is probably truer for girls. When Rosa's daughter-in-law was expecting her first child, Rosa found her pregnancy an optimal time to "practice" her Spanish in preparation for motherhood. Nevertheless, work by the Language Policy Task Force (1982) and by Zentella (1997) and my own work all suggest a substantial shift away from Spanish over the last fifteen years. Luis Molina and Marilyn Mojica, who were adolescents in my first study and parents in my second, noticed this pattern in their own lives.

Instilling a Spanish metalinguistic sense is seen as an important parental responsibility. As Rosa Rivera put it:

> I hate mothers who say "I don't want them to learn Spanish." Why? Why? It's your language, you know, it's beautiful for them to learn. Mine don't know it that good but they understand it. If a kid is born here and grows up here, and he talks to me in English and not in Spanish and says to me "I don't know Spanish," it's their parents' fault. Because if I want my kids to learn Spanish, I teach them. Then, if they say a word bad in Spanish, I correct them. And sometimes they come to me and say, "Mami, how do you say this in Spanish?"

Most parents shared Rosa's feelings. A few, like Luz Guzmán, did not:

> It really doesn't make any difference to me if they learn [Spanish] or not. My mother's the one who wants them to learn [it]. But it really doesn't make any difference. See, I hear all the mothers say that they show their kids Spanish first because they're Puerto Ricans. But when they go to school, then they're fighting because the kids don't learn anything, because they don't know English at all. 'Cause Spanish, they could learn it at home. But when they go to school, the teacher's not going to be speaking Spanish.

Parents' linguistic ideology and the contexts in which children experience Spanish and English affect the ways in which their metalinguistic perceptions develop. The linguistic patterns that children learn to call English and Spanish are not neatly bounded. Spanish is the family-oriented baseline language, with varied and increasing amounts of English that complement or are borrowed into Spanish; some of it may even be perceived as Spanish. Bilinguals growing up in New York do not have many opportunities to develop a dictionary-and-grammar awareness of Spanish that can match that awareness of English. Furthermore, as the next chapter demonstrates, many develop a sense that "good" English is the opposite of what they speak.

A Public Place for Real Spanish: The Pentecostal Church

Public Spanish is used in churches and community-based organizations, in bilingual education and in the Spanish media. The Spanish language press in the United States, including Puerto Rican oriented papers like *El Diario La Prensa,* provides an important means to imagine a Spanish-speaking community, both within the

United States and beyond its borders. But as García, Fishman, Gertner, and Burunat (1985) show, the fact that there are relatively few Spanish language newspapers also means that they have considerably less opportunity to be stylistically innovative than does the press in Puerto Rico or Mexico.

Bilingual education is meant in part to validate Latin identity by recognizing Spanish as a public language. Such intentions are undercut when children's authority over their own language is denied in the classroom. As Zentella (1981a) points out, Puerto Rican children frequently hear the double-bind message that their Spanish is not "real" Spanish, but that they are "lazy" if they take Spanish in school because they "already know it." Such messages devalue code-switching and reinforce the idea that linguistic competence can only be measured against academic standards. They also undermine students' authority over their own linguistic experience (Walsh 1991; Language Policy Task Force 1982). Moreover, bilingual education programs continually face budget shortages, curricular problems, and an unending public perception that they keep children away from English.

There are Spanish-speaking services, particularly Catholic masses, in many churches of major religious denominations, and this is an important venue for Spanish. But to some degree this Spanish is a linguistic concession from Anglophone authority. The Spanish-speaking Pentecostal churches stand out as a strikingly grass-roots phenomenon, a place in which Spanish is performed with authority, ceding no ground to English or Americans. I had an opportunity to see this in action on a Saturday evening in March 1978, when Chente Mendoza, Adelina's eighteen-year-old son, invited the project director and me to accompany him to a *campaña,* a preaching and healing meeting jointly sponsored by six Pentecostal churches. It was held in a building on the corner of Essex and Houston. We arrived at 7:30 to find a large, crowded room in which, as far as we could tell, we were the only non-Latino whites. The six sponsoring pastors were seated along the front of the room with a lectern for the person preaching and a platform to which members of the congregation would come to be prayed over and healed.

The service started with hymns in Spanish. For the next couple of hours, hymns alternated with *predicando* (preaching) until each pastor had preached. The themes were healing and powerful, as was evident in the passage from Luke read by the first pastor, in which Christ heals the servant of the centurion who was convinced of His power and authority. The words "power" *(poder)* and "powerful" *(poderoso)* were frequently repeated in all the preaching. Five of the six preachers spoke only Spanish; one spoke in both Spanish and English. The congregants spoke only Spanish when calling out spontaneous public responses to the preachings: *Hay poder, Señor, Santo, Gloria a Dios.* English could be heard in private conversation, especially among mothers telling children to behave. As the services progressed, the response became livelier and more frequent, with people calling out and clapping and occasionally becoming glossalalic.

The preacher who broke this pattern was a woman in her early twenties. She began in Spanish but, seeing us, switched to English, saying that she saw people in the congregation who might not know Spanish and that we must have been moved by the power of Christ to come so she would speak to us in English to help us continue to find Christ. She continued in English for perhaps five minutes, despite a few congregants calling out *"en español"* and *"no en inglés"* (in Spanish, not in English). She came up to us afterward, asking if we had understood the whole *campaña* and hoping we would return. We introduced ourselves and thanked her for her concern, assuring her we had understood most of it; "Oh, you know Spanish?" she said. Chente later commented that she had done as the spirit moved her, and people should have let her preach in English.

In the final preaching, the pastor developed most strongly the connection between power, faith, healing, and miracles. He then led the laying-on of hands. People lined up at the platform and he asked their complaint. If they had none, he called down God's blessing. If they had a problem, he laid on hands and after asking if the pain had gone, announced the results. For example, *"Esta señora tenía un terrible dolor en la pierna pero gracias a Dios no lo tiene ahora"* (This lady had a terrible pain in her leg but thank God she has it no more.) Chente urged us to go up and be prayed over, and the woman in front of us added her encouragement (in English) saying, "Don't be afraid. He won't eat you." So we went up. As I approached, the pastor said to Chente, *"¿Ella es Americana? ¿Ella entiende?"* (She's American? She understands?) Chente assured him, *"Yo le expliqué"* (I explained it to her). We returned to our seats, and there was a wind-down to mundane reality as announcements for the coming week were read.

The Pentecostal Church and the Catholic Church are the two religious organizations with sizeable Puerto Rican congregations. But there are important differences between them that help explain the power of Spanish Pentecostalism. As a charismatic religion, Pentecostalism makes a far more immediate connection between the public and the private than do routinized institutions like the Catholic Church. Pentecostalism embraces, defines, and allows one to transform one's fundamental persona; the Catholic Church provides an institutional framework of life-events. One is usually born into the Catholic Church, and the church becomes most manifest as part of one's life in sacraments and rituals: baptism, first communion, confirmation, weddings, funerals, *rosarios* (post-funeral rosary recitations), feast days, and holy days. Pentecostals actively and successfully recruit through friends and relations by appealing to the kind of person one wants to be or should be. Such factors invest participation in Pentecostal ritual with a more sharply focused emotive quality that does participation in Catholic ritual.

Pentecostalism promotes a sense of personal worth and effort immediately rewarded. Participation and promotion are far less rigidly hierarchized than in the Catholic church. There is no confession. People are baptized as adults, at the age of reason. Membership, participation, the experience of religious reality are all immediate. The Catholic Church's attempts to engage Puerto Ricans in an ethnic Catholicism has been somewhat tenuous, not least because of an often conservative Chancery (Stevens-Arroyo 1980). As a result, Pentecostalism has become an important way to enact, in public, a Latin identity through the language of a defining institution. The response *"en español"* to the pastor's well-intentioned English is a call to protect the integrity of a rare venue for such enactment. For Chente, the Pentecostal Church connects him to Spanish in ways that he is unlikely to find in another public institution. This was evident in his use of Spanish for concepts like *predicando, pastor, Espíritu Santo,* words that he said he did not know in English—this from someone who spoke mostly English.

Keeping Between the Linguistic Lines in the Outer Sphere

The inner sphere is the place where, ideologically, Spanish and English can "mix" or co-exist as code-switching. As Rosa Rivera put it:

> Don't mix, it's awful—well, it don't sound to *me* awful, but it would sound awful to a teacher, if I have a teacher visiting me.

This statement neatly sums up the distinction between inner-sphere language, which is transparently intelligible and acceptable, and outer-sphere language, which is seen as a body of rules. What is normal to "us" is a mistake to "them," that is, to a "teacher" as exemplar and monitor of order and correctness.[7]

The outer sphere is the sphere of an imposed order. It is the 180-degree opposite of inner-sphere life in which people see their "real" selves emerge as subtle, complex, and multifaceted. In outer-sphere relations, people must act as client, employee, patient, tenant, their personas bounded by the requirements of these roles. In speech-event terms, the setting and participant structure (organization of interaction) must fit authorized requirements. What people refer to must fit the goals of the transaction. These structural parameters shape outer-sphere interactions even when the authority representative is kind and helpful. When the state is involved, "right" and "wrong" language is laid out as a set of rules, and information is tightly coded (see also Attinasi 1983, Romaine 1989). Above all, the structural inequality makes people subject to an imposed metacommunication in which race, class, and language markers conflate in a tangle of "mistakes" and "bad accents" in which anything one says can put one at risk.

At this point, the English/Spanish boundary emerges with a vengeance. Code becomes critical: either one defends oneself in English or one retreats to Spanish and relies on a translator. (This creates structural invisibility, which is at times an advantage.) Defending oneself means negotiating an English defined entirely by rules for correctness, which is not an issue in inner-sphere English. The problem is, again, metalinguistic awareness—how does one know what the correct forms are and whether one "has" them. When I asked if she worried about her English when talking to her children's teacher, Luz Guzmán said:

> Oh my God! I don't feel very comfortable. I might say something stupid, like it's going to come out wrong. . . . I go to them hoping they won't correct me. I get outside and I think, did I say what I was supposed to say? Did I come to say

something and I didn't say it? Like if I think of something in Spanish that I want to tell her, maybe I said something else, translated it differently. That always gets me, because in Spanish I could think of a lot of things but when I say it in English it comes out all wrong.

While she sometimes found that her English blocked her Spanish, as when she talked to her mother, she saw this as merely an annoyance, a minor problem of routine interaction. It did not create the dead-end that talking to a social worker could create:

If they ask me about things, I start to talk to them, and then it doesn't come out, period. Something else comes out, not what I'm thinking but something else just by itself leaks out. And what I'm thinking just stays there.

Luisa Muñiz describes a similar dynamic:

Well, say like I go to face-to-face interviews from the welfare, when I have to talk to a social worker. I get nervous of what I'm going to say or if what I'm going to say makes sense to the person. I be saying sentences and the words I'm going to say, they don't come out right.

Rosa Rivera is explicit about the formal aspects:

You say things everyday in English but when I get in front of this kind of people, that you have to—you know—then I completely forgot English. I had to start myself up and then think, think, how am I gonna say this word? And I *used* that word before! It happens to me almost all the time. I forget everything. I forgot where I have to put the word, the endings, the plurals, I forgot everything. I doesn't know English at that moment. I seen people going to the welfare, these people who doesn't know English that much, go to these people in the welfare, social workers. And they try to explain themselves, and I see the social workers laughing at their faces, and they made me nervous. If one of them laugh at my face, I just run out of there because, you know, you feel embarrassed. Even if they have so much study, so much education, they just laugh in your face.

This never happened to her "around here." With American neighbors like Lena, she could "try to make them understand." If a store owner reacted critically, she reasoned, "Well, I'm going to buy with my money, so what I have to be nervous about?"

Information Control and Class Control

These women see their confusion and frustration as a language issue, but the more basic issue is control: whoever controls the terms of interaction controls information. This is made clear in the following incidents recorded in my 1978–79 field-notes. Let me start with two situations in which Spanish was not the issue, to make the basic dynamics more clearly visible.

June 9, 1978: Lena Johnson and I are going running but she wants to stop and pay her rent at the landlord's office. When we stop, she asks him what to do about her lease when it comes up for renewal. He says to leave it until the time comes. She says she just wants to know what to do. He hedges. She asks a third time. He says "you aren't planning to have any more kids, are you?" She says no. She says she has a plumbing fixture that needs repair. He says to tell the super. We leave. She lets it out: where does he get off asking if she was going to have more kids?!

The landlord (white, middle-class, male, a Westchester resident) controls information given to the (black, working-class woman) tenant. He does not comply with a straightforward request for information. He makes a comment (about having more kids) that sets up a racialized interpretive frame that undermines her right to ask for information. There is nothing she can say to him that will get the information she wants. Now let us add two factors: a landlord who is not simply withholding information but trying to evict the tenant, and a tenant who speaks no English. The tenant, Mrs. Fonseca, speaks no English:

> June 1, 1978: Aurelia Fonseca is having problems with her landlord. He is convinced that one of her children's friends called a false alarm in to the fire department, who came and broke the downstairs door. He wants the Fonsecas out, now. Mrs. Fonseca asks if I would go with her to talk to him. We find him in front of the building. He is large and blonde and, guessing from his last name, Ukrainian. I ask if he is the landlord and introduce myself, saying that Mrs. Fonseca has asked me to come and clear up a misunderstanding. He informs me there is no misunderstanding. He wants the Fonsecas out of the building. He complains that the older daughter brings in "all sorts of ethnic groups, Spanish, black, what have you," who hang out in the entrance and smoke pot. The neighbors are complaining and he wants them out. They're wrecking his property, his building, the only way to handle it is for them to leave and did she understand that? They could use May and June rent to find a place. He wants them out at the end of June. Each time he enlarges on the alleged misdemeanors, two of her children who are present defend their sister and mother and try to correct his account. He finishes his monolog, issues one last warning and takes off. The exchange has been between him and me. Mrs. Fonseca would tell me what she wanted said, I would translate, he would respond to me and I would translate back to her. After he leaves, Mrs. Fonseca and her children go into the office and talk over what he has said. They are enraged. To them he is, "that whitey, that Jew, *ese judío.*" A week later they receive a dispossess and are soon househunting.[8]

The landlord's power is directly exposed by the threat of eviction. Information control is a central issue, as only the landlord's interpretation counts. The landlord racializes the Fonsecas when he equates "all sorts of ethnic groups, Spanish, black, what have you" with pot-smoking loiterers. Mrs. Fonseca's children try to defend her, but the landlord ignores them. My presence as translator makes it possible for the landlord to bypass direct contact with the Fonseca family; he addresses and listens to only me and controls Mrs. Fonseca by making her a non-person.

Carmen, the study project assistant, contacted a lawyer at a nearby legal aid agency:

June 1, 1978: Carmen, Mrs. Fonseca and I go to see John Brown at legal aid. Mrs. Fonseca brought her rent receipts. Brown knew no Spanish. Carmen introduced herself, Mrs. Fonseca and me and outlined the problem. He took down general information and then focussed on the matter of rent: how much had she been paying, for how long, etc. He directed all questions at Carmen: "ask her if . . . "; "does she know . . . "; "how much does she pay . . ." He asked about the current rent, how much it used to be, under what terms did it go up, had the landlord given Mrs. Fonseca a copy of the lease; what exactly were his complaints about the children. Brown said that the landlord had no basis for evicting them. If she received any dispossess notice or other legal papers from the landlord she should bring them straight to Brown, who would send a letter to the landlord and specify what the landlord could and could not do and what his tenant's rights were. The interview lasted about 30 minutes and was entirely between Carmen and the lawyer. She would turn to Mrs. Fonseca to translate what the lawyer had said and to get confirmation or other information.

June 11, 1978: Mrs. Fonseca came by to say she was still having a rent dispute with the landlord. He had partially finished some promised repairs. How much of her rent should she pay? I called Mr. Brown and gave her his answer.

The information Mrs. Fonseca needs is available but it is directed at her advocate, not at her. Nor is she a direct participant. She and Mr. Brown take for granted that they deal with each other by proxy. Similarly, when I went as translator with Mrs. Fonseca to see her son's teacher, the teacher addressed me and I addressed Mrs. Fonseca. In both cases, everyone involved appeared to assume that English speakers would participate directly. I took this so for granted I was actually surprised by the following display of consideration:

October 3, 1978: Sister Jean from the Catholic school up the street came by this afternoon and introduced me to Mrs. Ortiz and her daughter Ana, who will be coming to the project office for tutoring. Sister Jean does not speak Spanish. She addressed Mrs. Ortiz in English, explaining our tutoring program, who I was and what I would be doing. Mrs. Ortiz seemed to understand her but when I spoke to her in Spanish she responded in Spanish only. Sister Jean spoke slowly, apologizing for not being able to speak Spanish, and looking at Mrs. Ortiz while Ana translated to her mother.

As I got to know Mrs. Ortiz, I realized she understood English phrases and sentences in her children's speech. Perhaps Sister Jean knew this. The point is that when Anglophones address non-English speakers through a translator, they almost always treat the translator as the interlocutor. Sister Jean treated Mrs. Ortiz as her interlocutor.

The information barriers in outer-sphere encounters are often exacerbated by long waiting processes, especially at understaffed and overbooked public services. Making people wait, like controlling what they find out, signifies the distribution of social power. Waiting in particular signals the disparity between the value of the service provided by the state bureaucracy and the private citizen's time (Schwartz 1975), a disparity compounded by the routinely underfunded and understaffed condition of public facilities. Schwartz shows in detail how waiting and delay maintain status boundaries and control over the conduct of others and shape perceptions of person; the same may be said about information control. These principles inform the following bureaucratic encounter.

> June 19, 1978: Lena Johnson asked me to go to the 13th St. Social Security Office to see about a problem with her daughter's S.S.I., saying I might be able to "help her talk to those people." Rows of chairs were set out for waiting clients. The place was full. A police officer at the front desk called out numbers. Mrs. Johnson said there were always police there in case an argument "or something" breaks out; she said there were even more at welfare, five or six. Several caseworkers were Latino. As the wait got longer and longer she said she figured there was no point in my staying. I left after an hour. She stayed another hour and told me later that all they did was "fill out stuff" and get ready to send for hospital records.[9]

She faced neither an emergency nor an English–Spanish barrier. She asked me to come because she wanted someone familiar with institutional language as insurance in case an information snag arose. The next incident shows what happens when the client maps the information barrier onto code. The interaction is by document and the interlocutor is an institution. The potential cost to a person unable to negotiate the information barrier is loss of services—income, food stamps, Medicaid.

> September 15, 1978: Adelina Mendoza received a letter from the welfare department saying that information she had put on one of their forms did not match information she had given them last summer. She was instructed to fill out the enclosed form so that welfare would not take steps to close her case. She told me she was afraid she had made a mistake, afraid to talk to them, afraid she would say the wrong thing and they would close her case. Would I call? I did. The person I spoke to said that Mrs. Mendoza had received a standard form letter sent to all clients to double-check information. There was no threat to close her case. She just needed to enter the name of each of her children, with birthdate, and send it back in the return envelope. She asked me to fill it out in case she made a mistake, and to enclose a letter from her doctor explaining that her oldest son was off the budget. I offered to write a note explaining the doctor's letter but this clearly made her uneasy (would I be doing something wrong?). After we finished, we had a cup of coffee and talked about her situation. She said that no matter how careful she was, she would make a mistake, or someone would lose something and she'd have another family problem.

Mrs. Mendoza's situation is like that of a traveler who knows there is quicksand somewhere out there in the fog, but where? The performative quicksand— the word that may be a disastrous deed—is the potential threat hidden in the document. If she cannot distinguish between the institutionally routine and a true warning, she must assume a worst case scenario. All she knows is that not following correct procedure (to "make a mistake" or "say the wrong thing") may have serious consequences. She is like a computer beginner terrified of typing in the wrong command and watching files delete; to her the system is equally unforgiving. She sees this as a problem of her English grammar and vocabulary, over which she feels little control. She has gained some confidence through the English adult education night classes that she has attended for the past two years, but there is a wide gap between basic literacy skills and the ability to decode "legalese." She wants someone who will tell the institution only and exactly what they need to know, no less and no more. I make her uneasy when I offer an explanation that may be extraneous and may amount to an unknown transgression that could put her at risk. The safest path is the most literal.

Another common outer-sphere venue is the courtroom. Here, Nilsa Buon, the project secretary, helps Jenny Molina bring a layaway problem to Small Claims Court.

> February 9, 1978: Jenny Molina bought some furniture on layaway at Avon House. She finished paying for the furniture but it had never been delivered, nor could she get them to return the money. Nilsa recruits me to help write a letter to the company explaining that if they don't deliver the furniture the matter goes to Small Claims Court. We deliver the letter personally the next day.

> March 28, 1978: Mrs. Molina still has not heard from Avon House so Nilsa and Mrs. Molina are taking the matter to Small Claims Court. The notice of court action must be served to the business owner by someone other than the plaintiff (Mrs. Molina) or a police officer. Nilsa and Mrs. Molina elect me because I don't "look Spanish" so the Avon House people might not guess why I was there. I am supposed to serve the notice to Mr. Miller (the owner) personally. I ask for Mr. Miller. One clerk says he isn't in. Another asks if he can help me. I say I am looking for the owner, Mr. Miller. The clerk says Mr. Miller isn't in. I ask when he would be in. The clerk says he doesn't work there any more. I asked who the owner is. The clerk says Mr. Green. I ask if Mr. Green is in. The clerk says no and what do you want him for. I say I need the information for a friend and when would Mr. Green be in. The clerk says oh, he's in and out. I say I'll check back.

In Small Claims Court, the burden of effort is on the plaintiff, who must do the bureaucratic work and fit his or her complaint into the categories of evidence upon which a judge can rule. As Conley and O'Barr (1990) show in their study of small claims cases, the conversion of everyday perception into legal formulae is tricky. The unfamiliar bureaucratic procedures are even trickier when the plaintiff is at a linguistic disadvantage. As Merry (1990) shows, although the system is supposed to be open to everyone, working-class plaintiffs often find it slipping out of their grasp. Latinos in particular shy away from going to court, feeling out of place there. Jenny eventually won her claim, but without Nilsa to find out and explain the procedures, to translate technical information into Spanish, to write letters and walk Jenny through the hearings, and to make sure Jenny had the necessary documents, nothing would have been accomplished. The investment of time by both women was disproportionate to the tiny response of the furniture company, which took another year (and another trip to Small Claims Court) to deliver. Installment plans make large purchases feasible for people who cannot pay in full or use credit but they also put the buyer at a disadvantage. Whether redress is possible depends on the resources and time available to them and to an advocate like Nilsa.

The unwieldiness of state bureaucracy exacerbates information control: state agencies have far too many clients or patients for their staff and resources to handle. People are reduced to roles (customer, tenant, client) and compartmentalized into a set of needs that are often displaced onto an advocate, especially if one does not trust one's own language. As all this happens, the client or patient increasingly becomes a non-person. Most of this involves women. Poor women are especially vulnerable to this process because of the ways in which poverty has been bureaucratically feminized, with family interests structurally represented by women.

Public-aid bureaucracies and legal systems involve highly codified sets of relations brought into being by a state-authorized language. Citizens in such relations must comply with all obligations and requirements or risk specific, codified consequences. Bureaucracies and courts utilize a strictly linear time frame reified in clocks, calendars, and schedules. The private citizen must give up time to the state, coordinating personal and cultural ways of thinking about experience with the conceptual rhythms and sequences of legal and bureaucratic information structures. Every action has a potential legal consequence, and the cause-and-effect sequencing is crucial. Failure to come up with the right information at the right time can result in loss of services or case closure. The problem is how to know that one has the "right" information.

The information barrier creates a pragmatic problem that people classify in metalinguistic terms. When so much depends on one's dealings with institutions and when those dealings are measured in language terms by "what works," people's perceptions of English competence will be affected accordingly. This perception of English—the right word for the right purpose in the right order—is construed in direct opposition to what does not work or what gets one ridiculed. This also shapes people's perception of an English more "real" than the English of home and neighborhood so easily mixed with Spanish. Small wonder that so many women attend night school class in order to take control of the spelling and grammar that is, for them, "proper" English.

Conclusion

If, as Gal (1987) argues, the place of a code in a political economy is mediated by cultural concepts, then the English of the inner sphere, which is the only English most working-class bilinguals know, occupies a pretty shaky place. The value of a code proceeds from what Irvine terms the "allocation of resources, coordination of production, distribution of goods and services" (1989:249). Correct English is tested by its results. When inner-sphere English is used around the neighborhood, it has no material results to offer. When inner-sphere English is used in outer-sphere dealings, its material results are undependable and all too often it draws down racializing judgments and reactions. As Hill and Hill (1986) and Mannheim

(1991) have shown, people's metalinguistic sense—what they see as "really" Mexicano versus Spanish, or Quechua versus Spanish—cannot be divorced from the matrices of verbal and social exchanges that define contrastive linguistic ecologies. Neither, for the people in this study, can their sense of "real" English.

When people do not trust their own linguistic knowledge, they opt for translators to help them navigate bureaucratic encounters in hospitals, social agencies, and legal services. They do so at some risk. The translator may not be any more expert than the patient or client at technical knowledge or terminology and may misapproximate what the client or patient intends to say (Díaz-Duque 1989; Berk-Seligson 1990). As Shuman (1986:77ff) and Vásquez, Shannon, and Pease Alvarez (1994:96ff) point out, children are most often relied on as translators since they are likely to be seen by parents as fluent English speakers. But again, parents are not always in a position to assess their children's abilities in terms of outer-sphere function, of information management and exchange, and children do not have much control over the kinds of verbal devices that give their parents social credibility.

For working-class bilinguals, the outer sphere is where language rules and measurements manifest symbolic power. Fabian (1986:137ff) argues that devices of symbolic power align and reinforce the ability of powerful institutions to override the complexities and contradictions of routine social life. Here, language is assumed to be an entity whose space in the individual brain can be measured in increments like a measuring cup (Romaine 1989:236ff). If language competence is really all about correct answers, then the complex communicative competences involved in playing, teasing, and other everyday language modes dissolve to nothing. As the next two chapters show, the bases of such symbolic domination run right through the conflation of language difference with race and class.

Notes

1. Switching does appear to be a particularly Caribbean-Spanish mode. García, Evangelista, Martínez, Disla, and Paulino (1988) find that South and Central Americans compartmentalize function by code considerably more than do Puerto Ricans, and they also tend to see switching not only as typically Puerto Rican (or Caribbean), but as marked for class and race.

2. Zentella (1996, Chapter 7) produces evidence that suggests the conclusions drawn by Pousada and Poplack do not take into account the linguistic life histories of English-dominant bilinguals born in the continental United States.

3. *Cabrón* (literally, "cuckold") is not always an insult. In "*Cabrón*, it stinks" it might be translated along the lines of "you asshole." In "*¿Cabrón, qué pasa?*" it is closer to the sense of "dude" or "bro," about as expletive as the word "shit" in phrases like ". . . and shit" which means (roughly) ". . . and stuff."

4. Transcriptions are by Jacqueline Vargas, Rupert Maura, and me. The translation follows the Spanish in brackets [ ]. A long dash (—) indicate that the speaker's voice trails off or is interrupted. Double brackets indicate unintelligible syllables [[xx xx]] or approximate transcription. Speakers generally exhibit the following features of Puerto Rican Spanish: /s/ is deleted before voiceless stops or word-final; the first syllable /es/ in all forms of *estar* drops

so that, for example, *están* becomes *tan*; *para* becomes *pa'*, and *todo, to'*; final nasals are deleted and the preceding vowel nasalized; word-final /d/ is deleted and syllable-final /r/ becomes [l], for example, *verdad* becomes *velda*.

5. The figures that follow are based on the total number of functions per speaker (often more than one per turn).

6. While transcribing, Rupert Maura noted that Camy has a familiar manner with both Leo and Luis but "home familiar" with Leo (which may explain the tendency to Spanish) and "street familiar" with Luis (which may explain the tendency toward English). He notes that throughout the hour of tape, her manner and Spanish toward Leo is like her manner and Spanish toward Jenny and Iris. He further notes a contrast between the English Camy uses throughout the hour of tape with Luis ("street colloquial") and with me (more formal and polite, with a tendency to explain to me what has just been said in Spanish).

7. See also Gal (1979:105) citing an informant's statement that "we don't speak either right"; Hill and Hill (1986:99) on Mexicano perceptions of "error and mixing" versus an idealized "authentic" Mexicano and Spanish; Romaine (1989:213) on social prohibitions against switching as uninhibited and incorrect.

Switching is not always regarded as error. The Language Policy Task Force (Attinasi 1983) found that East Harlem teachers do not generally see switching as wrong but do see it in formal semantic terms, a non-innovative combination of existing systems. East Harlem parents, however, see it as innovative and culturally distinctive, valuing its pragmatic potential.

8. The conflation of *Jewish* and *white,* although less frequent than the conflation of *American* and *white,* was often vehemently expressed. Lena's landlord was Jewish, and I often heard "Jewish landlord" comments about him from his tenants. I doubt whether the Fonsecas's landlord was Jewish (his children attended Catholic school), but the conflation is powerfully stereotypic and likely to emerge at moments when a landlord exercises what seems like raw power. This is racializing from the other side: *Jewish* and *white* as categories that "naturally" explain control.

9. Her daughter received SSI (disability insurance) for a severe learning disability resulting from lead paint ingestion.

Chapter 4

Good English as Symbolic Capital

Mapping Voices

As we have seen, bilinguals do not always treat English and Spanish as absolutely separate entities. They are most likely to do so when they have to communicate across inequalities of race, class, and authority. These are the situations in which "good English" becomes most crucial, and if people feel they cannot speak or write it themselves, they will find an advocate who can. The question that then arises is, what does good English mean to the bilinguals in this study?

Good English is not a clearly definable object. It is however, a powerful social fact. When people talk about good or correct English, they refer to language forms (words and sounds) in ways that highlight their nature as cultural capital, that is, as skills and knowledge through which people can enhance their social situation. Using such forms should bring people symbolic capital in the form of prestige and material rewards (Bourdieu 1991). It is not simply the forms themselves that carry symbolic capital, but the way forms are used in specific times and places. Because symbolic capital is tied to context, it is indexical. How it is used can affect people's social situation, which makes it performative.[1] For the people in this study, good English means having the right words and saying them clearly. The payoff is to gain respect and escape race/class stereotyping. The problem is, using the right words and accent cannot guarantee respect because one might also be judged by one's skin or name.

To understand how good English becomes symbolic capital, we must examine both the political topography of people's lives (the subject of Chapter 3) and the ways in which people typify and segment language (the subject of this chapter). The people in this study talk about language in semiotically complex ways. They construct images: voices, accents, or dialects are said to "sound like" a certain kind of person. They infer causal relations: how someone talks is said to be caused by his or her native language or country. They sort out words and sounds as discrete segments which can be correct or incorrect and which reflect race and class. Above all, people's sense of language is deictically shaped: people talk about who does or does not sound familiar, like "me" or "us."[2]

These issues came to the foreground in my second fieldwork. I had been unsatisfied with the ways in which I had written about bilingualism in my 1984 dissertation and returned to New York in 1988. Working with Nilsa Buon, Marilyn and José Mojica, Jenny Pacheco (formerly Molina), Luis Molina and his wife, Rosalina (Rosie), Rosie's mother Generosa (Tay) Román, Millie Wright and her daughter Cathy Wright, I shifted focus from people's linguistic behavior to their constructions of language, race, and class. We explored these issues in the interviews that form the basis of this chapter and the next[3] and in a procedure designed to show how people perceive, typify, and map language differences.[4]

This procedure, the subject of the first half of this chapter, was intended to serve as a starting point for further discussion. I tape recorded snippets of conversation from seventeen sample speakers, all New Yorkers, nine women and eight men, ages twenty to sixty, Puerto Rican and Dominican, African American, ethnic white and Anglo.[5] In these snippets, I had sample speakers talk about unhappy experiences with public transportation, a topic that deeply concerns New Yorkers. I then selected 30 to 45 seconds of recorded material per snippet, deleting as many references as possible to the speaker's identity or background. The respondent's job was to listen to the sample and design a persona to match the voice, assigning the voice a class and race/ethnic background, a job and a neighborhood, and to imagine how the hypothetical owner of the voice might be encountered (as neighbor, co-worker, boss, and so on).

I opted for this approach because it provided speech that would seem natural, that is, respondents could readily imagine relationships and contexts in which such talk seemed routine. Natural-seeming speech is hard to achieve by having people read written texts. However, opting for naturalism meant I was unable to gauge whether respondents reacted to the topic, the accent or the grammar. Nevertheless, by using the procedure as a way to evoke reactions rather than measure and compare variables, the respondents and I could concentrate on the interpretive process.

I transcribed each sample and read the transcription to the respondents to get a sense of cues available without the voice. Then I played the taped sample and asked respondents to assess the speaker's ethnic/race background, where the speaker grew up, what neighborhood the speaker might live in now, might they know the speaker and if so, where and how, what job the speaker might have, how the speaker makes them feel; whether the speaker is likely to know Spanish, what cues led them to think so, and would they speak Spanish, English or both with the speaker?[6] Descriptions of the seventeen sample speakers and transcriptions of their snippets are provided in the Appendix.

Ordinarily, when people make assessments about language varieties and accents, they assess linguistic and visual cues at the same time. In this case, since I was probing to see how people typify verbal cues alone, there were no visual cues. Nevertheless, respondents talked about what they heard as if they were watching someone do it. They typified the speech samples as *actions* and as *things*. Actions include how people talk or sound and what people talk about. Things like voice, sound, tone, and tune generally manifest a category of person and contain a strong sense of a person acting. Things like words, grammar, and letters strongly manifest a sense of language as an entity. Accents typify both person and language. This metalinguistic discussion was saturated with ideas about correct English, although I did not explicitly ask for them. Such ideas emerged readily in the context of these interviews which foregrounded outer sphere issues. I intended to do the procedure as a kind of game but at the conclusion of each sample, everyone wanted to know how many answers they had gotten "right." The ensuing discussions were at least as illuminating as the answers to the questions I did ask.

How People Talk or Sound

Comments on how people talk were prompted partly, but only partly, by my asking how the speaker made the respondent feel; people often volunteered such comments. Descriptions of how people talk or sound cast the speaker in images of personality or social types. For example, to Millie, speaker #1 "talked street." Nilsa, Millie, Marilyn, and José described #2 as sounding pleasant, Nilsa adding "he sounds cute" and Millie adding "he sounds fine!" Millie described #3 as sounding "civilized." José heard #8 as a "street talker." Nilsa said #9 "sounds trashy." To Marilyn #12 "sounds black, kind of boring." Jenny heard #13 as "vulgar."

When asked if the speaker sounded like someone the respondent might know, people were quick to give examples. José said #5 sounded like Marilyn's Dominican friend; Marilyn said #5 sounded even more familiar: "The way she talked. She talks like us. That's Puerto Rican." Also, #7 was similarly familiar to her:

BU: Could you see her living on N Street?
MM: Yeah.
BU: Does she sound like someone you might ordinarily meet?
MM: Yes.
BU: Where might you meet? Who might introduce you?
MM: I might meet her in my mother's building, there's a lady that sounds just like her.

Millie located #11 on her social map without prompting:

MW: Sounds like Chris, right Cathy? Between Jan and Chris?
CW: No.
BU: Who's Jan and Chris?
MW: Chris's a nurse that works up in X Hospital, Cathy's friend. She's old enough to be my friend but she's Cathy's friend. And Jan is Cathy's long-lost cousin, distant relative.

Routinely, sample speakers were said to sound Spanish, black, or white, for example, to Nilsa #13 "sounded black." José expanded this typification of #13 into an active image:

> She like—talked like a black person, like how [proud], the way they speak out. . . .
> I've heard it like that.

Speakers were also said to "sound like" they knew another language. José thought #14 was Jamaican but heard something that suggested, say, Chinese; at any rate "it sounded like he had more than one language." People also sound like their place of origin. As Millie said of #11: "I'd say she's white. She sounds like a New Yorker."

What People Talk About

People listened for signs of emotional honesty or stinginess, openness or fear. For examples, speaker #1 drew critical reactions from Luis, Rosie, Marilyn, and José in large part because she spoke disapprovingly about people carrying things on the train and did so with a noticeable Spanish accent—a linguistic performance resonating with the stereotype of a class-mobile Latin woman who looks down on working-class Latins. Marilyn and José thought she sounded like a social worker. Luis heard her as "one of these snob types, too good for herself" and at first thought she might be white because she reacted as she did to people carrying things on the train, something "Spanish people" typically do. Rosie said she'd *like* to put her to work cleaning the subway but could imagine her, say, in politics. By contrast Luis saw in #4's topic a clue that he was both Latin and a sympatico person:

> Because he adjusted to seeing everything in life, the way it really goes. You know what I'm saying? The speaker seems to be taking it very well, you know, since he must have experienced it a couple of times before.

Tay thought #14 might be middle class because he expressed fear of the street. Marilyn and José thought #17 might be Puerto Rican from the way she talked about children in need. Luis added that #17:

> LM: Let out a lot of feelings when she spoke, and compared to Americans, Spanish
>   people have the tendency to—
> RM: To give more.
> LM: —show more love and affection when they speak.

This sympathetic figure could easily be imagined living next door. Luis, who saw himself speaking English with most sample speakers, saw himself speaking Spanish with her:

> I can relate to her in Spanish because she seems to let out a lot of emotion and I wouldn't feel frightened.

Voice, Sound, and Tone

Voices are perceived as people talking, not as disembodied sounds. They manifest action. They have defining properties, high, deep, clear, and so on. At the heart of the voice lies a tone "caused" by some quality of the speaker, a causality that invokes the idea of someone acting. Voices may reflect a speaker's origins. Millie connected #14's "sexy" voice to his being Latin and #2's "deep voice" to his being Italian-American. Vocal qualities can also allow for finer distinctions within a category: Nilsa finds that #9 "sounds trashy, I don't know why. . . . It doesn't sound like a sophisticated white person."

Nilsa and Tay connected clarity of voice to class and race. Nilsa heard #5's voice as unclear, a quality she ascribed to #5's English not being native, and she expressed surprise that #5 was a college student. Tay heard #4 as Latin or black or both, and a "street person":

> The way he talks . . . I cannot get the whole idea what he's talking about, I cannot hear very well when he's talking. He talks like *rrrrrrrrr*, he doesn't speak clear.

When I said #4 was an academic, Tay said (much as Nilsa had of #5), "Then why he speak like that? . . . Because an academic person should speak clear." Tay particularly saw black speakers' voices as unclear. She commented that #6 "speak clear for a colored man." Similarly she said of #7, "And for me she sounds black, but she speak very clear."

Describing #8, Tay elaborates on the defining qualities of black people's voices:

> I don't know because . . . I hear in colored people, I hear something like they have their voice, they don't have their voice like we have our voice. When they speak, I don't know—you know what *ronca* means? Like when you have a cold, that your voice change? That's the way I hear colored people, and I hear him that way too. But I hear something that he could be Spanish too.

Nilsa related #5's voice to her linguistic history:

> It sounded sometimes, her voice, as though she came here and then learned English. The voice sounds as though it's—she speaks slow Spanish, and doesn't sound very clear. . . . The English doesn't sound as sharp as I think it should for someone that, you know, was born here and grew up here.

Marilyn and Nilsa both described #10 as Latin or black from his voice. Jenny said of #12: "*Tiene el sonido hispano y sonido negro.*" [He has a Spanish and black sound].

Voice is routinely related to accent. Millie on #5:

> The sound of her voice. . . . even though she didn't say anything in Spanish but she has that accent.

At the same time, the voice is not reducible to accent, nor is it always easily categorized. Tay said of #6:

> I don't think he's Puerto Rican. His voice, it's like Dominican or Cuban but he has no accent at all . . . He has no accent. You made me think that he's a colored guy or Spanish guy but I have to choose one. But he speak clear for a colored man. Let's put that he's Spanish.

Repeatedly we get a sense of voice as more something one does or enacts than a discrete definable object. Tay hears in #7's voice a dynamic image:

> She sounds black. Maybe I'm wrong but I hear and I start putting a picture in my mind. And for me she sounds black, but she speak very clear. She speak very clear, she sounds black. She sounds about in her thirties and she could be working in an office.

Millie described #4 in terms of his linguistic history, as "Spanish" (Latin) but with "something in his voice that sounded like he hung out with black guys," which meant he probably knew little Spanish.

When people talk about vocal properties they often talk about *tone* and *tune*. *Tone* tends to imply a mood or state of mind or personality feature, whereas *tune* tends to imply a melody reflecting one's native language, though people often interchange the terms. People also talk about the *music* of a language, especially the "singing" tune or tone of Spanish. For example, in #1, Luis heard a singing tone that suggested Spanish origins: "English doesn't sound like you're singing." Rosie described #16 as follows:

> RM: You could know, yeah, you feel the sound of Spanish, you could notice it.
> BU: If you pinned it down to one thing, is it this tune?
> RM: Yes!
> BU: What people talk about as a tune?
> RM: Yes. That sound, it's like music.

That music can also distinguish among varieties of Spanish, for example, between Puerto Rican and Dominican Spanish:

> LM: OK, I understand what you're saying, because when Dominicans speak, they speak—when we speak Spanish, we speak—
> RM: Music.
> LM: In a sound-like thing. But the Dominicans speak in another different sound.

Jenny made a similar appraisal of #17:

> Because *los dominicanos hablan cantando. Y todo lo hacen como "ii-ii-ii."* [Because the Dominicans speak (as if they are) singing. And they all do it like *"ii-ii-ii."*]

José and Marilyn are surprised to find that #17 is Dominican:

> JM: I don't hear Dominican. . . . Marilyn's friend is Dominican and I could hear it.
> MM: I could tell.
> BU: In Spanish or in English?
> JM: Spanish and English.
> MM: Both.
> JM: She's probably a light-skinned Dominican.

People often speak of *tone* when talking about an emotional reaction or attitude, as when Nilsa expressed discomfort with "the tone of [#9's] voice" and José described in #1 a tone that was "not so nice." Marilyn in particular related tone of voice to personality or social type. She described #1 as having a "tone (of voice) like a social worker" and referred to #12's "boring tone of voice."

When people talk about race/ethnic and language identity they may use either *tone* or *tune*. For example, in explaining why #4 seemed Latin, Rosie and Luis described a Spanish *tone* of voice whereas Nilsa described a slight *tune*. In this complex description of #5, José treats tone of voice as a social action that does not reduce simply to race/ethnicity:

> It was hard to pin down between—I could tell she was Puerto Rican but in a way the way she acts, the way she speaks, the tone of voice, it's kind of more white. But I could tell she's Puerto Rican.[7]

Luis thought #9 might know Spanish based on her "tone of voice." Marilyn heard in #13 a "tone" that sounded black. Marilyn and José heard in #17 an unambiguously Puerto Rican Spanish "tune," like someone right here on this block. Nilsa expresses a similarly deictic connection:

> Just the tone of her voice, that sounds, you know, someone that grew up here, speaks Spanish.

Accents

Like voice, sound and tune/tone, accents can manifest a person acting or rather a history of action. Accents are things people have in their voices that tell how they have come to be what they are. Thus accents are fundamentally locative. When people have "no accent" they are nearly impossible to place. If an accent is easily identified, it provides an immediate sign of connection. Millie describes #5:

> The sound of her voice. . . . even though she didn't say anything in Spanish but she has that accent.

Accents come in increments: Jenny and José picked out "just a little" Spanish accent in #2 and, for Millie, #16 "doesn't have that much of an accent. Sounded more Italian, didn't he?" Even a little accent can be an origin marker though whether it indicates knowledge of another language may depend on its size or strength. Millie describes how an accent "sticks" to a speaker:

> BU: If you do have a little accent, you would speak Spanish?
> MW: I think she (#7) would, even if it's not that great.
> BU: Why is that?
> MW: I don't think you could get that accent without knowing that language first. Just like a French person can speak English very well but when he talks to you, you hear all those little things. That accent is just there, even if it's subtle it's still there. If he's been here for a lot of—if he came here as a kid and he learned to speak French at home and then when he came here he learned to speak English—but usually it stays with you. To get rid of it is difficult.

Accents can be thin or thick, subtle or heavy. Millie, Nilsa, and Luis had trouble pinning down #10's accent, Millie describing it as "very subtle, it's very subtle, it's like underneath. It's like a very calm undercurrent." By contrast she heard in #14 a "heavy-duty accent," which she found quite attractive. Above all, accents mark origins, which means they may contain a tone or tune that signals one's origins. People are said to have Spanish accents, Puerto Rican accents, Dominican accents, white accents, black accents, southern accents, Irish accents, Jamaican accents. All these are location devices, though they are not always entirely determinate. When the boundaries are fuzzy, people may explain the speaker's location in other ways such as a complicating personal history in which one acquired a non-native accent from friends. Millie elaborates on #10's "calm undercurrent" of an accent:

> It was real subtle, it might have been there and it might not have been there, and it could have been a situation where he was black and he had some Spanish friends and he picked up a little something.

When people cannot locate an accent, they may look for an exotic locale in which to place the speaker. Jenny, Millie, and Cathy immediately heard #14 as Dominican, and Marilyn heard him as Puerto Rican. Rosie, Nilsa, and José found #14's accent strange and placed him in an "exotic other" category, as Pakistani, Italian "like really from Italy," or Jamaican with a touch of Chinese. Luis could not locate #14's accent so looked for clues in his grammar and decided he was white. Tay could not decide if #14 was black or white so looked for clues in what he talked about and since he seemed afraid of the street, placed him as middle-class white. People similarly exoticized #15. Tay elaborated:

> Yes, she have an accent of—like from Pakistan, like that kind of people. . . . I couldn't guess [Irish] because I don't know the accent of those people.

Luis heard her as possibly Cuban (who might therefore speak a little Spanish), Rosie as Jewish ("I knew she wasn't Spanish and I knew she wasn't white, so I put her Jewish.") Marilyn heard her as Jamaican, and José as Italian ("I don't know, she sounded Italian to me. She didn't even say those 'mama mia' expression things. But it sounded Italian.") To Nilsa, Millie, and Cathy, #15's accent and location were obvious: they heard her as Irish and in short order placed her on Bainbridge Avenue in the most Irish part of the Bronx and in a stereotypic Irish role or occupation: maid or church worker. They guessed accurately: I met #15 in a Catholic church on Bainbridge Avenue.

Accents are also heard as discrete language segments, as words, letters, and sounds. Listening to #4, José and Marilyn described "that Puerto Rican accent" in "sounding out letters" or when he "says certain words." Luis described how #11 "knew where to put the letters where they belong" and José said that #11 "speaks out the words clearly." Two people gave instances of specific sounds. Tay characterized #4's lack of clarity as "He talks like *rrrrrrrrr*," and Marilyn described #2:

> One thing that tells me that he seems white to me is because of his "s," when he says "something" and that sound "s" comes out? And a lot of white people that I've heard have that "s" sound.

Words and Grammar

Metalanguage (how people define and analyze language) intersects pointedly with race and class. People's characterizations of correct words and grammar are shaped by the polarities of class and race. When people judge voices or speech as clear or unclear, they map class and race onto an idealized language. When people judge voices as sophisticated, civilized, street-talking, or snobby, they map race and class onto social and personality types. Yet people also judge voices as sexy, boring, strange, familiar, cute. These qualities are not about class, race, and correctness. In other words, voices and accents and how people talk can be assessed along multiple axes, not all of which are polarized. Language judgments become most sharp-edged when correctness is mapped onto class and race: language segments are either correct or incorrect; if they are incorrect, they can and should be corrected to mask class and race markedness. Correctability is central to the ways in which words, grammar, and letters are codified in dictionaries and textbooks as the objects that define language and test linguistic expertise.

Specific words can be race indexes. Before she heard the tape, Nilsa assessed the transcribed samples of #3 and #6 as the work of white speakers based on the wording. Pointing out what specifically had led her to this conclusion, she said of #6:

> By the "they would always sweep the sidewalk," "the curb," "rather," you know, correcting herself. "Drivers are," "the new breed of sanitation," I would consider clues. Some little phrases that I—Hispanics don't normally use. A student.

Marilyn took #6 to be a white teacher:

> BU: What's his English like?
> MM: He talks English like a little bit of high-class, like when he says "congestion."
> BU: So you notice certain words in particular?
> MM: Yeah.

Some "white" vocabulary is not specifically marked for class: Marilyn noted that #9 said "God" and added "a lot of white old ladies say 'God.'"

Nilsa quotes specific things said by #10 which seemed non-standard. Echoing the assessments she and Tay made of non-standard accents as unclear, she describes #10's speech as "awkward":

> "I don't like", "you know what I don't like is when the people be." It's when people "are," rather than saying that "people be." Just the wording, awkward.

Along the same lines, Luis assessed #11 as putting the right pieces of English in the right places.

> LM: She's so squeaky, I hear it. She's good, she is good. . . . She's white, she's well-educated—
> RM: Yes!
> LM: She uses her [xxx] fine, very articulated, and she uses very very good words, like "chronically"—

RM: And her voice is soft.

LM: Here, here (consulting transcript)—the word "chronically," "efficient," "incoming," "delay," "cruel"—she's white. She's very educated and chances are she could be a teacher. . . . Because she knew where to put the letters where they belong, her English, her grammar was so good.

Luis makes a similar assessment of #12:

It's words. He used the proper English, like "ran." If a Hispanic person would say that, he would say "run."

José assessed #10's non-standard phrasing as a class index:

JM: When he said "You know how long it is that ride?"

BU: What did that tell you?

JM: That he was lower class.

BU: I talk like that sometimes.

JM: But he sounds like he did it on purpose, like he meant it.

While words and sound may be assessed separately, they are judged synergetically. Millie assessed #2's usage along with his voice, drawing a class/ethnic conclusion: "he said he was seven *foot* tall, he didn't say he was seven *feet* tall." That plus his deep voice brought to her mind a vision of Italian-American guys hanging out. Millie made a similar assessment of #17, concluding "Spanish. Definitely Spanish. Got an accent and everything." She had also guessed from the text:

A couple of words that you said there, "onto" and "like" and there was another one too, "like, you know." What number is this? Seventeen? "Like I mean," that's the one. Must have been [xx xx] where she said "like." And "I can't stand it."

People's perceptions of errors are strongly affected by their perceptions of accents. I had read #8's transcript to Luis who did not comment on #8's use of habitual *be*. When I played the tape he stopped me at the words "where I be at to catch the train," looked at the printed text and circled the *be*.

LM: He's black! Because he used that *be* and he was like, you know, "yo bro", you know.

BU: But you didn't pick it up from my reading?

LM: I didn't.

RM: Me neither.

LM: You know why? Because the way you read it. . . . because when I read it, I pin it down. When you read it it slipped through because—I don't know, it just seems different when a person—

RM: She's white.

BU: Because I have a white accent?

LM: Right!

BU: And it makes you hear different things?

LM: It sounds proper when you say it. It's weird because I was reading through it and the first part was, where did that *be's* come from? And there's no such thing as *be's*, unless you say *bees* like the ones that sting you. But I caught it, I said wait a minute, this is wrong, *be's*.

On the other hand, Nilsa noticed habitual *be* when I read the text and noted it as a feature that could be Hispanic or black, along with "wrong things like 'the crowd of people seen him.'"

Two interesting points arise here. First, the speaker's voice can affect perception of specific words so that perception of correct English is a function of both accent and wording. Second, the combination of a "black" accent and "mistakes" like habitual *be* is highly metacommunicative. Number 8 is repeatedly seen to be going nowhere. Luis thought he might be a drug dealer. Rosie saw him working at a factory. José saw him hanging out and probably mugging people. Millie saw him on the corner running numbers. Cathy noted "as much as he used *be*" as a sign that "he's not educated" though she thought he might have ambition.

Cursing was twice mentioned as a race index. Marilyn described #2:

> If it was Puerto Rican or black he would just come out like cursing without no respect.

Cathy heard #10's vocabulary as understated, saying that a black speaker would at least have said something like "the damn train." Millie at first objected "I don't think Bonnie wanted people to be cursing on the tape" but added "the cursing helps you to know too" though perhaps "that would be too much of a giveaway."

The phrase which people found most strikingly indexical was "you know." People heard it as an index of race (Spanish/black), class (poor education), and locale (New York). It was most striking in #5's speech, which was taken as quintessentially local and Latin: Tay, Rosie, Luis, Jenny, Millie and Marilyn all picked out her "you know" (she said it nine times). Millie picked out #1's "you know" as typically "Spanish." Nilsa heard good vocabulary and no "you know"—signs of education—from #2. Millie thought #3 (whom she heard as black) must have picked up her "you know" from living in New York. She said the same of #9: "They must be from New York, I see that 'you know' again. They must live up in the Bronx." Jenny described #6 as *hispano* based on "*Como habla, el acento y el* 'you know'" [how he talks, the accent and the 'you know']. Luis and Rosie made the same assessment, adding "You know that's funny, because we say it but we stay unaware that we're saying it." Rosie assessed #7 on "you know" and "OK":

> I think she's black or Puerto Rican, one of the two, because she has "OK" and "you know." . . . I think it's the "OKs" . . . I want to tell you, she's Puerto Rican. . . . She has the "OK."

Jenny characterized the same thing:

> BU: *Cual palabra* [which word]—you were pointing to one word?
> JP: Yeah, I pointed to "OK." *Cuando ella dice una palabra, una oración, ella dice el* "OK," *el* "you know." [When she says a word, a sentence, she says the "OK," the "you know."]
> BU: *Este* "OK," "you know," *es hispana*? [This "OK," "you know," is she Spanish?]
> JP: *Es hispana. Ése es*—[She is Spanish. That is—]

Luis found #13 "a very articulated person, she seems to speak very well English"; the only sign he saw in #13 as Hispanic was her use of "you know."

Luis spells out the synergy of correctness, race, class, and the use of "you know":

> LM: We black and Hispanic have the tendency to always say "you know."
> RM: [laughing]: That's true!
> LM: To cut the conversation short, you say "you know what I mean, you know." And it's always "you know." But you know one day I said—one day in school, Bonnie, right? I went and I gave a speech on a subject, I can't remember exactly and I started to say things and I kept on saying to the teacher "You know what I mean" you know—you know what I'm saying, you know? And finally the teacher says, "Luis I don't know, tell me." And I says "you know" and she kept on telling me "I don't know, I want you to tell me." And she was actually making fun of the fact that I kept on saying "you know."

Luis's teacher's criticism is based on the clarity and precision principle: correct language is explicit, leaving no meaning in the dark, an ideology that clearly resonates with Bernstein's (1971) elaborated code model. As with habitual *be*, Luis and Rosie did not notice the "you know" when I read them the transcribed text of #5. They heard it when #5 spoke on tape:

> BU: I say "you know" all the time, I don't think you pick it up.
> LM: So why is it so noticeable on us—
> RM: —and not on them?
> BU: I don't know.
> LM: Why would—you know, why would somebody make fun of it even though they use it often?

The answer is, what gets noticed is not simply the phrase "you know" but the fact that it is used by a speaker already marked in other ways.

Good English

Good English emerges from these typifications as a clear and exact use of the right pieces (words, letters) in the right order. Thus, Tay describes #3 as speaking good English because her speech was clear, she had no accent and made only "one little mistake." Nilsa saw #5's English as bad because it was "not sharp." Luis specified the race-class-correctness nexus in his appraisal of #10's English as "extremely poor . . . I don't mean very extremely poor but it sounds like Hispanic English" (compare Luis's assessment of #11). When Luis listened to #10 on tape, he added, "I'd say he's black, he's definitely black, and he has that sort of like street-talk English, the way we use it with very poor grammar. That's why I say his English is very poor." His use of "we" suggests that insofar as working-class blacks and Hispanics are equally excluded from the middle-class white world, neither quite excludes the other.

Correct white English creates self-consciousness and distance. Nilsa, Millie, Marilyn, and José all found #11's persona discomfiting. Rosie commented that "she sounded too good to be true" and Rosie and Luis concurred that talking to her would make them very self-conscious. Luis says much the same about #3, whom he also heard as middle-class white:

> LM: I would feel strange. I feel strange when I'm talking to Ann or Mary.[8] You—(pause).
>
> BU: Because we go back awhile?
>
> LM: No, not only that, maybe you have become as I say adjusted to the way I speak, and their English sounds so—
>
> RM: I don't know why because Luis's English is very good.
>
> LM: Their English sounds so professional compared to my English, I don't think my English is that professional. Maybe this is what I—what we were taught to believe.
>
> BU: Wow. Would you feel funny talking to this woman?
>
> RM: I don't think so. If I know English and she could understand me, I would think that's enough.

When Luis characterizes such English as "sounding professional," he imputes to Ann and Mary the ability to pattern their speech so that, in effect, it sounds scripted. Learning to produce this literacized "good" English requires the kind of schooling to which Luis feels he has had limited access. At the same time, he sees the relative arbitrariness of the ideology ("maybe this is what I—what we were taught to believe") but the world he has to live and work in does not allow that insight to give him much confidence. Luis goes to work every day in a mostly white workplace and it does not let him forget who he "really" is.

Correctness as Cultural and Symbolic Capital

The idea of correctness links the race/class conflation to language segments as cultural capital. If the same sign that reads "this speaker is Puerto Rican" also reads "this speaker doesn't know which pieces of language to put where," then perceptions of "low" class (typified as poor education) are conflated with racial markedness. The linguistic object that indexes such a conflation cannot operate as cultural capital because of the way it is put together and rationalized as a sign. For example, an accent is a thing with size, substance, and explicit connections to words and letters. As a result it is an object which its possessor, that is, the speaker, should be able to control. If the connections to the letters are wrong, the speaker should be able to correct them by applying rules learned in books made available through public schooling. If an accent is too strong, it can be diminished bit by bit. Not only can this be done, it should be done. Any bilingual with a public school education should have the knowledge and ability to control his or her language. In this way one disconnects race and class, ethnicizing one's identity in front of people who count—bosses, teachers, co-workers, anyone with whom one needs cultural capital. Control of language is thus read as a sign of education, which is a sign of investment in class mobility.

The correctness ideology is effectively outlined in the first paragraph of the widely used high school text, *English Grammar and Composition* by Warriner and Griffith:

> Success comes to the person who has at his command the words he needs and the necessary knowledge of his language to help him use these words as he wishes. A person's ideas, no matter how good, are of little practical importance unless he can express them clearly. Incorrect and awkward English is a social and business handicap and a frequent cause of failure in school. (Warriner and Griffith 1963:2)

Grammars like this are organized by topics like "Grammar Review: The Parts of Speech, The Parts of a Sentence, The Phrase, The Clause"; "Writing Correct Sentences: What is Good English?, The Completed Sentence, Agreement, Correct Use of Pronouns, Correct Form and Use of Verbs, Correct Use of Modifiers" and so on (pp. v–vi). The chapters are laid out as principles, rules and examples, explanations, and exercises. Correctness is explained as motivated, not arbitrary, and is rationalized in terms of function, logic, efficiency, precision, and economy. The key to efficient written usage is to avoid the linguistic devices most characteristic of *spoken* language. The use of subordinated clauses is preferred to clauses connected by "and." Run-on sentences should be avoided (pp. 238ff). Colloquial formulae are considered trite and ineffective (p. 263). At the same time one should sound natural by avoiding the *explicitly* literary. The aim is to achieve a written style that appears natural and logical. The line between good written and good spoken English becomes tenuous. Correct pronunciation is exemplified by standard *spelling*. Dialect or rapid speech, exemplified by variant spelling, is cast by Warriner and Griffith as mispronunciation (p. 531):

> The substitution of one sound for another is a frequent fault: *ciddy* for *city*; *dis* for *this*; *tree* for *three*.

Such rationales shape the idea that clarity and "knowing where to put the letters" are criteria for judging good English.

Milroy and Milroy (1985) argue that the ideologies expressed in complaints about English correctness serve to maintain one dialect over others as the "standard." In particular, the codification and prescription of written and published usage legitimized such formal registers as normative for any English, written or spoken, in any context. Much of the "logic" ascribed to standardized forms comes after the fact of standardization ("illogical" variants were widespread in previous centuries).

The ways in which people talk about "good" English, as grammar, words, pronunciation, letters, and accents, are not isomorphic with syntax, morphemes, or phonemes, the objects of linguistic analysis. Grammar, accents, and so on are constituted in the politics of everyday routines in which the bottom line is metacommunication. The concern with purity is explained by Silverstein (1987:9): "good" American English has a natural, pure logic unmarked by "lots of crusted impurities" and unconnected to any specific social group. Above all, it is interpreted as *clear*. Signs of origins in a stigmatized group are interpreted as unclear, impure, unacceptable, which is the message people in this study live with. Their local linguistic identity contrasts sharply with middle-class, white English, which is largely characterized by its *lack* of localizing features ("OK?" "you know?"), its lack of mistakes, and its lack of accent.

Language objects do not exist in a vacuum. They emerge in a consciousness of language as words, grammar, letters, and sounds that are correctable and isolable. The polarity between incorrect and correct matches the polarity between the stereotypic Puerto Rican or black street-talking lowlife and the Hispanic-American or African American model citizen. Voice and tone, the language elements least subject to correctability, represent social, ethnic, and personality types that do not reduce to educated versus lowlife, white versus Hispanic/black. Correct forms should be able to overcome racial marking; in effect, they should ethnicize. This is the prestige, the symbolic capital that correct segments should bring. Yet correct segments only bring symbolic capital when the prestige is enough to overcome other signs of racial marking in the speaker. Unfortunately, correct forms by themselves do not guarantee prestige: that depends on other dynamics in the speech situation such as who judges what.

Accents as Complex Signs

Accents are semiotically complex. Drawing from Peirce (1956), they are iconic in that they invoke images, indexical in that they are understood as causal or coexistential, and symbolic in that all this is culturally learned. Moreover, accents have a deictic quality in that people's assessments of them presuppose comparison with those who sound like "us" or "me." Above all, accents are modes of social action.

Respondents frequently talk about they "saw" as well as "heard." Tay is most explicit about this iconicity:

> The way I was hearing, at the same time I was putting the image in my mind. . . . they have something in the voice that tells you . . . the last one (#17) I put in my mind, I was hearing—I couldn't hear it too good but the image was there and I saw her young and I saw her that—I told you, she speaks Spanish, right? See, all that I saw here in my mind.

Images crystalize around the interplay of sound and topics, reinforcing the oppositions that define people's social and moral geography. People were especially tuned to the moral aspects of topics: how do speakers react to crowded trains, homeless people, noise, smells, all the things that make up real life as these people know it and from which they cannot afford to distance themselves.[9] The way linguistic indexes work in social action is inextricable from such iconicity, for accents, voices, sounds, words, and grammar index where people are *from*. Respondents look at where sample speakers are from, compare it to their own *here* and *us*, their deictic reference points, their habitus, and make sense of speakers' actions and motives on that basis. Without a known place-from-which, assessment lacks substance. We see this in people's attempts to make sense of #14 and #15 by exoticizing them. The substance of a known place means the *kind* of people who live there, how they look, sound, act and feel, their goals, desires, and moral center.

Listening to the taped voices, people inferred images and actions that they might actually encounter. The actions and objects of language are realized in flesh-and-blood contexts where they are performative, creating, solidifying, and shifting the terms by which people know and deal with each other. These linguistic actions and objects are metacommunicative, influencing the terms by which people interpret and *act* toward each other. Given the politics of race and class, the speakers whose accents respondents are most likely to feel comfortable with are also the speakers most likely to be assigned a low-level job, or to be seen as "stuck in place." This is not linguistic or ethnic/race self-hatred. This is a recognition of the race/class conflation that lies at the basis of their everyday reality.

For example, everyone heard #5 as Latin and five people heard her as Puerto Rican. Everyone thought she knew Spanish based on her accent and the fact that she said "you know" several times; most would speak Spanish or both English and Spanish with her. When it came to a job, people saw her as a sales clerk or counter worker, a neighbor, a mother waiting for her kids after school, perhaps still in school herself. Number 17, whom everyone heard as Puerto Rican, was assessed in similar linguistic terms and in similar job terms: a clerk or receptionist or secretary or factory worker—or on welfare. People phrase their linguistic perceptions of these women in terms of trust, *confianza*. To Marilyn, #5 "talks like us." To Luis and Rosie, #17 sounded warm and kind. These women would be nice to know, but no one can assume they have good jobs, given where they come from.

The male speaker that people heard as most local came across more ambiguously. Five people heard him as Latin, two as Latin and/or black, one as black, and one as white. At the same time seven people thought he knew Spanish based on his accent; given the local perception that young African American men might well learn Spanish from Latin friends, this assessment makes sense. Everyone who heard #4 as non-white thought him a pleasant person but generally unsuccessful. Tay for example heard his "unclear" English as the sign of a Latin and/or black street person. Most people assigned him an unskilled working-class job. As Marilyn explained it:

For me, Puerto Ricans—they try to move up but they don't get so high. It's only like a lot of blacks now are getting higher than Puerto Ricans especially.

The interesting exception here was Luis, who immediately saw #4 as a neighbor, co-worker, and someone who has "come up in the world." When we'd finished and I said that #4 was in fact an academic, he responded, "Nice!" He reacted sharply to the conventional race/class connection and metacommunicative implications voiced by Rosie:

> BU: How about a job, a teacher? A mechanic?
> RM: Factory. He's Spanish.
> LM: No, he doesn't have to, there's a lot of Spanish people don't work for a factory. You can't take that attitude.
> BU: Bank clerk?
> LM: I would say—
> RM: I say factory.
> BU: Store manager?
> LM: Yes. I would say a store manager type of guy.

The iconic and deictic process of building a persona starts with the points of reference least marked to the respondent, or as Marilyn said of #5, "She talks like us. That's Puerto Rican." People find points where they can compare and contrast, as when Millie said of #11, "Sounds like Chris, right Cathy? Between Jan and Chris?" The elements of persona cannot cohere unless there is a voice around which to "start putting a picture in my mind," as Tay said of #7. Linguistic action depends on that picture. In the neighborhood, on the local scene, relations of *confianza* are signalled by unmarked language. Unmarked can be Spanish, English, or both: the real point is whether the English is an English that *sounds* local. There are local relationships in which Spanish would be marked. Nilsa, who generally prefers English, explained when she would use Spanish:

> I would have to hear a real difficult, a really thick accent. And, if I would feel very uncomfortable in listening to the person, and trying to speak it, and the person were trying to speak English, it would definitely feel uncomfortable. If it sounds to me that the person is definitely uncomfortable then I would definitely turn off English and turn on Spanish.

These observations raises some points of concern about the limits of correlationist sociolinguistics. An accent is not reducible to pronunciation per se and certainly not to a set of phonological variables in Labov's sense of frequently occurring discrete units that can be quantified on a linear scale and correlated with social characteristics (1982[1966]:32). Since Labov first outlined the field of quantitative sociolinguistics in 1966, there have been a number of refinements and innovations. Milroy's (1980) study of network structure and speech patterns has been particularly important, but the emphasis on quantitative relations between linguistic items and social groups has remained constant. Such a model can provide a fine-grained representation of social structure and linguistic behavior but does not get at the interpretation of variability. The sociolinguistic index is a sophisticated and useful analytic construct but it does not belong to a voice.

Social actors hear voices—manifestations of social action—not strings of phonemes. Accents do not reduce to phonemes for the same reason that kinship does not reduce to blood or sex, nor race to physiognomy or genes. As Schneider (1980 [1968]) explains kinship:

> There are certain cultural notions which are put, phrased, expressed, symbolized by cultural notions *depicting* biological facts, or what purport to be biological facts. Sexual intercourse and the attendant elements which are said to be biological facts *insofar as they concern kinship* as a cultural system are of this order. Kinship is *not* a theory about biology; but biology serves to formulate a theory about kinship. (p. 115; italics in original)

And as Gould (1979:232) explains race:

> Geographic variability, not race, is self-evident. No one can deny that *homo sapiens* is a strongly differentiated species; few will quarrel with the observation that differences in skin color are the most striking outward sign of this variability. But the fact of variability does not require the designation of races.

An accent, like kinship and race, is a category of location which proceeds from a center, a point of reference from which people as social actors orient their sense of who they are, where they belong, and what their actions mean to each other in Weber's sense of social action (1978:385–395). In the United States, the heart of a person's social world is made of relations with people who look and sound like oneself, who share origins, language(s) and accent, and who, above all, share common blood as kin. Shared race/ethnicity is meaningful when it designates people who could be kin through common descent. All these axes connect people in primary ways to a world that existed before them and that will continue after them. The signs that mark categories of belonging mean different things to those sharing lifelong routine experience than they do to those looking in from the outside, such as social analysts. The same signs may be interpreted differently depending on the interpreter's point of reference: people hear me as white, American, Northern, Eastern, or central New York.

An accent implies the existence of boundaries, but boundaries are much harder to locate than are centers or focal points. Accents have a deictic quality, pointing out from the speaker's "zero point" in time and space, so the center is fixed in a way that boundaries are not. This sense of pointing out from the speaker is missing from the sociolinguistic phoneme variable. The variable indexes a category of person (e.g., a certain percent of lower-middle-class males will pronounce the first sound of the word "that" as [d] in certain environments), but this indexes a point in an abstract structure, not a point in a situation of speaking. As Benveniste

(1971[1956]) argues, language only becomes discourse when it does index the moment of speaking, at which point the indexical also becomes the deictic. Once that happens, the interpretation of deictic elements—pronouns, tense markers, time and space adverbs—depends on who, when, and where the speaker is.

The deictic quality that gives accents their indeterminate nature has important consequences for analysis. Variables and variable rules were designed for a relatively static model in which the primary concern is statistical probability of behavior in tightly defined contexts. As Dittmar (1983), Romaine (1982:240ff), Pousada and Greenlee (1988), and Mannheim (1991) have variously argued, the appropriate unit for sociolinguistic study is that which starts from the problem of social meaning, not that which is most readily quantified. Pousada and Greenlee, who worked with bilingual Puerto Ricans in East Harlem, are particularly critical of the asocial, ahistorical, and aprocessual aspects of conventional sociolinguistics.[10] The problem is not with multivariate analysis, which characterizes current variable rule work, but with the ways in which social factors are formulated to fit the analysis of variables. Gould's point on race is well taken here: multivariate analysis of human genetic variation confirms the impossibility of understanding race as anything other than a social construct. Similarly, multivariate analysis in sociolinguistics can show a social complexity of linguistic practice that does not correlate isomorphically with social categories. This raises the important question of how categories of person are constructed and how they fit into the local political/symbolic economy.[11]

Metacommunicative Politics

Irvine argues that analysts should examine the ways in which specific code properties are meaningful to speakers, both as discrete, autonomous, or rule-ordered linguistic elements and as "ideas about social relations, including ideas about the history of persons and groups" (1989:253). Linguistic elements and ideas form a system in which:

> Verbal skills and performances are among the resources and activities forming a socioeconomic system; and the relevant knowledge, talent and use-rights are not evenly, randomly and fortuitously distributed. (p. 255)

The code properties of English, as experienced and understood by the people in this study, carry race/class risk insofar as they figure into an American ideology of correctness. Not all language segments are subject to correction, nor is correctness always an issue. Correctness lies not in the forms per se but in their relation to the politics of context. What works fine in the inner sphere, metacommunicating safety and familiarity, is a "mistake" in the outer, sending very risky messages. It is no surprise that Ryan and Carranza (1975) found Mexican-American students much more likely to rate a "Mexican" accent as solidarity at home than in the classroom, where students are most aware of accents as cultural capital. If correction is possible, it is (ideologically speaking) the individual's responsibility to know what to correct and how to do it. People who do not correct their language cannot disconnect race from class or rewrite race as ethnicity. They abdicate any hope of metacommunicative control. Where "mistakes" reinforce white ideas about "lowlife" Puerto Ricans, correct language provides a chance to challenge that stereotype, to be seen instead as a hard-working Hispanic-American and to open the closed doors of a class-structured social environment. For Rosie and Luis Molina, metacommunicative control is what schooling should be all about. They stress the merits of their children's new school:

> RM: That's why I like this school that the kids are at because they give them proper—what is it called? They're teaching them how to speak English, proper words, no mistakes—
>
> LM: Grammar and pronunciation—
>
> RM: Grammar, that they cannot know what race you are.

Metacommunicating Exclusion

When Nilsa Buon started her current job, she said she made a conscious effort to keep English and Spanish absolutely separate. She succeeded at first to the extent that her boss did not know she was Hispanic. But the effort was tiring. After a few months she could not keep it up, and she felt the two languages start to scramble. She said she had always been painfully conscious of how she sounds and how she might be judged at work. She finds it exhausting to stay in English if she is talking to someone "very educated" such as "my boss or sometimes even you." At such times she feels her "Spanish accent" just "slipping under the door," as if something were oozing through the cracks. Her imagery is straight out of *Purity and Danger* (Douglas 1966): language pollution, matter out of place, uncontrolled, and unpurified.

Tay Román explains the importance of knowing "right words" in controlling others' perceptions of her:

> TR: We want to explain something and we can't. And we try and we try and we try and we can't explain what we want to say. And I get nervous. I get—you know, I would like to sometimes to disappear because like it just seems something against me. And I want to defend myself. I don't have the right words to explain myself. I need somebody else to do it for me, you know? Maybe I would be able to do it but I get nervous and I'm afraid. Maybe what I'm gonna say is not right.
>
> BU: And what would happen if it wasn't right, what would be the result?
>
> TR: Well, it could be a lot of things, because if I say something—I mean, if I think I am saying something that would be helpful for me and maybe I'm saying something that is gonna be against me. I don't know because—I don't know—maybe I don't know what I'm saying.

Saying the right words casts her in a positive light ("helpful for me"); saying the wrong words casts her in a negative light ("against me"). She conveys a sense of struggling with unwieldy pieces that do not quite fit together:

BU: So . . . that's when you find yourself in a position when it's hard to defend yourself—

TR: Yes, it's hard. If you don't speak good English, if you don't know how to explain yourself, how to say things clear, it's difficult. That's why you get nervous and you get confused and everything.

She stresses the importance of clarity. Clarity and order define boundaries when status is on the line; what is orderly *enough* depends on context. Responsibility for getting it right is not an issue when people talk about understandable things and when the terms of understanding can be negotiated, as is more likely to be the case with neighbors:

> Well, I have a friend here that she's a colored lady, and uh, if I say something that is not right, she will correct me. And if she says something that I don't understand she will explain me. I will ask, you know, what you mean with that word, and she will explain to me. I don't have no problem.

Metalinguistic recourse is available: she can ask her neighbor to explain things. But when there is a status difference, the responsibility for negotiating meaning is hers alone:

> Because I feel that that person is on top of me. You know, I think that that person, not—I don't mean that she is better than me. But I think that is a person that is on top of me and I'm afraid to, you know, I don't have the confidence. If she says something and I don't understand it, maybe I will ask her once. But twice, I'm afraid to do it. Because some persons, you know, they don't like a person to ask a question more than once. . . . If I ask them a question and they answer me and I don't understand them and I ask them a question twice and I see some kind of faces that they do or, like, oooh you know, she asks me the same question again, then I feel—I feel bad. That's why I am afraid to ask questions twice.

"Good" English is always implicitly, usually explicitly, measured against the written standard. Tay has taken classes for some years with just that standard in mind. Formal schooling is one's primary, perhaps only, access to explicitly codified rules. But "getting the degree" takes a considerable investment of time and effort that can be a real hardship for working-class people, especially women. Jenny Pacheco's story is particularly vivid and painful. She had been taking courses at Hostos Junior College in the Bronx and had been doing well, when her son was killed. She decided to drop her courses rather than risk failing. She went to see one of her professors (translated from Spanish, see endnote for original):

> He told me, "The best thing you did was not come to take the exams because if so, you would have failed." So then, here I am with the pain of my son's death. And he hits me with this, when he was the first professor I talked to. Because he wanted to. He was one of the harshest ones that made me suffer with English. He's black. He said to me "why don't you know how to read English well? You

know that I make you read" . . . I almost never raised my hand to talk because I was scared of saying something wrong and having them laugh at me, you know—no, not that. But when he made me read, I had to do it. And I read English badly because I didn't—I understand everything but I don't read it right. So he told me "why do you read English so poorly?" Then I left and that gave me such grief that I'm squeezing myself [rubbing her chest with grief]. Because I came back from Puerto Rico [after her son's funeral] with that pain to face this bullshit that I didn't go see any (other) professor, I came back crying, I came back here. And because of him, I let them throw me out. . . . Without knowing if I could pass the test, because he—the fact that I couldn't read English fast and fluently in front of the class didn't mean that I couldn't read it to myself and figure out what you're trying to tell me on paper. I could have done that exam and I could've gotten, God only knows, if maybe even perfect, because I could read it for myself, what I didn't have was the fluency to read it aloud.[12]

Jenny's dilemma is as follows. As far as this teacher is concerned, the metacommunicative bottom line, shaping his perception of everything she does and says, is her classroom and test performance. In effect, she is her test score. So she wants to give school her best shot. She must do so in a system that makes minimal allowance for emergencies, for grief and loss, for travel and funeral arrangements that must be made with limited funds. Her story is not unusual and not particularly extreme. Working-class women in night school are constantly faced with demands made on their time, energy, and resources by the lives for which they are responsible. Moreover, working-class urban-minority people are generally at greater risk from accidents, inadequate health care arrangements, and violence than are middle-class white people, and their lives are laced with a disproportionate degree of death and illness. One of the especially pernicious "hidden injuries of class" is sheer lack of protection from complex and difficult circumstances. Class advantage brings not only money and status but far greater financial and social resources for handling emergencies, illness, and grief (see Rapp 1987).

When people face situations where they may be stigmatized, accents become risky, as Nilsa described above; when people do not face such situations, accents are not risky. Luis and Rosie Molina describe this contrast:

BU: Does [your accent] come out all the time or do you just feel it sometimes?
RM: *No entiendo.* [I don't understand.]
LM: To me, to me it comes out—
RM: Explain to me.
LM: OK, to me it comes out when I'm dealing with just mostly—
RM: —white folks.
LM: —white folks. Okay, like in my job.
BU: When do people make you really conscious of how you talk?
LM: When I'm dealing with white folks. Where I work now? They always, always, these guys, A is white, B, he's from Guyana, . . . then there is C who is also white, Irish white.[13] And they let me know the fact that they—in a way they sort of remind me who I am. . . . You know, it's like when I speak they let me know that I am Hispanic.

BU: You sound like you don't experience that much.

RM: No, not very much.

LM: Because she doesn't deal with people—

RM: I don't deal with white folks. . . . I just deal with teachers.

LM: And this thing's been going on for years and years and it can continue to go on for years. They sort of like, they see you, oh, look at him talk, you know, listen to him speak, we can put him down because his language, it's not English so it's constantly wrong because of the things he say because of the interference between the two languages. . . . We get discriminated from that. . . . We get put down. We get put down.

Luis, like Nilsa, has constant contact with whites in a work situation where race and class differences are much sharper and language a much riskier issue than around the neighborhood. Luis sees the leaky-accent issue in terms of his co-workers' perceptions of his speech. They seem to Luis to look for ways to distance his speech from their standard so as to highlight their perception of his worth as a person. Race ("Hispanic") frames notions of linguistic impurity and blurred boundary ("interference"); hence Luis feels judged as *not trying hard enough* to overcome the limits of race and be a good ethnic American. Such linguistic morality is central to ethnicizing discourses and is a yardstick that minoritized people often use against each other. It is no accident that Luis mentions a Guyanese along with two white co-workers. If what Luis speaks is not "really" English (due to interference), he can be regarded as not "really" American.

The inability to control language boundaries is most risky when a person is faced with a difference in status and authority. When Nilsa Buon talks to someone who speaks much less English than she does, she does not face a sense of confusion or loss of control. When faced with the opposite situation, someone whose Spanish is better than hers, she feels fine about her English yet may well find her Spanish inadequate. But in those situations, she does not face the same consequences. The fluent Spanish speaker is unlikely to be in a position to hire, promote, pass, fail, or grade her. Marilyn Mojica describes the same phenomenon and nicely lays out the dynamics of outer-sphere English:

BU: Is the way you feel about being teased about Spanish in Puerto Rico the same as how you feel if the landlord got on you about your accent?

MM: No, because we only get Spanish from our parents but we get English from everyplace here, the schools and everywhere so if you make a mistake in English, you feel worse.

Metacommunicating Solidarity

The other side of exclusion is the mutual solidarity that can be felt among the excluded. José typifies this in terms of "good" versus "accented" English (notes):

JM: When I have friends that speak OK, good English, I get to not like it anymore. I like to be with people who have an accent because otherwise I feel strange—they all have that same tone, the same voice.

BU: How does that make you feel?

JM: Angry, kind of.

BU: Is there a barrier? Do they seem like different people?

JM: They seem like all the same people, not their personality, but all the same race, even though they're not, even if they're Chinese or Jewish or Italian.

BU: Is it that they all start to sound white?

JM: Yes, and I get the feeling that I don't like this language anymore, like it's getting too difficult, out of hand.

BU: (to MM): Would you have the same reaction?

MM: In a way. It's good to learn English but if you come from another place where they don't speak English you have that in you too. And you shouldn't let it slide just to be the same as everyone here.

JM: And if you lose that accent, and start to sound like everyone else I feel like I'm not going to understand you anymore. Like I have a friend who's Russian or German, it makes him easier to listen to.

BU: Is it that the words are easier to understand or that he seems more real?

JM: He seems more real?

BU: Like the sound, the accent?

JM: He's got this accent from another country and it makes me feel that because he's from another country we are friends.

BU: Because he's not just another American?

JM: Right.

When everyone has "that same tone, the same voice" they are "all the same *race*" and, implicitly, all the same class. One trades one's distinct identity for status. To José, there is a real sense of loss, even if the identity one gives up is, in white eyes, stigmatized. Labov calls this a covert norm in that José attributes "positive values to the vernacular" (1972:249). Labov's assessment is too simplistic. It misses the political dimension of solidarity, the sense of shared exclusion, as relationships as well as language start "getting too difficult, out of hand." Moreover, while numerous linguistic studies have talked about power and solidarity in broad code terms (i.e. Spanish or English), José's focus on tone, voice, and accent is significantly closer to the Brown and Gilman (1960) argument that power and solidarity relations are indexed by specific elements such as pronouns. Furthermore, as Friedrich (1979[1966]) showed, context is central: pronouns can index social relations precisely because they relate to situations of speaking in complex and unpredictably nuanced ways. In the same sense, accents and other boundary-marking objects relate to context-specific, constantly fluctuating relations in complex, unpredictable ways. The full pragmatic meaning of an accent emerges every time a judgment is made. What José's classmates and teacher "like to hear" is as much part of his accent as is the pronunciation itself:

JM: Where I go now the kids in the program like to joke around with my accent, and the teacher too, and I say I don't have an accent, it's that I say things that aren't the way they like to hear it.

BU: Everyone's been reporting the same thing, that you have to tell people what they want to hear.

JM: You have to know what to leave out.

Accents mark people's origins and original language but these can fade from view, as Rosie explains:

> You see a Puerto Rican when he's born here, I think you don't know the differ-
> ence with English, because baby Luis doesn't have an accent. I have—you could
> know I'm Puerto Rican because I have my accent, and Luis but not him. He
> doesn't have an accent because he don't speak Spanish. It's because of that. He
> don't speak the language that he learned plus English—it's not that I don't speak
> Spanish in the house. I do, I see soap operas in Spanish, they see it all the time, I
> put Latin music. But it's because I put them when he was three years old and I
> stopped. He picked up the English and not the Spanish. He started speaking
> English and everybody speaks to him in English and the problem with his sister is
> everybody speaks to her English. The only ones that speak to her in Spanish are
> me or Luis or Mami.

José and Marilyn Mojica add that one picks up an accent from people to whom one is closest (notes):

> JM: Besides, the way people speak when they come from Puerto Rico is different
>   from here. They have an accent almost like Dominicans, it sounds funny to me.
> MM: So you pick up the way people talk if you're with them. Like my friend who's
>   Dominican, I come home and [my husband] says why do you sound
>   Dominican? And it's because I'm with my friend. *Que se pega.* [It sticks.]

Marilyn elaborates this theme in a later interview:

> MM: And that's the way I see it, I say wait a minute, what's going on, why is every-
>   body looking at us? Because we talking Spanish? I mean, not Spanish,
>   Dominican. Because they have like an accent.
> BU: Sure. Where do you think accents come from? The language you speak? The
>   place you come from?
> MM: The place you come from. Because people from Santo Domingo always have
>   an accent. And if you hear it, that's the way you're going to talk it.
> BU: Especially if it's somebody close to you.
> MM: Because if I talk to my friend, I try to talk the way she talks so we can always
>   have, you know, like a communication going. And when she talks to me she
>   tries to talk Puerto Rican like I do, you know?

Marilyn raises much the same point that José made earlier. An accent is solidarity because it is phatic, creating a bond. People who sound alike feel that they resonate with each other. The accent opens a communication channel that links selves together at a point of common experience:

> BU: So it's almost like the accent and the way you talk—it's more than just the
>   words, it's like a channel between people? It's like if you were getting to know
>   me, it opens up a channel between us? Like a pipe that you put water through?
>   A little piece of yourself and a little piece of your friend flow together?
> MM: Yeah!

BU: And like with the language. And other things too, your feelings about things, your attitudes, what you like—

MM: And to make them comfortable. You know, I talk Dominican with her, it's to make her comfortable, "yeah, I can talk Dominican too," you know? So I'm proud to talk like that too.

BU: So it becomes a thing you share.

MM: Yeah. But her mother don't like it. Cause when—you know, she's hanging around with me a lot, so when she goes to her house she goes "*Miiraa!*"—a lot of us Puerto Ricans when we're calling somebody and they don't respond, we go "*Miiraa!*" So she does that in her house. And her mother says "stop trying to talk like a Puerto Rican!" Then she goes—she don't like it, she just don't like it. And then she gets very upset with her daughter? And she goes, "You know that Puerto Rican? They got like a song to their words?" I don't know, I think that's nice what she said there, you know? But she don't like it.

BU: But she don't like it?

MM: No, she say *que*, you know, "*déjate de hablar como la puertorriqueña*" ["stop talking like a Puerto Rican"]. And I don't understand that. I don't know why she don't like it. Maybe because she's not used to her daughter talking like that.

What Marilyn describes here is the same sense of shared self and shared perspective that emerges in playful language. Marilyn's friend's mother was probably quite aware of this dynamic and not particularly happy about it.

Millie Wright's daughter Cathy develops the same theme; a shared accent marks a shared location and shared self, and people may find it desirable for just that reason:

CW: If you have a white kid and he lives in a poor neighborhood which is majority black then I guess he feels compelled or, I don't know, he just picks it up and it grows on him or whatever, then you have him walking around and he bops—

MW: There's a guy around here—

CW: Yeah, there's a white guy, he has blond hair, blue eyes, he bops, he, even his voice has gotten deeper.

BU: Do women do that?

CW: Yeah. A white woman—

MW: I don't know about that—

CW: If she dates a black guy, to fit in with the family, she definitely feels compelled—

BU: So it'd be like learning Spanish—

MW: Yeah—

CW: All she'd have to is imitate the accent.

BU: Well it's not the same as learning a language but I see.

CW: She'd feel compelled because she'd feel as though the guy's sisters, if she goes within the house, she cannot go in there acting white, they're not going to accept her. They're going to say hi and bye, but they're not going to let her in on the dirt, let her in on the conversation—

BU: They're not going to see her as being there.

CW: Right, whenever she's there the conversation is limited. And she knows it. You know when people are not being themselves. So she after a while it's like she's one of the family and she comes in and she's like, "Where's Julia" and it grows on her, and then after a while they see it's no longer an act and she's got it down pat, OK now you're going to fit in. So it happens vice versa, I've seen it that way.

Conclusion

This chapter has presented a complex picture of linguistic typification and objectification. At many points it is clear that linguistic variants stigmatized in the outer sphere are valued and enjoyed in the inner sphere. The problem is, there is no point where inner-sphere life is truly free of outer-sphere structuring. If, as is the case for the people in this study, the correctness model can be avoided only by staying within the inner sphere, then it really cannot be avoided at all. The outer sphere fences in one's life. As soon as one seeks a path to class mobility, the correctness model surfaces.

Correctness means the ability to negotiate the language required by status-oriented interaction with metacommunicative success. People typify this communicative competence metalinguistically as "good English," but there is a functional tradeoff. The language functions that make inner-sphere English and Spanish comfortable and familiar—the aesthetic/playful, the expressive, the phatic—have no place in this English. What does count are the functions referable to dictionaries and grammars: the referential (being clear and exact) and the metalinguistic (knowing the rules and explaining them when tested). Any phatic or expressive or aesthetic usages must support these functions; the playful, the heart of inner-sphere life, has no place at all.

Notes

1. Indexes are signs of connection, often interpreted as signs of cause and effect. Race/class indexes such as skin color, accents, and so on are read as "natural" signs of one's origins. "Good" or "correct" English forms are (hopefully) read as indexes of education and class mobility. Indexes are creative (performative) when they establish "the parameters of the interactions" including "the social relations of the individuals" (Silverstein 1976:36); indexes are presupposing insofar as they do not change those parameters.

2. Deixis is the process of "pointing outward" from one's locus in time and space. Benveniste (1971[1956]; 1971[1958]) argued that people can appropriate language to themselves as a system of *discourse* because the grammatical categories of language encode an egocentric or subjective perspective. English deixis is lexicalized and grammaticalized in time and space adverbs, demonstrative adjectives and pronouns, and verb tense (see Lyons 1977:636ff for discussion). It encodes such oppositions as *here-there*, *then-now*, *this-that*, and so on. Most linguistic attention paid to deixis has been paid to its formal codification. But deixis informs all human action because all human action assumes a locus, a point from which *I* am *here* and *now*. This is not only temporal and spacial in the ordinary sense but cultural and moral as well: where do I belong, who do I belong with, what is my normative time and place, how do I align myself with an *us* that

I find sensible and intelligible, right and good—people who think and act like me. The end-points of such oppositions may be a great deal clearer and more determinate than the boundary between them.

3. Most interviews were transcribed verbatim from tape recorded interviews. Those marked as "notes" were not tape recorded but were transcribed directly onto my computer during the interview. All interviews in this chapter were done in 1988.

4. This bears a superficial resemblance to the matched guise procedure of Lambert et al. (1960) but, unlike Lambert's work, was not meant to be formally analyzed or quantified. In fact, my procedure is much closer in spirit to Preston's (1989), in which he asked people in different parts of the United States to map and classify American-English dialect boundaries. In response, people matched accents and speech styles with states, cities, regions, local history (Spanish influence), local stereotypes (hillbilly), national stereotypes ("no real accent, like TV anchorpeople"), famous figures (Kennedy), and speech qualities that invoked a social type (drawl, twang). These responses form a vivid range of images typifying place and person. Moreover, these images and evaluations point to where their makers are from and how those places are valued. For example, Preston's Indiana informants consistently rated their own English as both correct and "nicer": clearly they are comfortable with their social location and see their English as a fund of cultural capital.

5. I met these sample speakers in any way I could. Most were students of my New York colleagues or friends of friends.

6. Based on numerous conversations, these questions approximate as closely as possible the ways in which the participants in this study actually talked about these topics.

7. Most were surprised to hear #5 *wasn't* Puerto Rican.

8. Ann and Mary were white friends of mine whom Luis had met.

9. Thus, while it is methodologically feasible to set up a non-topical control for accent (like getting a good dialect actor to read the same text in several accents), in ordinary interaction topic and accent are not separable: people talk *about* things and since images form in interaction, images do crystalize around the interplay of topic and accent.

10. Nor, as Hymes (1980) points out, does such theory deal with the ways in which a variable may or may not be psychologically salient. For example, Nilsa, Luis, and José all know that a "Puerto Rican accent" can be read as stigma, but they do not each find it equally stigmatizing in all relationships. José in particular finds the potentially stigmatized accents of others both comforting and individuating.

11. For example, Mannheim (1991:95) argues that Quechuan speakers are not sensitive to "subsegmental phonological variation within Quechua," and so do not categorize accents in the ways that Europeans and Americans do. He also argues that, in Peru, the linguistic ecologies of indigenous languages differ from those in contact with Spanish in ways that "correspond to the differences in productive relationships and wage structures." It is certainly possible that in the United States (and similarly industrialized and stratified nations), the ways in which accents are cultural/symbolic capital may have co-evolved with the political economy. Moreoever, ideas about accents in the United States are tied into moralistic discourses about correctness. Such discourses have become so entrenched in the economy that considerable money is spent on accent therapy in the form of speech classes, and people with nonstandard accents can be legally refused employment in the electronic media (Matsuda 1991).

12. Spanish original: Y él me dijo, "lo mejor que hiciste fue no venir a coger los exámenes porque si no, yo te hubiera colgado." Entonces al yo llegar con el dolor de mi hijo y él salirme con eso, que fue el primer maestro que yo fui, porque él quería. Ahí fue uno de los fuertes que me hizo sufrir a mí por el inglés, es prieto. Me dijo "porque tú no sabes leer

buen inglés. Sabes que te mando leer—". . . Yo casi nunca levantaba la mano para hablar temiendo que dijiera algo mal dicho y se rieran, you know—no, eso no. Pero cuando él me mandaba a leer, tenía que leerlo obligado. Y yo leia mal el inglés porque yo no—lo entiendo todo, pero no lo leo bien. Entonces me dijo, "porque tú lees muy mal el inglés?" Entonces yo me fui y eso me dio tanto sentimiento que yo venía, que me estoy esprimiendo—porque yo venía con ese dolor de Puerto Rico y al entonces salirme con esa bacheta que yo entonces no fui adonde ningun maestro, me vine llorando, me vine para aqui. Y por él yo deje que me botaran. . . . sin saber si yo pasaba el examen, porque—el que yo no leyera el inglés en frente de la clase rápido y con fluidez, no dejaba dicho que yo no podía leer esto para mí persona y saber lo que tú me estás diciendo en ese papel. Yo podía haber hecho el examen y lo pudiera haber sacado, que sabrá Dios, si hasta perfecto, porque lo podía leer para mí, lo que no tenía era la fluidez de leerlo.

13. A, B, and C represent names deleted.

Chapter 5

The Race/Class/ Language Map

How to Be American

As the 1988 fieldwork proceeded, it became increasingly obvious that how people perceive and talk about language must be connected to how they perceive and talk about race and class. People frequently brought up experiences like the following from Nilsa Buon (1988[1]), Jenny Pacheco (1988), and Luis Molina (1988 notes):

> **NB:** I feel the name of Puerto Ricans are dragged down . . .And I take it personally when I hear it, even airing on the CBs, "You Puerto Rican slime," this and that, and it hurts, it really does . . . I'm more conscious of other people's behavior that will reflect on Puerto Ricans who are not like that, are really trying to struggle and get ahead. And it really makes me angry.
>
> **JP:** "Ah but if you Hispanics always live shamefully, you never want to get ahead, never want to progress—" No, their phrase "You Hispanics" is always there.[2]
>
> **LM:** Valley Stream is so white, I'm scared to drive around in there because even though I work and I'm entitled and pay taxes just like a white person I'm scared, because I feel like I'm in another world.

People's experience and analysis of class became the focus of interviews in 1991. They often spoke about progress and personal responsibility, locating themselves in a fundamentally American model. They have internalized much of that model, as have all of us who have lived our lives within it. But they have also seen, as many Americans have never had to or wanted to, how mobility is systematically denied to racialized people.

American classifications of kinship, race, ethnicity, class, gender, and language are embodied in the person which is, in Schneider's terms, the major unit of American culture (1980 [1968]:57). None of these classifications are experienced

137

apart from any other. Each figures into the ideologically unmarked American citizen, the white, Anglo, middle-class, English-speaking male to whom people routinely compare themselves and their kin. Class mobility has become central to the idea of the good citizen, and perceptions of language are tightly tied to ideas about class mobility. Race/ethnicity and gender may be accidents of birth but, ideologically, people should be able to control class mobility and language.

Shklar (1991) argues that the idea of the citizen in the United States. has, since the country was founded, stood in opposition to the slave on the one hand and the aristocrat on the other. Unlike the slave, the citizen controls his own labor; unlike the aristocrat, the citizen does not live off the labor of others. The opposition between slave and citizen is racially significant since U.S. slaves were of African descent. Where the slave's station in life was fixed by nature and economics, the citizen's station was or should be mobile. Rising in life is not only a right but "a necessary corollary of the duty to contribute to the progress and prosperity of the republic" (p. 68). How much individuals rise can be scaled by how educated they are and much they earn—the familiar stratification model—which is also deeply suffused with cultural morality. Moral worth is literally measurable in increments marking class mobility. This attitude is internalized early in life, as Rosie Molina's story (1991) shows:

> There's these little girls in the church, they're white, they . . . have a house . . . And my daughter's speaking to them and they tell [her], "Get out of here because you're poor." She doesn't know what's poor. She comes to me, "Mami—" crying, you know, hysterical, "Mami, am I poor? Am I poor?" And I look at her and tell her, "No, why, why are you saying that?" And she tells me "because they told me that I was poor." And she made me cry so much. It was—I just wanted to pick her up and leave. And she cried until she fell asleep. And I looked at the little girls and I didn't say anything. And the next day—[our] car was brand new—the next day we drop by and we were in the car. . . . and she walks out of the car and the little girl comes to her, "Could I play with you?" And she said, "how can you play with a poor girl?" . . . But it really hurted her and it really hurted me, you know? . . . I told her, "You think poor people could have a home? A decent home? Ain't that what you have?" And she looks at me, she was around four years old, I think . . . I tell her, "You don't have to be ashamed, it doesn't matter if you're rich or not. But you're not poor." She looked at me and she got really happy because she's not poor. And then Luis comes out and says, "Hey, here's the poor girl's car."

The pressure to ethnicize through achievement is constant. Nilsa (1991) expands on the connections among stratification, progress, and moral worth:

> BU: What's the difference between poor and middle class?
> NB: I would say obviously the money to begin with. The person who is middle class is living much better, tends to be better educated . . . They're more Americanized. . . . depending upon your class, you're exposed to different things, you're more open minded . . . because you're better educated, obviously, you're on a different social level, so you tend to be more Americanized I think, and more mutual and less critical. . . . while the people that are of lower classes

tend not to—I'll give an example. I met a couple recently that did not have any objections about having a pet and having the pet breed over and over again, while I thought that was the most outrageous thing, that someone should actually have a pet, allowed to breed and just continuously, without being concerned about what will eventually happen to these kittens. I think because I'm in a different social class, I'm more concerned about the environment, things that other Hispanics who are lower class, who are not quite as, you know, [xx xx] don't consider at all, don't consider the garbage outside, don't consider the appearance of the place outside, you know so there is a big difference.

BU: So you see class not just as money but a set of attitudes about organizing your life?

NB: Exactly. . . . A person who is middle class will tend to really want to progress, while the person who really isn't, it's like they're very laid back, they're not thinking about their possible future, having a job that's secure and eventually will provide a decent pension . . . they would be more content with just making some money, as opposed to making good money and having good benefits and having a good pension. So we see things very different, we're more secure, more ambitious.

BU: And you wouldn't even necessarily need to have a lot of money to be middle class?

NB: Not at all.

BU: More attitude, do you think?

NB: Exactly.

Planning for the future, thinking about appearances, being tolerant, and displaying rational intention and action, all middle-class status values, may not automatically come with money but they can and should be learned. Nilsa summarizes what Rapp (1987) calls the U.S. normative middle-class perspective. As she and I discussed elsewhere, Nilsa does not equate "white" and "middle class," nor does she see "Hispanic" and "American" as mutually exclusive identities. Yet becoming Americanized is an achieved status, and in order to achieve it, one gives up some things that mark one as both poor and Hispanic.

Marilyn (1991) also distinguishes among poor, middle-class and rich by both economic and moral criteria. But, as she points out, these criteria create a space where she does not quite fit:

MM: I see middle class as people working and trying to get what they need and what they want. For me, that's middle class. Now the rich, for me, is they don't have to work and they have everything they need and want. So that's—for me that's the rich. And the poor . . . some poor people being lazy and not caring whether they have it or they don't have it. So I feel I don't fit in none of those categories. Because I'm not working, I'm not rich, and I'm not poor. Because I do have a home and I do have food to eat and I know the government is supplying—

JM: I would consider myself poor if there was a place like no schooling, no free clinics, if there wasn't free lunch, you know and all that.

MM: But we have all those free things because the government is paying for it. . . . I don't put myself in none of the categories.

BU: But your husband's working, or was working—

MM: Then, at the time, yeah, we were I'd say in the middle class. At the time. But now I don't know what to call myself.

The criteria for middle class are not just what one gets "for free" but how one gets it, that is, by working (earning money) for it. So where does this leave Marilyn? Meanwhile, José introduces a new element, how one's persona is seen and judged.

BU: Do you see middle class in part as goals people have or stuff they're trying to achieve?
JM: I see it as they're trying as hard as they could [to present] what people accept . . . you have to do this all on your own and make you present yourself and how you look in middle class.
BU: You're nodding your head, Marilyn.
MM: Yeah, it's what society wants to see.

One thing that society "wants to see" is an acceptable language, which Marilyn explicitly links to class distinction. One learns a style appropriate for public presentation, "working," and one saves potentially stigmatizing behavior for "personal" time. The implication is that the poor have nothing but personal time:

MM: The poor people, they don't care how they talk, to other poor people or to the middle class. But when you're trying to get up to that middle stage, then you try to be more—I'd say, more respectful to them, not to say a lot of curses. And I see that the middle class—they do say it only like maybe in their personal time, in their homes. But when they're out there working, you can't see it as much.

The same actions or behaviors may carry a different class message for Americans and for Puerto Ricans:

MM: I see it a different way cause some Americans they don't dress too good and it's because they just saving.
BU: Saving?
MM: Uh-huh. But that's the way I see it.
JM: Oh, I see, I see.
MM: They just saving it. But us Puerto Ricans we have—I'd say we want to let people know that we're not that poor, because we like to go out there and shop around. But the ones that do have the money to shop around don't do it as much, that's the way I see it.
BU: So the people who don't do it as much are—are what?
MM: Are saving for better things, for more education, or for what they want in the future.
BU: And is that a way that people are trying to be more middle class?
MM: Yeah, in a way, because . . . middle class they work a lot, and they save but they gotta spend too for their living. And the rich don't have to work that much, so they don't care if they lose a job or not, because they have it all. And the poor, like I said before, some poor just—they don't want to get themselves up there.

José demurs, seeing the poor as exploited and unable to compete:

JM: Or they work—I think they work much harder than us.
BU: The poor do?
JM: I mean, they try their best.
MM: Some of them try. There's others that don't.
JM: They try their best. And there's so much that people want from them. I see it that they can't compete, because there's so much that people want from them, and they don't see nobody giving them for what they are, you know? They're human beings only.

Luis Molina (1991) also sees being poor as being stuck in a place where efforts are futile. He elaborates on the structural disconnection that characterizes the place of the poor:

LM: We don't have the resources to plug in, unlike the middle class. . . . The lower class . . . cannot support itself, because it cannot connect to anybody . . . There's no connection. . . . The lower class cannot plug into the middle class because the middle class needs help itself. So where do we wind up? At the end of the stick. We're never able to keep our heads above water.
BU: Where would you put yourselves in this system?
LM: Economically speaking? Or—
BU: Any way you want to put it.
LM: OK, as far as race is concerned we're at the poor [level]. As far as economically, we're at the poor.
BU: But with aspirations?
LM: Yeah. With desires to some day get out of the level if we are given the opportunity, because I find it—one of the things I've most noticed, and I mentioned this to you before, is the fact our society does not allow us to move up. They tell us you have the opportunity, there is an opportunity—
RM: But they don't give it to you.
LM: But there's nothing to plug into. It's like if you tell me, Luis, get the toaster running, but there's no outlet. . . . They tell us hey, you have the opportunity, you could do whatever you want, nobody's telling you to be poor. But they don't [say] . . . look, we're going to provide you with a loan for a house or we're going to provide this, you're a taxpayer, to get you on your feet so you can—
RM: They won't do that for a Hispanic person.
BU: You see that as making it more complicated?
LM: Yeah.

Luis' toaster analogy ("nowhere to plug in") nicely illustrates the lack of fit between ideology (class mobility as a matter of free will) and structure (what does "having opportunity" mean when race makes it harder to get a loan). They agree that it is not possible to disconnect poverty from race where race makes it so hard to find somewhere to "plug in." When Rosie spoke of wanting a house and yard, Luis said, "They talk about the American dream. What about the Hispanic dream, the black dream?"

Millie Wright (1991) also sees the American dream as racially marked and emphasizes the tradeoff required to live that dream:

BU: Do you see middle class as making a certain amount of money? Having a certain kind of job? Advancing?

MW: Well, I think being middle class is more the amount of money that you make and the kind of car that you drive . . . And then if you have a husband and all that, you can get a home . . . stuff like that, then you're like middle class America, you know? The American Dream, supposedly. But it seems like somewhere along the line you give up something. You have to. You give up one thing to get something else. . . . because you have to act a certain way. . . . when somebody goes from one stage to another, they've changed, ... they start talking differently. They don't talk slang or street stuff anymore. They talk like business people . . . you live in a different neighborhood so you have different neighbors. . . . And then you start acting a certain way, you talk differently and you start acting differently. Oh, you have to be prim and proper and you can't do this and you can't do that and you can't go outside and yell out the window "Hey, Joe, what the—hey, come down here" or something like that. . . . you got to go ring the bell . . . all this etiquette comes into play. . . . And usually when a black or Spanish person goes from being a poor person to a middle-class person, then everybody says—then it's like they can't come back to the old friends that they had because it's like "Oh! You act like you white! You know? What's the matter with you act like you white? What's the matter, what's happening, hey, ain't no mo' bro'? What's this 'how are you doing, and how are you feeling?' When the fuck you learn to talk like that?"

José Mojica (1988) comments on nation, race, and hierarchy:

JM: (commenting on actors in TV commercials) See how white they are? (Laughing) Whatever white is. It must be skin, but it's not just skin.

BU: So what is it, what's white?

JM: Maybe an attitude a person has about themselves? They're real American or—I don't know what the word is, like they feel into America, they're more into their history and proud, they do what their fellow man wants them to do. If that man's American and I'm American, I'm the same race, I want to be at the same level, the same position. It's like if we were both in the army. If he was a captain I want to be a captain too, not just a private.

"What their fellow man wants them to do" suggests actions that Americans would expect and approve, much as an acceptable accent is "what people want to hear," as José put it in the previous chapter. It is not simply a moral imperative that impels one to move up, but a search for approval from others "at the same level"—levels which are racially marked.

In a 1991 interview, Luis recalled a conversation we had had a couple of years earlier, in which he described himself as "really middle class" because of his aspirations for himself and his family (Urciuoli 1993). He now rethought his position as he and Rosie expanded on the ways in which racial marking weigh against upward movement through class levels:

LM: Society had me believing that being middle class had more dignity, had more respect. And what is being middle class? Always it's a game, whoever winds up with the most toys wins. That's not true . . . for instance, I guess that this is middle class, . . . when you step off the low class into middle class: getting credit cards.

RM: No, that's only debts!

LM: But this is the picture of being your typical average middle class, at whose expense? Your own expense, again, you know? Having credit cards, having a car, being able to have a good income, let's say making between $20,000 and $25,000, that's middle class enough for you; having a reasonable education, not no doctor's degree or master's degree, but just enough education to get you by—

RM: Diploma.

LM: Even a few years of college. Just enough to get you by. That's what I thought getting to that middle-class stage would be. But I found out that even getting to the middle class: it was nothing. . . . Because again, you get to the middle class, you don't lose your language barrier, you don't lose your race. OK? And what you do is, you bring along the same things that kept you from becoming a middle class, right along with you, until you become an upper class. And you just continue to do that. There will never be a change, you follow what I'm saying? . . . It's like I'm Puerto Rican now, I'm making ends meet, I'm running, I'm making it, I'm doing this, I'm doing that. I'm gonna get to the middle class. What do I do with my skin color, do I go and dye my color? Do I go and dye my hair? Do I try to speak fluent English, use these sophisticated words? Is that what going from Stage 1 to Stage 2 is? Still, you bring the same economic problems, the same racial problems, the same language problems. And maybe if you do, your chances—if you become rich, then . . . there is no longer a language barrier, there's no race barrier, it's just your economic ability. If you can afford it, that's fine, you'll be all right. You're nothing else. But in the poor and in the middle class, it makes a difference, being whether black or Hispanic and not able to speak properly.

Race-marking is like gravity in that one needs to achieve escape velocity. One may escape the gravity of race-marking by becoming so rich that others' judgments do not count. For most people, even at the "middle-class level," one remains race-marked. Later in the interview, Luis and Rosie compared being Hispanic or black to having a disease: moving into the middle class is "like not finding the cure for the disease but finding something that's going to prolong your life."

This feeling of entrapment is made even more painful by the sense that recent immigrants are racing past Puerto Ricans, with Koreans "taking over" the produce business and Dominicans running the *bodegas* (small markets), coffee shops, and travel agencies in Hispanic neighborhoods that used to be run by Puerto Ricans. Here Luis identifies with the struggling individual who has sacrificed for the nation:

And where's the Puerto Rican? The Puerto Rican is being serviced by people who just came in, who have not struggled, who have not given their share to America. Unlike the Hispanic community. I mean, I'm not saying that I deserve—well as a matter of fact I *am* saying I deserve a piece of the pie—because after all, I struggled, I worked in America. Ever since I came in 1969 I've been working, my first job was pushing groceries in a shopping cart, through the snow, rain, sleet, winter.

In this moment, Luis claims ethnicity (not race) as the major defining axis of identity as he defines his moral worth as a Puerto Rican. In this discourse, Luis has little recourse but to talk in terms of struggle and ethnic sacrifice to the nation. No other American discourse clarifies moral worth so definitely: ironically, in the very act of criticizing the nation-state, one has few options except to use its terms of definition.

The Politics of Markedness: Acting White

People try to control prejudiced perceptions of themselves by editing the ways in which they may be seen as marked, through their name, hair or skin color, behavior, or language. This can be risky, but people take the risk because markedness so readily leads to closure when people find themselves stereotyped, judged, cut short, excluded, pigeonholed, or made invisible. Millie Wright talks about markedness and being judged (1988 notes):

I meet people and they try to guess what I am, black, white, East Indian—they *do* want to know because they want to know where to put you. . . . They judge who you are on the basis of your performance. . . . It's the frustration of not being able to change people's images of you. People see you a certain way and you're stuck with it. They set a limit on you and you can't get past it.

People look for unambiguous places on the social map "where to put you" and the person being judged has little control over where one is put. This issue is especially complex for Cathy whose father, Millie's late husband, was African American. Millie and Cathy describe how people poke at ambiguities to find out just how marked one *really* is:

BU: So is it that you're being judged?
MW: Because of the class you belong to. Like the people at work try to categorize me, keep trying to get out of me what I am *really*. Really Spanish? Really black? Really East Indian?
CW: Or people say, well, that person's OK for now but just wait. And then they'll sit and wait for you to do the thing that's going to be the great revelation and show your real true colors.
MW: And people keep trying to provoke that.
CW: And you know you're being provoked and you have to keep your guard up.

In these situations, one's markedness is not merely assumed but "provoked": one is pushed into one's place on the social map. What makes this so aggravating, as

Cathy put it, is the fact that "They're not real places. That's why I was going to say, what is your place?"

José and Marilyn describe the problem of protecting oneself from appearing marked, especially to those in authority (1988 notes):

> BU: It seems like it's both information and language, what you say and how you say it.
>
> JM: Like talking to a social worker: you have to tell them what they want to hear so they could respect you more, to respect the way you want to do it. If you tell them the wrong thing . . . I only tell my social worker certain things.
>
> MM: But that's different from what we were talking about before, which was only telling people what they want to hear if it's positive things. But other people want to hear the real you—
>
> JM: Negative things.
>
> MM: Negative things meaning the real you?
>
> JM: Positive things are the real you.
>
> MM: But it's both, you're both negative and positive.
>
> JM: If you do something wrong, it might be positive for you but for other people it might be negative, you don't want nothing that's negative for you.
>
> BU: Does it matter who the someone else is, your sister or a social worker? . . . the position the person is, a social worker versus a next-door neighbor?
>
> MM: The social worker could take away your benefits.

José points out that markedness is relative ("It might be positive for you but for other people it might be negative"). Those being judged carry the burden of figuring out and getting rid of the "negative" since, as Marilyn points out, there may be material consequences. Rosie Molina (1988 notes) makes a similar point, phrasing it explicitly as a problem of truth:

> They don't respect you. The [social worker] I have now is good, but you never know, you're afraid to go with the truth, to put a last name to your baby because you might get cut off.

Millie, Cathy, José, Marilyn, and Rosie all point out that it is a constant struggle to control what others see as one's marked "real" self. People have powerful reasons for wanting to edit their personas. But ethnicizing oneself creates a dilemma: one cannot be a worthy ethnic without acting in ways that appear "American" but how does one keep those ways from also appearing "white"? If one does not edit marked language and behavior, one risks future vertical mobility; if one does edit them, one risks present horizontal solidarity. This is the dilemma Fordham and Ogbu (1986) describe for black high school students with good grades who did not want to be seen by their friends as "acting white," a phenomenon that turns up in any area of achievement, casting the achiever as a kind of deserter. When I told Millie Wright about the Fordham and Ogbu study, she said (1991):

> MW: Cathy gets that a lot from black people.
>
> BU: I was afraid she would.

MW: "What are you doing, you think you're white? You think you're this? You think you're better than us? And you this?" She gets a lot of that, and it's kind of hard, you have to find ways of dealing with it. Or just telling them, "Yeah I think I'm white, so what? So what? What you want to do about it?" or something like that and just—the heck with it. When it comes to family or something like that, you can do that. But when it comes to other people it's not that easy.

How much "acting white" lies in the eye of the beholder becomes evident in this discussion with Millie and Cathy (1988):

MW: There's this girl Milagros in the hospital, and I don't know how you get a name like Milagros without being Spanish. You can get named Maria or Carmen— but Milagros is not a name that you can just get—and she tries to act like she's white.
  BU: How do you do that? I mean what—
  CW: Right! What is "acting white"?
MW: That's what she does—
  CW: Somebody told me I act white.
  BU: You act white?
  CW: Right, like I'm not black.
MW: She had this situation where she acts like she's better than you are, but if some-body else Spanish comes into the situation—
  LA: Well a lot of people act like they're better than everybody else—

Cathy separates others' interpretations from one's intentions. Millie insists that she is talking about one's intentions:

MW: And—no, no, I'm not saying that, I'm just saying that she wants to be, she'd rather have been white or whatever. So, OK, let's say another Spanish girl comes into the office—she's [i.e., Milagros] the secretary, and there's another Spanish girl comes into the office, and she's one of these, you know, Charo types, hootchie-coo and all that kind of stuff. . . . So she comes into the office and she's talking her little Spanish and she's talking English and she talks with an accent and all, OK? And Milagros, they call her Millie, Millie comes by and she wouldn't want to associate with her because she's like lower class or whatever. She [Milagros] speaks English very nicely . . . she sits there and talks differently and she acts differently than her [the Charo type] so she doesn't want to be asso-ciated with her. So the only girls in the office that she's really buddies with are white girls, because she didn't want to associate with anyone else that wasn't white. And the black people there, if she had to deal with you and she had to take something to your desk she'd put it down or whatever but I did not see her—the only people she'd associate with were the white people, that's it.
  BU: So is it like—to give another example, sort of the archetypal example, sort of the social worker who pretends she doesn't know Spanish, something like that?
MW: Yeah! You don't hear that girl talk Spanish and I bet you any amount of money she speaks Spanish. But when she comes to work, I bet you she tells people, "I never learned how to speak Spanish, they don't speak Spanish in my house."

One can control one's dress, language, and associates to avoid being "found out." If one's family name is Latin, one can deny speaking Spanish, as if it disappeared when the family "came up in the world." As Millie put it, "If they can possibly speak English without an accent, they do that . . . . If you ask where their parents are from they'll avoid it." One can hide any sign of a Latin family by changing one's name, names being the most "natural" (and so the riskiest) origin signs. Millie continues:

> Let's say this. When you're born in the United States and your parents are from Puerto Rico, they put white on your birth certificate because that's the color of your skin—if you're born that color. If a guy is white, has nice hair, if he has like grey eyes or green eyes . . . the only thing is he would have to change his name. If his name's Azevedo, there's no way he could sit there and pretend he's white. You can go there and act all the white you want but if someone asks him his name and he says "Jorge Azevedo," so much for that. But he would probably get the job because he knows how to speak properly and they figure he'd act accordingly . . . And they could pass him off if he wants to because he doesn't have to tell everybody his name.

People who "act white" unmark themselves so much that they no longer seem to be independent actors. They become reactors, shaping themselves to fit dominant standards, co-opted into a personhood no longer their own. The only way to get respect is to be class mobile, and yet the very things one does to be mobile make one unable to be proud of oneself (Sennett and Cobb 1972:32). Luis Molina (1988 notes) draws a similar conclusion:

> LM: If you take a Spanish person who starts acting like a black or white person he's forgetting who his family is.
> BU: "Acting" is trying to be something you're not?
> LM: "Acting" means putting on a front.
> BU: What do people mean by the term "hiding from your race"?
> LM: They're hiding the fact that they're Spanish or black.
> BU: White people don't hide their race?
> LM: They don't have to. They were born white. They hit the lottery when they were born.
> BU: How do you hide from your race?
> LM: In a material way, by not dressing like your own race, or by trying to speak the way whites do, or by trying to live in a way that you know you're not capable of living that way.

Luis contrasts "acting white" with the fact that whites do not have to act: hitting the lottery at birth neatly sums up race/class advantage. Luis sees an inherent opposition between race/class origin and structural location "in the system" (1991):

> LM: There is this story in the Bible between Esau and Jacob. Esau sold his birthright for a mess of pottage. That's exactly what some of the Puerto Ricans do when

they get in that position [of authority, as in a social agency]. They sell their birthright as far as their nationality, their custom, their religious belief and on and on and on. They strip themself away because they get to a situation where they're part of the system.

BU: Is that what you call "acting white"?

LM, RM: Yes! Yes!

Marilyn and José see "acting white" in the same terms (1988):

MM: They're trying to hide who they really are.

JM: Or they're trying to act as better than what they are. They're not going to try to act worse than what they are.

BU: So it's always like putting yourself up?

JM: Yeah!

Nilsa Buon (1988 notes) gives an example:

BU: What do people mean when by "acting white"?

NB: Acting white, for example, like a woman who doesn't value her own language enough to teach it to her children, she doesn't cook anything Hispanic, she's very judgmental to Hispanics. She has a white husband whose family may not act very proper. But she says nothing about them. Yet Hispanics doing the same thing are lowlifes. So it isn't the thing you're doing. It's who you are as you're doing it that makes it what it is.

Nilsa and her then-husband Jorge elaborate on the sense of up and down contained in the idea of "acting" (1988):

BU: Do you ever hear people talk about acting black or acting Spanish? Or do you usually hear "acting white"?

JB: Well, when someone acts like a minority, it's not really to upgrade them but to lowgrade them, really streetwise, no? If someone imitates a Hispanic—

NB: Like [X]'s girlfriend who's a white Canadian, who sounds like a black person.

JB: Which one?

NB: The one who was in prison. She sounded real black. It's usually the other way around, Bonnie.

BU: That's what I was going to ask, is when you talk about acting, does acting imply trying not just to act like something you're not but to act up a step?

NB: Exactly, that's what it is. Do you think when somebody's acting white, they're trying to act more—

JB: Superior? Definitely.

NB: More so than—

JB: More so than acting the other way around.

NB: Than a white person acting like a black, or a black accent.

JB: That's correct.

BU: What does the term "acting" mean to you here?

JB: Being someone you're really not.

BU: And it always carries the sense of trying to upgrade?

JB: Yes.

BU: So it's the same sense as "hiding from your race"?

JB: It's true. I guess in the minority world, which we're based on, we tend to be more like the white race, because we see them as superior to what we are. . . . I think it deals a lot with the way we were brought up, the way we were taught to believe in certain things or situations. We tend to copy somebody else's past, and try to live a dream and fulfill that dream, try to make it into reality.

Jenny Pacheco locates "denying the race" in embarrassment or shame about the way Latin origins have been subordinated (1988):

BU: What does that mean, denying the race?

JP: Well, there are some of us who come for one reason or another, go to work at welfare. To work in social service. So she feels bad about her language, her heritage and about the fact that we are kept under a lid, to put it vulgarly. So she tries to assimilate herself to the American way, because of the complex that has been created in terms of the language. Because we have a complex due to the English language, not because of ours. Because a Hispanic is just like an American. You are American and you get into the governor's office and since that is your language regardless of how bad you feel, that is your language and you are going to say it. That is the way that you learned it or it was taught to you or you learned it since you were a child. That is what happens with us. We speak our language, Spanish. But when we go to a meeting full of Americans, we want to assimilate, so that we will not be subject to racism because of our language.[3]

Jenny typifies the person "acting white" as both female and a social worker. The "snotty Spanish social worker" is a common, powerful, and very female stereotype. Not only are more women than men likely to hold such jobs, but there is no worse cultural travesty than a Latin woman who denies knowing Spanish to another Latin woman whose children have needs. The only difference between them is class, and denying Spanish to create distance is an illegitimate assertion of class status. Tay Román:

BU: Like with the social worker who's Spanish but they pretend they don't know any Spanish. They pretend they only know English. And somebody will say, well she's acting white. . . . what I'm trying to get at is the way they use "acting" there.

TR: Well, they act like that because they think that their level is different. They are up. I, I am under them.

BU: So what they're trying to do is—

TR: "I am better than you."

After one edits as much markedness as one can, one's "real" self, or what's left of it, remains buried inside. Millie (1988):

MW: A lot of times people will say I'll do it like this [i.e., like I am] and they go out
there and they're themselves and they keep getting turned down and turned
down and turned down, and [a person] feels "I'm not good enough, so maybe
I'm going to go home and I'm going to change." So he starts improving his
speech and doing this and that and the other and he goes out and ends up getting accepted because he's changed the way he's acting, he's no longer—you've
degraded the man because the man's no longer proud of what he is, he wants to
be something else.

BU: It's really a reaction to outside pressure?

MW: Yes!

Cathy (1988) recommends a strategy for reclaiming autonomy and control:

> Some people who are proud of what they are will . . . educate themselves, this
> way they'll be able to speak properly and be able to get their point across. But
> they won't let you forget what nationality they are. Because once you let a person
> know that you're trying to deny your nationality, they don't have respect for you
> for that one point there. So now you have a lot of people who are saying "I'm
> intelligent, I articulate very well, I go to a good school, and I'm not going to deny
> who I am."

The strategy is to define, not hide, one's nationality and then present a polished,
articulate image of that nationality. By clearly stating one's nationality, this strategy
makes obvious that one's intent is to foreground rather than hide. One still
unmarks oneself but one does so selectively:

BU: And I'm not going to fit into your stereotype of how I should be what I am?

CW: Right, because then you're controlling me by denying who I am, that makes me
less of a person right there so you've got me either way. So this way I've got
you. I am what I am. But I also fit in because I can communicate very well.
There's nothing you can do that I can't do, and I *am* Mexican and I *am* black
and I *am* Hispanic and I *am* Italian or Irish or whatever.

By setting up Puerto Rican, Mexican, black, Irish, and Italian as parallel nationali-
ties, Cathy proposes a strategy based on ethnic respectability as a contribution to
the nation-state. Millie (1988) proposes a related strategy: establishing one's ability
and achievement first and stating one's ethnicity afterward.

MW: In my particular experience, people usually think that most Spanish people are
very ignorant people. And they meet me and they don't find out right away
what I am.

CW: Poverty has a lot to do with it. If you don't have money, you cannot get the
right education.

MW: But I'm not rich and I have a pretty good education.

CW: But the majority—

BU: I think she's talking about making somebody outside your experience respect you.

MW: People respect me when I open my mouth and they find out I'm no airhead. . . .
they're thinking "I can't guess what she is so I'm going to ask her." And I tell

them, "I'm Spanish, I'm Puerto Rican." And they get that expression [of] big surprise, like "Oh, I didn't know." . . . And I do start getting respect after that.

All this is a tricky balancing act. Markedness by its very nature is segmentary.
Being unmarked in one group ("typically Puerto Rican" among Puerto Ricans)
may mean being marked in a larger group ("Americans"). If one unmarks oneself,
one risks being seen as "acting" and therefore marked among Puerto Ricans. There
is no simple or general solution, only a constant, painful, and risky struggle in
which people are hurt all the time. Social meaning is not determinate, and the
indeterminacy can be painful when one is caught between such opposed categories as "educating oneself" and "acting white," that is, when "one person's individual achievement in the eyes of authority becomes betrayal for the others"
(Sennett and Cobb 1972:149).

Racial Teasing and Other Pernicious Ambiguities

People are surrounded by reminders of their own markedness. Jenny Pacheco talks
about crime reporting (1988):

> When they give the news on American channels, they always say for example "a
> Cuban . . . a Honduran or a Colombian kills here." They say "the Hispanic."
> They almost always say "the Puerto Rican" because to a white, here all Hispanics
> are Puerto Ricans. It doesn't matter if it's a Cuban, a Colombian, a Honduran,
> from wherever, they say, "the Puerto Rican so and so killed John Doe." But when
> they give a story about a white, they never say to you "A white did this" or any-
> thing like that: "Mr. So-and-so committed this act."[4]

Marilyn Mojica describes an incident that hit home (1988 notes):

> I'll give an example. In my daughter's daycare they wanted a picture of kids to be
> in a magazine. So people came and looked around and said "What kind of chil-
> dren do you have here? Colored or something?" And we said, "ninety-five per-
> cent is black and Puerto Rican." And they said "We were looking for more white
> kids." They told them right in their face.

Such routinized stereotyping forms a kind of background noise. For people
who are unmarked, it becomes naturalized, laying the ground for everyday bits of
racializing. One such bit takes the form of racialized teasing: "I thought all you
people thought (or said or did) X." When the butt of this teasing reacts with anger
or hurt, the reaction is delegitimated by disclaimers like "I was only kidding, don't
overreact, don't be so sensitive, can't you take a joke?" In effect, the teaser hides
behind the cultural definition of humor. Jokes, teasing, wisecracks, and so on are
defined as meaning something other than what they refer to. In fact, people often
do mean what they are supposedly kidding about but when friends or equals tease

each other, they are in a position to call each other on it. People in a subordinate position rarely have this option so whatever the teaser's intent, what actually happens is that the stereotype is reinforced and the butt is left in an indefensible position pragmatically.[5] Cathy (1988) elaborates:

> This is about when you try to insult someone by putting them in their place . . . So you don't like a [black] person, you could just walk into the room and say, "you be whatever," and you say "you be," and that's all you have to say to make fun of them and to put them down. . . . And what will they turn around and do, how will they defend themselves? They don't want to say or they can't think of the quickest Jewish joke or whatever to defend themselves, so they just sit there with their hands in their pockets and after a while they get frustrated and they say, "fuck you, man!" And the first thing is, "Oh look at that person, it's typical that he would behave belligerantly. He really showed his true colors . . ." Well he pissed him off!

When teasers say "Can't you take a joke?" or "Why are you making a big deal out of it?" they control the definition of social reality. When play among equals gets out of hand, people can walk out and refuse to have their reality so defined, even if it disrupts the relationship (Basso 1979). Teasing someone who cannot tease back reinforces the stereotype. Trivializing someone for taking offense ("you're overreacting") casts that person as "out of control." The moralism driving such remarks is hard to miss, as Nilsa (1988 notes) points out:

> BU: Do you experience judgments disguised as jokes or comments like "you Hispanics are all alike"?
>
> NB: Especially from my boss. It's infuriating!
>
> BU: Can this ever be two way? Could you say back to him, "you [fill in blank] are all alike"?
>
> NB: It's strictly one-way. He acts like he knows everything, he's the only one fit to judge. And he judges just about everyone and everything. . . . like if my boss says "Oh, you Hispanics—" it's that you aren't coming up to the level of what he considers right.

The power play is made clear by the fact that such "joking" only goes in one direction. Millie Wright (1988 notes):

> Like when people make comments about big butts or they try to talk black and use expressions like "what it is" and it comes out wrong, and they say "Oh it's just a joke." But what if you drew a swastika on the table, would they take it as a joke?

Luis Molina (1988 notes) compares co-workers who make him the target of racialized teasing with the one co-worker who does not:

> LM: They joke about people in the Bronx. They call me "José" or "Jesús" because they think all Spanish people are named that. I become immune. . . . One nice

guy at work treats me like what I am, asks about my family, how'm I doing financially. He cares for people in general . . . [The others] joke about it but they're really trying to keep you in a spot.

BU: Do they say to you at work "you act Puerto Rican"?

LM: Like at work, when they make fun of my shirt, the kind with the pleats down the front, they'd say, "Oh you're dressing Puerto Rican." Well, what do they think I am?

I asked others what they made of this story. All recognized the dynamics, although only Nilsa and Cathy had directly experienced such remarks. This may have been because they, like Luis, had worked in places where most employees were white, making them especially marked. Marilyn and José Mojica, both of whom knew Luis, commented (1988 notes):

BU: How about when Luis Molina gets called "José" or "Jesús" for a joke, because that's a common Spanish name? Or when Luis wears the kind of shirts with pleats down the front and his boss says, "You look Puerto Rican today?"

JM: He [the boss] is putting himself on a higher level—it's nice to keep noticing what you are, I want people to know I'm Puerto Rican. But not to keep bothering.

José brings the idea of levels to bear on the distinction between what he sees as two different intents, "noticing" (implying acceptance rather than erasure of difference) and "bothering" (implying an illegitimate imposition of power in the definition of difference). The fact that this perception is about levels and therefore political, emerges in a feeling of loss of control over English:

BU: Luis says that when this happens to him, he feels like he's losing his English, like he can't control words. And you know he speaks English well.

JM: I would have that reaction. If it's a boss it's different from a friend.

BU: (to MM) Suppose José teased you about something you said funny, would it matter?

JM: No, because—

MM: But if it's one of those persons that have more education they could tease you and tell you the right way to say it.

I ask if this is a race problem. Marilyn sees it as a problem of authority relations:

BU: Is it a problem of dealing with white people in certain positions?

MM: It seems like it comes from working, a job, some kind of pressure. I haven't encountered much of that, not yet anyhow, and maybe it is a thing that you encounter as you move up. It's something I have to think about when I look for a job.

JM: He should just tell his boss.

BU: But can he?

MM: He could but then again he can't—he's trapped.

"Trapped" about summarizes the performative effect of racialized teasing. People frequently see this effect in terms of space and limits: "he's trapped"; "[they] keep you in a spot"; "not up to his level." Cathy Wright (1988 notes) spells out the dynamics:

> At work, people crack a joke about you and pretend they're kidding. But they're really not. It's a way of keeping you in your place, as if you're starting to fit in so I'll fix you, like you're not aware of who and what you are.

It is the ambiguity of intent in the wisecrack that serves to "keep you in your place." Such ambiguity can surface with equal effectiveness in non-teasing interactions. Millie describes an incident that happened when Cathy was twelve (1988):

> I took Cathy downtown to a gymnastics center because she was interested in gymnastics . . . I don't know, we must have looked like a sore thumb or something. I know we stood out. But . . . the only thing you saw in there—this was around East 70-something, and there was nothing there but whites, there wasn't a black soul in the place. The only black people that were there were the ones that were taking care of the kids, baby-sitting or whatever, picking them up. That was it. We went in and I—well I usually don't feel out of place but I think this place really went to an extreme. . . . the teacher said oh she [Cathy]'s very good and everything, but she thought she was too old to get involved in it. But that—I can see that because most of the kids were smaller and Cathy was pretty big compared to most of them. But it was a situation where you would feel a little funny. . . . I just felt a little peculiar. I usually don't feel this because I go into restaurants and forget it, I go everywhere and anywhere. I just fit in there in some kind of way, because I'm spending my money, that's all that I have to worry about. . . . And then Cathy said "Well I don't want to come here anyway" so I said "OK, you don't have to if you don't want to." And then we just left. But that was one situation where I wished I'd had some moral support.

Did the teacher demur because Cathy was too old or because Cathy was black? There is no way Millie could know, and the teacher could always have stated her intent as "all I meant was . . . " Cathy (1988) tells a story with a similar point about her white co-workers at a Friendly's Restaurant in Westchester:

> The girls were all rich, well, they were high class, they all had a lot of new, very expensive cars that their parents bought them and they always went on vacations, they always got their nails done and what-not. . . . They would invite me out to drink and go to their house and so on, and then I'd ask them why didn't they invite such-and-such [a black co-worker]. Nobody said anything. But there was one girl . . . She was white, I didn't know what nationality. I asked her, later on, and she said "About the question you asked, why don't we invite such-and-such, the other girl who was black, it's because they said we can tell she doesn't feel comfortable around us." That's all she said, "Why should we invite her knowing she would be uncomfortable around us?"

What makes such interactions so pernicious is that Cathy *might* have been mistaken in suspecting the intent behind "She doesn't feel comfortable around us" or Millie about "she's too old." By suspecting and perhaps acting on the worse interpretation, one leaves oneself open to, as Cathy put it, the accusation of "showing your true colors" by overreacting. In such ways, ambiguities provide an effective way to map race/class lines, to keep people "in their place" without admitting any such explicit intent.[6]

Respect and Defense: Resisting Control

When people talk about resisting judgment, they talk in terms of getting respect and defending themselves. These concepts are closely related. In his study of Puerto Rican social discourse, Lauria (1964:54) defines *respeto* as "a quality of self which must be presented in all interpersonal treatment":

> The element of *respeto* which must be communicated in the most minimal message of this ceremonial idiom concerns the person's basic right to a self. This element of *respeto* obtains between those who are, otherwise, social equals, superiors and subordinates. One's very social existence is predicated upon the bonds of *respeto*. (p. 57)

Millie Wright (1988) defines respect:

> MW: To give a mutual feeling you would want to return . . . almost like saying hello. . . . you should respect older people, your neighbor like it's yourself . . . You recognize that that person deserves to be acknowledged. . . . having respect for an older person would be having respect for that person because they have lived longer than you have and there's a lot of things they know that you should give them time to explain to you. . . . you figure this person has lived all this time, they must know something. . . . And . . . then for somebody your own age that's kind of a mutual respect. You know, you give respect, you get respect.

Tay Román (1988) comments on respect and race:

> I am not against anybody. I don't care what color it is, the person, if the person is black, but the person respect me. Because I always ask for respect, but I always give respect. Because if I want you to respect me, I have to respect you. Right?

Luis Molina (1988 notes) describes mutuality as a fundamental principle of linguistic respect:

> BU: So how do you show respect through language?
> LM: If someone speaks two languages, the proper way to show respect is to speak the same language they speak.

One does not force linguistic choices onto others. One respects their preferences, abilities, and limits. Younger people should respect the choices of older people. Children growing up in New York can plead incompetence in Spanish without *falta de respeto* (lack of respect), especially if they manage a greeting formula or at least an apology. This is not the case for those who "make believe" not to know Spanish and so "hide from their race."[7]

Younger people should respect the choices and abilities of older people. Men should respect women. Uninvited visitors, however powerful, should respect the rules of the house. Rosie Molina (1988) describes the violation of all these principles by her building manager:

> [The building] manager . . . came to talk to a widow downstairs and he told that lady off in her apartment. I got so upset because she doesn't know English, I told him "You have to respect her. This is her apartment and she pays rent here, all right? If you're going to talk to her nasty, you get out on the street and you talk to her nasty but you respect her. You are a very nasty man." Then you see she couldn't defend herself. . . . He didn't respect her. He even tell her "shit" in her house, that he was not going to eat her shit anymore. And I—my blood just went up and then you see she doesn't know how to speak English and the only thing she told him is in Spanish, "You have to respect my house." That's it. And I got so upset that she didn't understood what he was telling her. One day I told him off. I told him, "You know what's wrong with you? Because she can't speak English and you get her rent . . . you must respect her. She's a human being like you are." "Ah, no miss." I said "No miss nothing, alright? You speaking to her very nasty and when I go to the [landlord's] office, I'm going to report you."

Marilyn (1988 notes) tells a similar story of her own experience:

BU: What's respect? How do you show respect?

MM: To see the person you are inside and outside, don't judge them for anything else, just what they really are.

JM: Marilyn put it so good. I was thinking, "mind your business." Don't push it, respect what they are.

BU: What's a way in which people show disrespect?

MM: Like the way the landlord comes and tries to put me down in words and even if I don't know the words I can tell from his voice and if I respond to him—the only words I know are bad [i.e., not fancy] words, I can't talk to him in big words like on his level, so he might be thinking I'm a lowlife, "she's a lowlife girl."

BU: Does he do this a lot?

MM: Over the phone, not personally, he didn't come out with bad [i.e., rude] words, but I could tell from his tone of voice he was angry. And I feel like I don't know what to say back to him and I can't say anything back to him anyway because he could throw me out of the apartment because of welfare.

BU: That's disrespect?

MM: It is disrespect too because if you're in the welfare they have all this opportunity to take advantage of you. Or like with housing, they think you're not working, we're supporting you, we can't give you a good apartment.

Marilyn and Rosie both link disrespect to language. Rosie sees disrespect in the manager's "nasty" talk and disregard for the neighbor's Spanish. Marilyn sees disrespect in her landlord's manipulation of social capital ("big words") which she cannot match. She is further silenced by the possible material consequences: her status as an AFDC client makes her practically a non-participant to begin with.

Tay Román (1988) looks to education for social capital. As an AFDC client, she feels linguistically defenseless against the ways in which the state can manipulate her—"we can fool her." Disrespect grows from there:

> TR: You know, that's why I want to study. I want to be somebody, I don't want to stay just like that. They [AFDC] treat people like, like they are nothing.
>
> BU: Like—with no respect?
>
> TR: Yeah. Like they are nothing.
>
> BU: Unless you can talk to them a certain way, they act like you're not there?
>
> TR: They don't give a fuck. . . . They don't respect, they don't respect. They see that, that, ohhh, this lady, she doesn't speak English. We can fool her, you know. We can fool her.

Even when one gives deference, one should be respected for (in Marilyn's terms) "the person you are." This does not happen when race/class conflation defines who is or is not worthy of respect. Nilsa (1988 notes) examines this point:

> It's easiest to respect position in a situation like at work where the boss's position is defined. In general, socially, respect comes hard in situations where you are on the offensive as much as the defensive, scrapping for a little space shopping or whatever. Socially you always feel vulnerable to being judged or in a position to be put down and categorized, especially by other Hispanics and double especially if they're South American.

Puerto Ricans carry the burden of proving that they are not "lowlifes" and that they deserve respect. Where there should be some kind of linguistic or historical solidarity, none exists: "other Hispanics and double especially if they're South American" fear being seen conflated with Puerto Ricans.

If respect is based on each accepting the other's personhood ("being accepted for what you are"), defending oneself reclaims respect by establishing one's personhood in the face of power. Marilyn and José Mojica explain (1988 notes):

> BU: When people talk about using language to defend yourself, what does this expression mean to you?
>
> JM: It's like the level thing. If someone speaks English well, you'd like to speak that way too.
>
> BU: And if you can't?
>
> JM: You get lost in your environment.
>
> MM: You get lost. That's why my mother brings one of us with her when she has to go somewhere. Even if she understands she doesn't know how to answer in English. So we do.

The "level thing" refers to the fact those who are more marked by race and class carry the burden of matching language skills with those who are less marked. When people cannot do that they can indeed "get lost in your environment," in a sea of disorder. Defending oneself by getting to "their" level means controlling both information and perception. José and Marilyn expand (1988):

> BU: What does it mean when people talk about speaking English well to defend themselves?
>
> JM: I don't understand.
>
> MM: What I'd say is, to get to their level of speaking.
>
> JM: You mean like if you want to, like you go down to—an example, you go down to face-to-face [welfare] or to housing and you want to have the right words or the right things to say so you want to defend yourself and actually have those words.
>
> MM: Explain yourself clearly to them.
>
> JM: Right.
>
> BU: Do you ever think about having to defend yourself in Spanish the same way? Or would that be different?
>
> MM: No, the same to me, because there's a lot of people, if I'm talking to a Puerto Rican, like myself, a lot of people know more Spanish than I do so they come up with all these big vocabulary words that I don't understand them.
>
> BU: So the idea of defending yourself always has this idea of bringing to an equal level?
>
> MM, JM: Yes.
>
> BU: And making people respect you?
>
> MM: Yeah.
>
> BU: Like they won't respect you if you can't defend yourself?
>
> JM: I always think about that whenever I go to housing.
>
> BU: Really?
>
> JM: Yeah, they just think about the computer, that's it, they don't think about the person behind the wall they're talking to.

Nilsa's ex-husband also sees defense in terms of levels but prefers distance to verbal engagement (1988):

> I know that [Nilsa] knows how to defend herself with these higher professional people. As far as me, I'm more aggressive, I either give you a "fuck-you" or I turn my back to you. That's the way I would defend myself in that situation. But she would defend herself verbally.

Nilsa herself sees defense as explicitly verbal (1988 notes):

> You defend yourself by just speaking out and standing up for yourself. The hell with self-consciousness.

Luis and Rosie Molina connect English clarity and control to self-confidence and emotional status (1988 notes):

> LM: You defend yourself when you are in a situation where it's important to get your point across. That's when you go to your own language. It's not always necessary.
>
> BU: Is it something you do more in Spanish than English?
>
> LM: I try to defend myself in Spanish. If the person understands Spanish then I'll argue and dispute the situation in Spanish. If the person doesn't know Spanish I have no other choice but to fight my battle the best way I can in English.
>
> BU: What's the problem with English?
>
> LM: It's lack of confidence. You know the words but you're put in a situation where the words don't come out as clear and understandable as if we were just talking.

Rosie later added,

> RM: I think I defend myself better in Spanish, because it's my language and when you're upset, you know, words twist and you start English and you finish Spanish or [vice versa].

Rosie describes how much easier control and defense are among equals (1988):

> RM: *Pues* [Well], I went to store once, Bonnie, and there was black girls, four black girls and we were going out, right? . . . [One] said in English—she thought I didn't know no English—she said in English, "I bet you I could take her makeup off." Right? And they were laughing. She said, "Look guys, she didn't understand what we said, right?" And they walked out of the store. . . . I told them "That's what you think, that I don't understand. I might be Puerto Rican, but I know what you're talking."

Like Marilyn, Rosie connects "big words" to unequal relations:

> BU: If it's like your landlord or boss?
>
> RM: They use such big words sometimes, you don't understand them. If I was going to speak English, I could defend myself with the English that I know. You know, if you told me whatever you're going to tell me, if I could, I would answer you. I could defend myself with the English I know, yes, I do. But if it's those people that give you—(Pauses)
>
> BU: So it's really not differences in English but differences in power?
>
> RM: In power, you're right. Yes.
>
> BU: And with a neighbor that's really equal?
>
> RM: That's easy, it's so easy to speak to a neighbor. And in the building it's all Spanish, there's about three black womans, that's about it where you have to speak English. And the black lady from the third floor, she understands Spanish, she

doesn't speak it but she understands it. You tell her this, she understands it. Because I tell her a lot of things in Spanish dirty, she gets real mad at me! She understands a lot.

When class is equal, defense can be a two-way street. There are fewer information barriers and they are less crucial: an African American can find a Puerto Rican friend to negotiate a tricky situation and vice versa. Race ceases to equalize when authority differences come into play. When I asked for an example of defense, Jenny Pacheco narrated a story connecting respect, defense, race, class markers, and authority (1988):

> JP: [Defending myself] means for example since I am Hispanic, I go to work, I have four black supervisors, and an Irish one. They are all Americans. They are two managers, both Hispanics. But at no time do they ever speak Spanish to us. They want to pass themselves off as Americans too. One is Puerto Rican and the other one is Honduran. But he has a very important position within the area where I work . . . housekeeping. So then, if one of the black women comes, the supervisor, and tells me in English, "No, Pacheco you have to do this." . . . Then I'm going to defend myself because I know the rules and I can tell her "Clean that blood? I am not supposed to clean blood." So if she comes and tells me that I have to do it, I have enough English so I can say to her "No, I don't have to do it."
>
> BU: So it's like . . . [saying] in effect, look, I'm a person and you have to—how do I want to say this? You have to give me—
>
> JP: Respect.
>
> BU: It seems the biggest problem . . . is respect because if you don't respect how someone else talks, how—
>
> JP: If someone expresses herself to me like that I'll do the same. If she doesn't respect me, then I can't respect her. . . . I had that problem. My Irish supervisor came up to me one day to tell me, "You have to do all the general cleaning on this floor, from top to bottom, beds, everything, everything, everything." Then I said no, that I cannot do in one day a job that is supposed to take six days. He told me that I had to do it. Then he gave me a warning. So when he gave me the warning, when I told him I wasn't going to do it, he took my cleaning rag from me and shook it like this in my hair—I still had long hair, I hadn't cut it. He shook it in my hair. So when he told me the warning, that's why I told him in English, "You did that because you think I am garbage here because I clean. That is not so. . . . I'm going to be disrespectful now, I am going to say what you told me. Because you treated me bad, and the way you treated me is the way I'm going to treat you. Now if you respect me, I'll respect you because you are my supervisor, but you are an employee just like me. You have no reason to disrespect." So the union delegate told me, "Well, what happened? And explain your reasons and what happened to them." "Well, this and this happened and he . . . snatched the rag from me and shook it in my hair. So he does not respect me. For that reason, I don't respect him either, and you have to tear up that warning," and . . . I told him [the supervisor], "If you don't tear up that warning that you gave me, I'm going to take you to court." Because . . . as supervisor and

since he speaks English, he could defend himself with the other two who, although they are Hispanics, don't want to get their arm twisted speaking Spanish. "Well," he said "I'm going to win here and she is going to lose her job." But he couldn't because—I can't defend myself very well with my English but neither do I allow anyone to be disrespectful to me. My English is poor, but the little I've been able to learn I defend myself with.[8]

Jenny's supervisors have no authority to make her exceed her job description, but they have the power to try to intimidate her into doing so. To defend herself, she must know her job description and union rights. She must be able to explain herself in English to the union delegate. She must make her presentation as authoritative and convincing as that of her supervisors and do it in a way that outweighs their perceptions of her as a Puerto Rican cleaning woman. In her situation, race can only work to her disadvantage, since her supervisors' status negates any racial equality. Puerto Rican/black solidarity goes by the board as the black and Irish supervisors both try to make Jenny do unauthorized work. So does Latin solidarity: the Puerto Rican and Honduran managers "act white" by putting status above race in refusing to speak Spanish. Respect disappears in a situation that typifies white authority, even with players who are not themselves white. Jenny summarizes, "In other words, they think that their skin and their English makes them better than us. But that's not how it is."[9]

The more unequal the situation, the more one is held to a measure of behavior that does not come into play among equals. One can defend what one sees as truth but people who control situations have a good deal more influence over what counts as true. When one is judged on accuracy and logic, one's version of events is only as convincing as one's English. Nervousness, loss of control, and incoherence in the face of authority are a running problem. Luis gives an example (1988 notes):

LM: I'm supposed to get overtime for Saturdays and [my boss] claims that he's already paying me for Saturday. When I'm nervous and I argue with them, I can't remember the words to put them in their spot.

BU: So when you're with those people you're not a person?

RM: You're nothing.

LM: You're not allowed to think, like my boss saying "You're not paid to think." He actually said that to me once, he came in when I was sitting like this [demonstrates] and asked me what I was doing and I said "Just thinking" and he said "You're not paid to think."

BU: What happens to your language in those situations?

LM: I get so nervous. I know I can speak English, I know I can control it but I get so nervous. I cannot defend myself in English. I can in Spanish, I can use Spanish as a sword, the way you would use English to defend yourself, like with a weapon. Your weapon is English, and you fight me with something I cannot fight you with. I start fighting you in Spanish and you're lost. White folks try to bring us down with your language.

BU: What happens when you get nervous?

LM: You lose track of your grammar, your vocabulary, the words you normally know and say. You become so nervous that you put yourself in a bad position. And that's the position where they get you.

RM: Like one time when baby Luis (their son) fell at school, and the white office worker called and asked how he fell and I told her and she said then it's not our responsibility. I got so mad my English went blank. I just went off in Spanish.

LM: The same happens to me, and who has time to think when you're arguing?

RM: You get nervous, uptight, and your English goes blank.

LM: It's because we speak Spanish, because Spanish is our real language. . . . You defend youself with the only language you know which is Spanish for us.

"Our real language" goes beyond form to linguistic function in speech events and participant structures. When speakers are in comfortable control of function and participation, language forms fall neatly into place. When others control function and participation, making speakers socially—and emotionally—vulnerable, language forms lose coherence. When others also control key bits of information (e.g., Luis's boss's claim that Luis is already being paid for Saturday or the office worker's disclaimer of responsibility for Luis Jr.) language form dissolves to nothing: "my English went blank." In the face of these dynamics, Spanish becomes all the more real.

Unfortunately, ideas like speech event and function and participant structure have no reality in the U.S. ideology of language, which is about individual control of form. So people take on terrible burdens in their attempt to prove themselves *as individuals* by conquering English. Tay Román (1988):

It is very important to me to know how to explain myself, how to defend myself. That's what I want, to speak good English and to understand it. Because . . . if I have to go to court, if I have to go to some place and I have my reasons, and I know I am right, I don't want you to go with me for you to, to talk to me. I want to talk, because I, what I want to say, maybe you won't say it. Maybe if I tell you, Bonnie, say this and this and this, maybe you won't say it, maybe you say something different. No, I want to explain myself. I want to say what I feel. It's very important to me to speak English and to understand it at the same time.

Tay went to court because she was accused of welfare fraud. Her only hope in court was to "tell the truth" by giving exactly the right words in the right order. But one does not just "tell the truth" in court. Court procedures set up the speech event, the functions and the participant structure in which truth is cast and, in the end, even rules on whose truth counts:

TR: Because like I told you the other day. I had one experience in court. I lost the case, and I even showed them the truth, that I was not guilty.

BU: That was [where] . . . somebody stole your Social Security card?

TR: Yeah. And they work[ed] with it, and everything. Then the welfare find out that I was working because the computer shows them the Social Security and the place where I was working. I was not that person. I was not there, and I showed them proof. I showed them even the check, the copy of the check [paid to the person working on her card] that they got. And I lost my case. Why I lost my case? Because I didn't have the vocabulary, the way of defend myself. . . .And I didn't take no lawyer with me, because I said I don't need no lawyer. Because I have the truth. I had proof, I showed them proof. They saw the proof.

BU: And they didn't believe it?

TR: They didn't believe it, they . . . on the last hearing, the judge told me, I am sorry I can do nothing. I say why you can do nothing? He said because the welfare changed the story. I said, but what do you mean they changed the story?

BU: They changed the story?

TR: They changed—that's what the judge told me. But I didn't have the ability to defend myself. I didn't have the ability to look for somebody. Then I went to the Grand Concourse [law offices] to look for a lady that she is supposed to help poor people like us. . . . I went there and the lady, the lady wants me to believe, no, not wants me to believe. She was trying to say that I was guilty. That I was that person.

BU: How did she know?

TR: I don't know. She said that the signature [on the check] was the same [as on the card]. I said it can't be the same because that's not my signature, I didn't write it. That is not me. And I have proof. I showed her my proof. And she was bullshitting, you know, and I stopped going there, and I said, I'm not gonna do nothing . . . I sent Rosie for her to send me the papers that she has. And she didn't want to send the papers and I didn't go to pick them up. I save them for her. . . . Why? Because of the language. . . . That's why—I don't know. I don't know what to think about the government or the people who are working for the government or for this agency, I don't know. Because if I show them proof, I even signed. I told them everything. They even called—they even called the boss [of the person working with the stolen card]. And the boss sent me a letter saying that I was not the person who was working for him. . . . I have the letter. I have the letter in the house. I have the copy of the checks.

Despite Tay's conviction that the non-matching signatures and the employer's testimony are self-evident truth, the truth that counts in court is established by institutional procedures. There are two sets of evidence, hers and AFDC's. When she sought help in organizing her experience into evidence, her advocate passed judgment on her rather than convert her story into evidence that counted. In the end, AFDC controlled the very meaning of her evidence by "changing their story." With the weight of legal performativity against her, she was fined $1900.

People on public assistance have little reliable access to information and protection from the consequences of actions. When I asked Tay if she had gone to Legal Aid when the problems with her Social Security card began, she and Rosie responded, how do you know you can trust them? Where do you get information about them? When asked by a tenants' group to join their rent strike, Marilyn expressed similar reservations. This is another manifestation of the information barrier. Luis Molina (1991) described Blue Cross, his private insurance carrier, as considerably more forthcoming with information than the publicly funded Medicaid had been:

With the Medicaid, a lot of people are not aware of the benefits, OK? Is it because they don't want to let people know that they have the medical capability to get whatever they want? Or is it that the Hispanic doesn't care? To me it seems like they have a line already drawn: "Hey, you know, you got Medicaid, be happy, stop complaining, you get this medical service, and that's it." What would be your attitude? You would just say, "Oh well I got Medicaid, I'm just gonna go in, check myself and I'll be all right." You know, one X-ray, the doctor checks you and says, "oh, you're OK," and in a couple of months you'll wind up getting sick again from the same thing, then again you don't have any—how can I put this? The system doesn't allow you to be aware of your rights as a human being, as a person. You know? Your rights get violated as far as what you're entitled to, Medicaid program, food stamp program, all that stuff. For some reason or another—OK, there is a lot of abuse in the system, ain't no doubt about that. But there are people who are trying to make ends meet, who are determined to survive, and to come out of that system to a better system. And again, our—not our economy— our society doesn't allow us. They have a cap on it.

Places on the Language Map

How do English and Spanish "feel" to people in this study: Did they keep English and Spanish separate? Which seems more "real"? When and why do people pretend not to know a language they know: when would a bilingual pretend not to know English? not to know Spanish? In outer-sphere relations, when is Spanish forbidden? What is it like when Americans speak Spanish to bilinguals? Each of these questions is about the definition and control of social space through code: when is it necessary to "control" code boundaries? how and why do people control the perception of their persona through control of code? what does it mean when people with the power to forbid the use of Spanish appropriate Spanish themselves? Here is what people had to say.

1. Do you keep English and Spanish separate?

Nearly everyone said that as a rule they did not, though most (Jenny in particular) felt that bilinguals should know how to keep them apart. Luis agreed with the ideal but said that as a rule, "If the words don't come out English, you go to Spanish and other way around" (1988 notes). Most said they actually spoke *lo que salga*, "whatever comes out." This is consistent with the inner-sphere ethnography of Chapter 3 and with the Language Policy Task Force survey. Nilsa (1988) added:

> Speaking Spanish here, it sounds like you're almost trying to push it out, get rid of the English and speak more clearly your Spanish. But when you're speaking English, you don't try to do that with Spanish. It doesn't work the other way around.

"Here" (where Spanish is the ideological baseline) the language that should be kept separate and clear is Spanish, even though that can be a lot of work for someone like Nilsa who sees herself as primarily an English speaker.

2. Which language is more real, more emotionally salient, English or Spanish?

For most people, Spanish is easier; for everyone it is more emotionally salient. Luis and Rosie (1988 notes):

> BU: Is there a different feel to the two languages? How does Spanish feel different from English?
>
> LM: I feel closer to Spanish, it feels prettier, sexier.
>
> BU: Does it make you feel connected to something? Your family?
>
> RM: Yes, definitely.

Marilyn and José (1988):

> BU: For you, which language seems more real to you, more like it's your language inside you?
>
> JM: Spanish.
>
> BU: Spanish? Or is it changing?
>
> MM: I can't really tell because I do speak a lot of English outside but when I'm in my house I speak a lot of Spanish. Not clearly but I do speak it. But I feel that Spanish is my language.
>
> BU: Like it's more inside? More you?
>
> MM: Yeah.
>
> JM: Yes, yes! Because when I talk to my mother Spanish, I feel like this is me, you know?
>
> MM: Yup!
>
> JM: I'm really Spanish, and I talk to her like if I knew everything, I mean everything. And sometimes it doesn't come out so—something happens and it drops.

Marilyn later adds:

> MM: I just—the English is like always outside, and the Spanish is inside, in my [mother's house]. Now here [in Marilyn's home] we talk a lot of English, but when my friend comes over I talk to her in Spanish because she knows more in Spanish than the English. But sometimes I feel like wait a minute, what's going on, why is everybody looking at me? 'Cause they're not used to people talking in Spanish in the home. Here! Like when I'm talking to my friend, [my husband] could come, pass over and like look at me and look at her, like "these girls are—I don't know!"

Marilyn, like José, Luis, and Rosie, perceives Spanish as stronger. Her husband, like Nilsa (and Nilsa's former husband), perceives English as stronger. Nilsa describes this (1988):

> I've even been asked what language do I think in? And it's definitely English. It's the language I definitely feel the most comfortable in. I think in English, I feel comfortable, it's more realistic, I mean it's more natural. . . . Spanish is sometimes—I have to think about what is being said, really give it a lot more attention.

I then asked,

> BU: Spanish would seem more closely connected emotionally?
> NB: It [Spanish] is important to me. But English is definitely the most comfortable language I feel with.

Millie Wright does not rank either one over the other (1988):

> BU: Do you feel as much at home in Spanish as in English?
> MW: Sure. I'm bilingual . . . I know that there's some words in Spanish, that I lose a word or something, but I don't take it as anything critical. Of course I feel more comfortable with the English because I've been speaking English such a long time. Does one supercede the other?
> BU: Does one feel more *real* than the other?
> MW: No, they're pretty equal.

3. What is your experience with bilinguals pretending not to speak English?

Women in particular pretend not to know English in outer-sphere situations with doctors, social workers, and similar gatekeepers. This strategy is the opposite of an active defense: instead of creating a strong social presence with the "right" English, people deliberately efface themselves to better monitor a situation. Many women prefer being invisible to risking the "nervousness" and "forgetting" induced by outer-sphere English: better to have no social presence than seem disordered. Rosie (1988) describes the strategy and explains how it can backfire:

> I understand everything they say. But I have done it. You know why? It's that I get so nervous especially when I go to court, like with the baby. So I always get someone American. They say "Do you understand English?" I say "No, a little bit." [But if] she's speaking so slowly, I come out speaking English. She tells me, "I thought you didn't speak English," I tell her I understand a little bit. You know they talk to you so much. And then for a person to help you, how you speak Spanish, it takes an hour. So I thought, let me throw my English, forget it. But I've done it in the welfare.

Tay Román (1988) described how she tried this strategy, how it backfired, and how she found a way to make being "out of control" work for her:

> Oh, yes. One time I did it and I hit the social worker. Luis was with me and Rosie was with me. I was in a bad shape. I was almost in the street. And I told Luis, "Luis, go with me, and I'm going to pretend that I don't speak English. Then when you speak to the social worker you speak to me in Spanish, then you will answer to her." We did it that way, I was very nervous. I was very sick. Then, Luis did it. And, like, I said that I didn't speak English. The lady, she sat down like this, and she told Luis, "You know what, that lady's lying". Oh, my God, she said that, and I stand up and I say "Who is lying? Mother-fucker, I am lying?" *Thwa*, I hit her with my pocketbook. Ohh! Two policemen came and they grabbed me and I was crazy, my God! The same day they gave me coupons and they gave me a check. You have to be rough, you have to be nasty with them. I am a very respect-

ful person, I respect everybody, but don't be dirty to me, because I am dirtier than you. Oh yes, that's the way I am, Bonnie. That's the way I am.

Pretending not to know English does place other bilingual women in the position of translator, which can be an imposition, as Marilyn (1988) describes:

> And I be like "I thought you didn't know English," and she goes "I know a little bit." I hate that, I can't stand that because for one thing I don't want to get into their business, you know? And another thing, I have my own problems to take care of in welfare, don't come bothering me to translate anything for you if you know a little bit of English. I don't like that. That's why I say, "*No, yo no sé,* [I don't know]" if somebody Spanish comes to me and asks me to interpret. I say, "*No sé muy bien, pero te puedo tratar de ayudar* [I don't know very well but I can try to help], I'll try to help you." And sometimes they get pissed off when I do that.

The imposition of code solidarity ("You know my language so you translate for me") overrides privacy, since it requires "getting into their business." The bilingual who would prefer not to translate is placed in the tricky position of being "Spanish" yet refusing to speak it. Nilsa's job has often placed her in this position. She objects even more forcefully than Marilyn (1988):

> Oh, Bonnie, I can't stand them. You know why? Because I translated for many years, and I had to deal with people who were denying they knew English so they wouldn't have to translate? And I had to sit in counseling sessions hundreds and hundreds and hundreds of times translating for a stupid bitch that didn't want to make any goddamn effort. That annoys the shit out of me. I feel that if I went to Italy today, I would learn Italian, and if I moved to France I would learn French, and if I moved to the Soviet Union I would learn Russian. It's [i.e., not speaking the local language] like really laid back: I feel that any country you're living in, you should make every effort. It annoys me. And I've actually translated for people that when I'm ready to tell them what it is, they'll say "Oh yeah, I understand." So what am I doing here? You have no idea. In genetic counseling? Tons! But if they would be put in a situation where there was no one to translate, I am certain that they would make one great effort to understand. Tons!

Nilsa's response resonates with her perception of class as a set of values: people should try to help themselves in all respects, whether speaking English or, more generally, trying to "better themselves."

4. What is your experience with bilinguals (especially social workers) who know Spanish and pretend not to?

"Acting white" by denying Spanish is a particular sore spot for women, who (because of the bureacratization of poverty) are more likely to encounter Hispanic gatekeepers who will not speak Spanish. Rosie Molina (1988) emphasizes that such gatekeepers make things even tougher for clients:

RM: Well, I get real nervous. And I saw his accent, and I said, do you talk Spanish, he tells me, no I don't understand Spanish. . . . He is Dominican. Spanish, he's Spanish. I tell him, I'd feel better if you speak to me in Spanish. He says do you want somebody to help you speak, you know, I tell him, no I speak very good English and I could defend myself. I just want to speak Spanish because I feel nervous. I tell him the truth. And he didn't spoke to me in Spanish.

BU: So he was pretending—?

RM: That he didn't know Spanish, no.

Tay Román (1988) spells out the politics of such interaction:

> Well . . . if I know they speak Spanish I speak Spanish then. I don't care. They have to answer me. They answer to me in English, I don't care. If I understand what they are speaking to me in English, I answer in Spanish. And they have to answer. Because they can't keep their mouth shut. They can't tell me "speak to me in English," because if I know they speak Spanish they will understand what I am talking about. . . .

She later adds:

> Yeah, I have a lot of experience. One day I have the same experience with Rosie. The man was Cuban and I didn't know he was a Spanish man. And he told me to wait, he told me, "go to the line and wait in that line." And I wait and wait and wait—the line was long—and wait and wait, and when my turn came, he told me "what are you doing in this line?" I say, "you told me to wait here." And he told me—I don't remember what he told me. And I start cursing him off in English, and somebody told me, "He's not American, he's Cuban." Oh, he's Cuban! Oh, he's Cuban! You speak my own language! Oh, I told him so many things! They brought me the police too. Oh, yeah, they brought me the police. They told me "Lady, lady!" I said, "Lady nothing! He did this and this and this to me and that's not fair!"

The "snotty Spanish social worker" is a stereotype powerfully rooted in women's experience. Men reported meeting people like them but had little to say except "they make me feel bad." The women I talked to in 1979 and 1988 had plenty to say and in much the same terms as these selections from 1979 interviews:

> Adelina Mendoza: When I see [that they're Spanish] . . . then I get mad. I speak to them in Spanish. And they have to answer back. Why should they hide themselves?

> Luisa Muñiz: They're passing as white and hiding from their race.

> Rosa Rivera: They're acting like they're American, like they're ashamed to be Puerto Rican, like I'm shit and they're so big.

> Jenny Molina (Pacheco): They make me so mad and they eat rice and beans the same as me. I just want to hit them in their face.

Luz Guzmán: They'll talk Spanish to each other but not to some old lady. Sometimes they even look for a translator so they don't have to show they know Spanish, like they're showing off and pretending not to be Puerto Rican. You could imagine, people hit the roof! Maybe they think they're better than we are, us lowly classes down here.

The idea that someone "just like me" with a "white" job would put "me" down to appear that much "whiter" is a cultural travesty. When people deny Spanish, they create illegitimate distance; forcing them to speak Spanish reorders social space properly. Nilsa describes how others' denial of Spanish puts her in an equivocal position: translate for people who may be bilingual anyway, or herself risk appearing to "hide from her race" (1988):

NB: I think it's infuriating, I can't stand them [people pretending not to know Spanish]. It may be so that they don't know Spanish, but it makes me very angry.
BU: What's the most typical situation of that happening, of a Hispanic pretending not to know Spanish?
NB: I found that to be much in the working setting, where other Hispanics have refused or have denied knowing how to speak it well, in order to not be used as translators, to just not be bothered by another Hispanic to translate. That has always made me upset, because everyone has been aware that I do know and I've been pulled in different directions to translate. And that makes me angry too, but it makes me more angry when—in the work setting and people refuse to speak it or just someone I meet that—like in the movie "La Bamba" the Spanish guy chasing after the white girl, not knowing a single word of Spanish. To me that's pathetic, I can't stand them, I can't stand people like that whether they're women or men. I hate their guts. Like the guy across the hall from my mother who was rooming there for a while, I can't stand him, he doesn't know a word of Spanish. . . . It's like to speak Spanish would make him inferior.

5. Have you been forbidden to use Spanish somewhere such as the workplace or classroom?

People answered a resounding "yes." Nearly everyone had had a boss or co-workers who asked them not to speak Spanish because "it's rude." All resented being told that. Everyone felt it was an illegitimate restriction on their social space. The commonest reaction was "How dare they? I'm not talking about 'them' and I'll speak what I want!" Nilsa's reaction (1988) is of special interest since she is English-dominant:

There's a little phrase that goes around, "Speak Spanish, you're in America." . . . You see when I was growing up, people would really try to put you down because you spoke Spanish. It was like [imitating snide tone of voice] "Don't speak Spanish, speak English," very nasty. Now very few people tell you that. I haven't been approached with that. I think if anybody today would tell me that, I'd tell them go fuck yourself, I'll speak whatever I want to.

However, José Mojica (1988) describes the same dynamic from outside, when the excluding language represents someone else's in-group:

> I be talking to—you know there's Chinese people also there [in his program] and I don't know what else, Italian people there too. And they be talking, right? And something stops and I start hearing Chinese. And I say, are they still—are we still communicating and stuff? . . I don't know what happens. Inside, I'm mad. But I don't want to show it, I don't want to say, "am I still in this?" Or maybe they just want to be themselves?

6. How do you feel about Americans speaking Spanish to you?

This is a question of defense against outer-sphere invasion by white Americans. Hardest hit are those who feel vulnerable in English. Jenny Pacheco and a neighbor (N) (1988):

> JP: With you I speak Spanish and however much you say to me, I understand you, and I'm someone interested in you learning it.
> N: But you know, most of all, also, this should be considered, the fact that you should feel proud when you're speaking a language that's not your normal language . . . it makes me feel good personally to speak the American language knowing behind that, that I know a second language.
> JP: But because of that—it's because of that that we feel proud [of speaking English] because we want to be at their same level. Because they want to make us [be] seen as Hispanics, as if we are under them.

Jenny adds:

> JP: If you—not you because I understand you very well—but someone who—an American who comes and makes some conversation and says a lot of words with a lot of effort. And I have to keep telling him what he's going to say to me. It's not in my interest for that person to learn Spanish because it's not a relation of mine. . . . No, it's the relationship of the person and it doesn't interest me whether or not they speak Spanish, so it bothers me.[10]

When the ability to defend yourself in English is an important source of symbolic capital, there is an important difference between speaking *no* English and speaking *some* English. If people can defend themselves in English but are forced to speak Spanish, they are robbed of the chance to acquire symbolic capital, or as Jenny put it, "We want to be at their same level." Moreover, if the American is less than fluent in Spanish, the Puerto Rican has to do the linguistic work for both and *still* gets no symbolic capital. José Mojica (1988 notes) further spells out the dynamic:

> Or like an American comes and talks to you in Spanish. You're already used to them in English but if they talk to you in Spanish it's like their personality

changes, like they're trying to make you feel less in life, less important. I don't like when they speak my language in a different [accent]. If everyone's going to speak English the accent is OK.

An American who speaks Spanish without invitation is invasive, as José and Marilyn explain:

> BU: So if an American social worker wanted to talk to you in Spanish, it would be like going into your house uninvited, it would make you feel—
> JM: Uncomfortable.
> MM: Unless they explained they wanted to practice, then it's OK. Otherwise no.

José elaborates:

> BU: Getting back to Americans speaking Spanish—is it an invasion?
> JM: Right. When my social worker speaks Spanish it's not so comfortable because of the English accent in the Spanish and it's hard to understand when they're talking your language with an accent. It's not the same with English, this is America, everyone's supposed to know English but you don't have to speak Spanish for me, English is OK, I talk English. If I go with my mother, it's OK for my mother to understand, but not for me.

"OK for my mother to understand but not for me" means the difference between his mother knowing *no* English (which makes defense a moot point) and him knowing *some* English (which allows him to play for symbolic capital). "Practicing" Spanish focuses on formal rather than social skill and is less invasive.

> BU: You told me this the last time I was here [in 1979], you told me I didn't sound real in Spanish.
> JM: I remember.
> BU: So the difference between an American asking to use Spanish to practice and an American just using Spanish is what?
> JM: Making fun of you.
> BU: If I just started to talk to you in Spanish and you knew I was American, how would you react?
> MM: I would tell you in Spanish and then a word in English so you would know I knew it and if they kept on in Spanish I would stay in Spanish.
> BU: Even if they seemed American?
> MM: Yes.
> JM: Not me. You go to their level, I wouldn't.

Luis and Rosie spell out a position very much like José's (1988 notes):

> BU: How do you feel about Americans who try to speak Spanish with you?
> RM: It doesn't bother me.

> LM: It bothers me, because it goes back to how I speak English.
> RM: If you know English, it's no good.
> LM: It's like listening to my boss abusing the language, when he's talking on the phone to Puerto Rico and I have to listen to him.
> BU: How about if it's a black person [instead of white] who wants to speak Spanish?
> RM: I know a black lady who speaks perfect Spanish.
> BU: How do you feel about that?
> LM: I'd feel more comfortable to be able to communicate with her in my own language.
> BU: Suppose someone wants to practice their Spanish?
> RM: It's OK if it's to practice . . .
> BU: So me speaking Spanish—
> LM: It doesn't fit.
> RM: Well—
> BU: Really, how do you feel about it?
> RM: Really? No.

Neither finds the idea of a Spanish-speaking black neighbor quite as disconcerting, for the neighbor is not in a position to judge their English. Furthermore, with whites (1988):

> LM: It's like trying to invade our—our lives. . . . When you do that, you threaten us. We feel threatened in a situation like that. . . . You threaten—when you go into someone else's language you're threatening their—how will I describe it?
> BU: Security?
> LM: Their security, their life . . . And that's where it becomes racist, and that's where it becomes a thing that you will constantly have when two people are from different backgrounds.

Luis elaborates:

> LM: It's different between us because we've known each other so many years.
> BU: So we can talk about it?
> LM: Yes! But let's say Bonnie just walks in and you know we hear her speak, we hear her trying to communicate in Spanish, we say wait a minute. Talk to us in English, you know we feel more comfortable talking to her in English than we would in Spanish, because when we speak to her in Spanish we're like selling the store or selling ourselves, instead of just, you know, keeping a wall between ourselves by speaking English . . . [English is] national. . . . It's big. Everybody can speak it, everybody is welcome to use it. It's like, we, everyone who comes to this country is authorized to use the English.

That "wall" makes it possible for Luis to defend himself and earn respect by showing he can speak his own language and at the same time "come up" to the public, national language.

Nilsa and Millie have no problem with the idea of an American speaking Spanish to them. However, both are extremely fluent in English and there is no question of their ability to defend themselves. Nilsa (1988):

> I'm glad they [Americans] are making the effort . . . See, I like it. I think it's nice that someone should make an effort to speak a language that I like.

Millie sees how someone less fluent might be affected and she translates symbolic capital into economic terms (1988):

> For myself personally it doesn't really bother me. Some people feel threatened, you're taking something away that they have, that they had gotten naturally or whatever. That's a plus for them, because like I said before you already have a plus because you have white skin, that's your plus that you have. And if you have that and you're able to talk like I talk too, and if we both go to get a job, they're going to give the job to you before they give it to me. So you've taken something away from me. That's a threat.

Limón (1979) describes how students from Mexican immigrant families appropriated the term "Chicano" as a public symbol of political/ethnic unity in ways that irritated working-class Mexican-Americans. "Chicano" was for them a private, multivalent symbol and making it public was exposing and invasive. Here, a private and multivalent Spanish is made public, and, what is worse, it appears to be appropriated by condescending outsiders who assume that any Puerto Rican must naturally want to speak Spanish with anyone who comes along. This is racializing, insofar as Spanish is seen to stand for being Puerto Rican: people are seen as part of a mass, with their individual skills and preferences ignored. People resent being denied the chance to ethnicize by defending themselves in English.

Conclusion

As the people in this study talk about their experiences of race, class, and language, control is a recurrent theme and a key element in the opposition between *Puerto Rican* and *white*. Control emerges as a feature of specific outer sphere relations: when white employers forbid Spanish on the job, when white bosses or co-workers engage in racialized jokes, when white landlords use "fancy language" that effectively silences back-talk, when bureaucratic officials are able to mandate "the real story," when Latin gatekeepers pretend not to know Spanish, when white gatekeepers address Puerto Ricans they do not know in Spanish. Respect encodes the sense that the client, tenant, or employee deserves equal footing and defense encodes a way in which that footing might be achieved. Outer-sphere institutions are, however, notably lacking in actual mechanisms for evening up the communicative footing. So bilinguals carry the burden of appearing ordered, unraced, ethnically controlled. But this burden leaves bilinguals in a delicate position: at what point are they seen to cross the line into "acting white"?

The hegemony that saturates these communicative actions stays in place because the Puerto Rican client, employee, or patient has little control over the metacommunicative frame. Much of what people recount in this chapter is their perception of the ways in which communicative routines reproduce a conflation

174   The Race/Class/Language Map

of race and class. As Foley (1990) documents in his study of the reproduction of class/race culture in a small town in South Texas, a "clear counter-hegemonic class consciousness" (p. 195) does not develop precisely because of the way class operates in America. If the terms of cultural definition are *explicitly* about class immobility and domination, then race cannot be turned into ethnicity, and domination is more readily recognized for what it is. When the terms of cultural definition are explicitly about class mobility as every individual's moral imperative and when race can be recast as ethnic-American identity, then social domination is not easily recognized, and it is much more difficult to resist. Onto this dynamic is mapped the English-Spanish boundary.

Notes

1. Dates in parentheses indicate which year the interviews were done. The word "Notes" indicates interviews written directly onto my laptop computer; otherwise interviews were recorded and transcribed. Jenny Pacheco's interviews are translated from Spanish; the Spanish originals are provided in footnotes.

2. Spanish original: "Ah, pero si ustedes los hispanos siempre viven en acomplejar, nunca quieren echar pa'lante, nunca quieren progresar—" No, siempre está la frase, "Ustedes los hispanos."

3. Spanish original: Bueno. Habremos personas que venimos y, por una razón o otra, nos vamos a trabajar, por ejemplo, en el welfare y se hace el social service. Entonces, ella se acompleja del idioma de que es hispano y que siempre nos tienen por debajo de tapete, como decimos nosotros vulgarmente, entonces ella trata de asimilarse al americano. Por el complejo que se ha creado por el idioma. Porque nosotros tenemos complejo por el idioma del inglés, no por el nuestro. Porque un hispano es como un americano. Tú eres americana y tú te metes adentro del governador y como ese es tu idioma, por mas que tú te sientas mal, ese es tu idioma y tú lo vas a decir. Tal es como tú lo aprendiste o te lo enseñaron o lo aprendiste de pequeña. Eso nos pasa a nosotros. Hablamos nuestro idioma, el español. Pero entonces, al ir en una reunión de americanos, queremos asimilarnos al americano, para que no nos den el racismo por la lengua.

4. Spanish original: Cuando dan la noticia en los canales americanos, ellos siempre dicen si, o por ejemplo, un cubano . . . un hondureño, o un colombiano, mata aquí, ellos dicen "el hispano" casi siempre dicen el puertorriqueño. Porque para el blanco, aquí los hispanos son puertorriqueños. No les importa que sea cubano, colombiano, hondureño, de donde sea, dicen "el boricua tal mato a fulano de tal". Pero cuando se da una noticia de un blanco, ellos nunca te dicen a tí "un blanco tal ni fulano de nada"; "Mr. Fulano de tal hizo este acto."

5. In my discussion of culturally encoded intent versus social results, I draw on Silverstein's (1976) notions of function$_1$ (roughly corresponding to Austin's 1962 illocutionary intent) and function$_2$ (Austin's perlocutionary force). I prefer Silverstein's formulation. Austin sought to account for the non-truth value effect of oaths, promises, and other "deeds done in words" and so concerned himself largely with classes of verbal formulae. Silverstein treats the performative as an indexical process. By doing so, he locates speech acts in defining cultural categories much more explicitly than Austin does, which makes his approach applicable to a wider range of linguistic phenomena and to a more general theory of cultural construction.

6. Sometimes the mapping is quite explicit. When Cathy's white supervisor at Friendly's told her she didn't "act black," she asked what he meant by black? He pointed to a co-worker who was, as she put it, "real dark, thick lips, not too bright."

7. As Adelina Mendoza put it (1979 interview), "I know they speak English and it's because they're raised here, sometimes it's hard for them to speak Spanish, so I try to follow them . . . but when I see somebody that they are not kids, and they just want to make believe, that's when I get mad."

8. Spanish original:

JP: Bueno, significa que, por ejemplo, yo, como soy hispana, voy a mi trabajo. Yo tengo cuatro supervisores morenos, y un supervisor irlandés. Todos son americanos. Hay dos managers, son hispanos. Pero ellos en ningún momento nos hablan español. Se quieren pasar por americanos también. Entonces, uno es boricua y el otro hondureño. Pero tiene un puesto bien importante dentro del área donde yo trabajo—te estoy hablando del housekeeping. So entonces, si viene, por ejemplo, una de las morenas, la supervisora, y me dice a mí en inglés, "no, Pacheco, tú tienes que hacer esto." Press, right? So, ella viene y tú lo tienes que hacer. Estoy yo—ya yo me voy a defender porque ya yo conozco mis leyes y yo le digo a ella, por ejemplo, "limpia esa sangre," yo en mi trabajo no estoy supuesta a limpiar sangre. Si ella viene y me dice, "tú lo tiene que hacer," ya yo tengo un poco de inglés que a ella le puedo decir "No, I don't have to do."

BU: So es como—lo que estoy pensando, es cuando una persona puede—se puede defender, puede decir en efecto, mira, soy una persona y tú me tienes que—how do I want to say this? Me tienes que—

JP: Respetar.

BU: Umm—hmm! Porque . . . me parece a mí que el mayor problema . . . es el problema del respeto, porque es que si uno no respeta a otra persona como habla, como—

JP: Si una persona se expresa así a mí, yo me expreso así a ella. Si ella no me respeta a mí, yo no le puedo respetar. . . . Yo tuve ese problema. El supervisor irlandés mío vino una vez donde mí a decirme, "tú tienes que hacer toda la limpieza general en este piso, desde arriba hasta abajo, el piso, camas, todo, todo, todo." Entonces yo le dije, "que no, que yo en un día no puedo hacer el trabajo que se supone que se haga en seis días que está del piso." Me dijo, "que tú lo tienes que hacer." Y él me dio un warning. So cuando me dio el warning, yo le dije que yo no lo iba hacer, él me quito un paño que yo tenía limpiando, y me sacudió así el pelo. Yo tenía el pelo largo, no me lo había cortado. Me sacudió el pelo. So cuando me dio el warning, por eso, yo le dije a él en inglés, aquel día, "tú lo hiciste porque tú te crees que yo aquí soy basura porque yo limpio. Pero no es así. . . . Te voy a faltar el respeto ahora, te voy a decir lo que tú me dijiste a mí. Porque tú me trataste a mí mal, y del way que me trataste a mí es como yo te voy a tratar a tí. Ahora si tú me respetas, yo te respeto porque tú eres mi supervisor. Pero tú eres trabajador igual que yo. Tú no tienes porque faltarme el respeto." So entonces, la delegada de la unión me dijo a mí, "bueno, qué pasó, y explica tus razones y qué lo que pasó a ellos." "Bueno, paso este y este, y me dio, no me dio que cogió el paño de la mano, pero me sacudió el paño de la mano y me rozó el pelo, [xx xx]. So no me respeta a mí. Por eso, yo no le respeto a él, y me tiene que romper ese warning," y . . . le dije a el, "y si tú no me rompes el warning que tú me dijiste a mí, yo te voy a llevar a tí a la corte. . . . Porque él, como supervisor y como hablaba en inglés, se podría defender con los otros dos que a pesar de que son hispanos no quieren dar a torcer su brazo y hablar el español. "Pues," él dijo aquí "yo me la voy a ganar y ella va a perder el trabajo." Pero entonces no pudo porque—yo no me puedo defender muy bien con el inglés. Pero tampoco me dejo que nadie me falta el respeto. Mi inglés es malo, y lo poco que he podido aprender, yo me defiendo con ello.

9. Spanish original: En otras palabras, ellos se creen que es por la piel y por su inglés que son mejores que nosotros. Pero no es así.

10. Spanish original:

JP: Contigo yo hablo español y por más que tú me lo digas, que te estoy entendiendo, y yo soy una que estoy interesada en que tú aprendas.

JP: Por eso, pero—es por eso porque nosotros nos sentimos orgullosos porque queremos estar al mismo nivel de ellos. Porque ellos nos quieren hacer ver a nosotros como hispanos, que estamos por debajo de ellos.

Si tú—no tú, porque a tí te entiendo bastante, pero alguien que, un americano que venga y me haga alguna conversación y me diga tantas palabras o tantos pro—trabajo. Y yo tengo que estarles diciendo lo que él me va a decir a mí. Y a mí no me interesa que esa persona aprenda español porque no está relacionado a mí. . . . No, es la relación de la persona y no me interesa que me hable español. Pues, me molesta.

Epilog

Chapters 3 through 5 follow the people in this study through thirteen years, from 1978 to 1988 to 1991. In that time their lives changed considerably. In 1978–1979, Nilsa Buon was our project secretary; she, her husband, and young son lived in the north Bronx. Millie Wright and her two daughters had recently moved to the block; they had been living out of state with her husband's family when he died. Jenny Molina, as she was then, lived upstairs from our project with four of her sons, including Luis, and one of her two daughters. They moved to the south-central Bronx in the summer of 1979, not long before Luis and Rosie started going together. Marilyn and José Mojica lived with their mother, sister, and two brothers around the corner from the project office. Luis was in high school. Marilyn, José, and Millie's daughter Cathy were in junior high. They were also all after-school tutees of mine at some point, which set an interesting and helpful precedent for our discussions in 1988 and 1991.

By 1988, Nilsa was in her early thirties, working as a hospital administrator, attending Lehman College part-time, and living in a co-op in the north-central Bronx with her three children and then-husband who worked for a chain grocery. Millie and Cathy lived in the north/central Bronx; Millie worked in a home for learning-disabled adults, and Cathy attended Lehman College and worked part time in clerical and restaurant jobs. Luis and Rosie lived in the central Bronx with their two children; Luis worked as a shipping clerk for a small textile firm on Long Island. Jenny lived a few blocks from them with one of her sons and worked in housekeeping in a Manhattan hospital. Tay Román, whom I met for the first time in 1988, lived with two of her grandchildren in the building where Luis and Rosie lived, and attended a local business college. Marilyn lived on the Lower East Side with her husband and daughter; her husband worked in construction. She attended a combination General Equivalency Diploma (GED) and job-training program. José attended a combination job-training and rehabilitation program.

By 1991, Nilsa and her husband had split up. She had moved elsewhere in the Bronx, continuing to work in hospital administration and taking classes when possible. Millie was working as a receptionist for an import/export firm. Cathy was about to graduate from Lehman College. Jenny had been laid off. Tay was still attending classes. Marilyn, her husband, and two daughters had moved to public housing in the south/central Bronx; work had become sporadic. José still lived on the Lower East Side and attended the program. Luis went to work for the city school system. He and Rosie joined a local unaffiliated church with a mixed Latino, African American, Asian, and white membership and sent their children to its school.

During these thirteen years, everyone had ups and downs. Nearly everyone went through episodes of job loss. Several went through episodes of illness and fragile mental/emotional health. Nearly everyone had taken in relatives or faced family emergencies caused by death, illness, jail sentences, or drug problems in their family. Two of Jenny's adult children died. The Mojica family faced a period of virtual homelessness. At the same time, everyone strove toward goals. Cathy now teaches high school history and is in a master's program. Nilsa, Luis, and Tay are well along toward their bachelor's degrees. Millie and Jenny have also taken college courses. Nearly everyone else has received their GED. Luis and Rosie are active in their church, which has been most supportive to them. For them it is a true community.

Ethnolinguistics or Real Data?

Chapters 4 and 5 are about experiences that people remember and describe rather than, as in Chapter 3, activities that I report on as ethnographer. Yet it is no less data, no less real. However good an observer I or any ethnographer might be, I cannot see what the people in this study see, or feel what they feel, or conclude what they conclude. The point to this book is to show how they theorize about the intersection of language, race, and class in ways that emerge from their location. Their perceptions, constructions, and assessments are consistent and coherent, forming a complex theoretical whole that importantly complements and expands standard social science thinking on class, race, and language. Above all, their reflections on their experience show how racializing operates within a specific sociohistorical frame.

Each non-white "race" in the United States has taken its own specific shape within its sociohistorical frame. Being Latino, black, Asian, or Native American are not equivalent categories of identity. But what each has in common is that each is always subject to scrutiny and assessment: achievers and a credit to their people, or a disorderly, welfare-dependent underclass. Being subject to scrutiny in this way is a structural issue. Americans in positions of institutional authority—teachers, counselors, supervisors—can be kind, sympathetic people. In the course of this study I met some educational program supervisors, people who put in long hours in trying conditions. They worked with clients and students under severe institutional restraints with little opportunity or incentive to step outside that context and its discourse. It was no surprise that when they talked about the difficulties that students and clients had in their respective programs, they focused on cultural explanations rather than on structural issues: if people dropped out of a program or failed tests or turned in work late it was "because of culture"—specifically, what supervisors and teachers saw as "Hispanic culture." Rarely did they talk about the class-based conditions that led to dropping out or turning in late work.

Policy, legislative, academic, and media discourses in the United States overwhelmingly map racial assessments onto perceptions of culture. They circumvent talk about how class is structured and instead talk about class as something individuals control, or should control. It is no particular surprise that such ways of speaking are endlessly repeated in private discourses, or that both public and private discourses have come to shape perceptions of social reality in the United States. In the light of such powerfully performative discourses, it is most important that people who are usually objects of scrutiny become interlocutors and co-theorists. What they know about the racialization of language, and the conflation of race and class is as much theory as data.

Appendix

Description of Sample Speakers and Transcriptions of Speech Samples

In the transcriptions of the speech samples, the punctuation " . . . " indicates where I deleted material in the sample tape to remove cues as to the speaker's identity, background, or location.

#1. Female, age 29, Puerto Rican, came to New York at age 14. Working her way through college as secretary.

> The most annoying thing that I find on the trains is the people, you know, people that they don't like public transportation and they don't want to be touched. That really annoys me. That's the most annoying thing I find. What annoys me is too when you get on a train and it's so crowded and you see these people coming in with TVs, they got boxes of TVs or a carriage or something, that really annoys me. . . . Or the ones that come up first and they say well I'm begging but you know I'm not stealing on the street, I'm not robbing of anybody.

#2. Male, age 30, Irish-American, born and raised in the Bronx. Working for telephone company.

> I'm on the subway and I got off at 125th Street and changed for the express. And it was very crowded and in a crowded train you're balanced up on someone's foot. So I stepped on this guy's foot, and he must have been about seven foot tall. This huge, huge man, seven foot tall. And it about—it was about seven o'clock in the morning and, I was, I don't know, I was just in a poor humor, getting up so early in the morning. And—so he's upset that I stepped on his foot and glared at me with a mean look on his face for the entire trip down to 42nd Street. And, well, I was getting off at Brooklyn Bridge and it winds up he was getting off close near there also so he's glaring at me [xx xx] and we glared at each other for—'cause even though

I'm much smaller, I was just in poor humor and willing to tear into this guy. And he had to duck to actually get on the train. He was a huge, huge man, far bigger than me. And it was funny. And even though it was crowded, I noticed the spaces that developed around us, and people expecting to see a fist fight.

#3. Female, age 30, African American, born in New York, spent much of her adolescence on military bases (father in service). Attending college part time and working as receptionist.

> Like I have an aunt and she won't get on the subway. I'm sure she has done it because she's lived in New York many many years. She does not like the subway and I asked her why, she says she does not like that idea of being underground and not knowing where she's going. . . . But that's what I was saying about the people make me more nervous than anything else. I was on the subway yesterday and this young boy, this young black boy had on a Walkman of some sort, I don't know if it was a Walkman but anyway he had on one of those tape players. And every so often he would shout, I mean he would just scream out, you know? And what surprised me is that for all intents and purposes, he looked like an average black teenage boy. But this person was, I don't know, anyway he was someplace else. I was reading, I was in no mood for that kind of foolishness. But it's something you have to deal with all the time on the subway 'cause you're with all these people, we all have places that we're—that we need to go and we have to make the most of it til we get off the track, I mean get out of the train. But that's the thing about the subway riding that really you know makes me nervous. But not the system itself.

#4. Male, 38, Puerto Rican, grew up in Bronx and Manhattan. An academic teaching in a city college.

> Like I was telling you the other day, since I've lived—moved to Manhattan, it hasn't been as bad as when I lived in the Bronx. And when I lived in the Bronx, that was eight years ago, the trains were in really, really bad shape because of—that was terrible. I remember that worst thing was that I had to—I was delayed three hours getting home and it was frequent that you'd have delays of a half hour, forty-five minutes. The trains were cold, and they were not heated in the winter sometimes, and in the summer they weren't air-conditioned. And once in a while, on occasion, you'd have somebody would throw themselves on the train, on the tracks. That happened—yeah, that happened quite a few times. This was—I don't know why this was never reported in the news media. I was still living in the Bronx at that time and at least three times, we were delayed because they had to cut off the electricity on the train, on the third rail, so everything stops because the men had to get in to take the person out. But I remember one day it was really gruesome, you know I was walking to the train station and the blood was dripping down from the elevated tracks, and it was dripping down to the street. And there was a crowd there and the ambulance was there and the police was there and everything. It was terrible. But since I've been in Manhattan, like I told you, it hasn't been too bad. The train service has improved somewhat and I don't have to travel that long a distance. Sometimes you'll get a delay where you have to

wait five or ten minutes for a train so it could take me sometimes as much as twenty-five minutes or half hour. But usually not much more than that.

#5. Female, 24, Cuban, family moved to New York at age 7. Working her way through college.

One thing I hate about the subway is really, is the people that go in it. You walk in, you know, you might be in a good mood and you walk in and you see all these people with faces from here to here, you know? And if you look at them, they're like "what are you looking at?" And no one is that friendly on the subway unless something happens you know that everybody gets together. Sometimes, any-way. . . . I read in the paper where this woman was—what was it, she was beat up and raped? Inside the train with all these people watching. Nobody dared to do anything, these people that they go, I don't want to get involved, you know. . . . I was rushing in the morning, the train was—was—you know, again, [xxx xxx] the train just left. I ran and thinking it was a puddle of water? It was oil. It looked black, you know, I figured the water was—you know, dirty water there? So I stepped over it and when I stepped over it, I went flying. I fell on my side and I had oil all down my leg. And then an undercover detective, he comes up to me, real close to me, I got scared, I was like, you know, what is this guy doing getting close to me and he shows me a badge he says, you should sue the subway. And I go, naw, that's OK. I was like—I was, aw man, I was in pain my leg, all this oil. That was terrible though, thinking it was water and it was oil?

#6. Male, 60, Puerto Rican, born and raised in Bronx and Manhattan. Works in accounting, attends evening college classes.

One of the things I can't understand is why whenever the trains stop between sta-tions, and you're wondering what's going on, and there's nobody announces you know what's happened or how long we're going to be there. And [it's that] really, it makes me even worry what's, you know, what it is. [xx xx] will someone say well there's a delay or there's congestion ahead or whatever. . . . Every—they would always sweep the sidewalk, the curb rather. And the streets were always clean. And then with the new breed of sanitation workers, it just disappeared. . . . I think the bus drivers are more cordial and more understanding, you know. Buses are pretty good, I think.

#7. Female, 50, Puerto Rican, born and raised in New York. Secretary, attending evening college classes.

Another thing I hate about the subways is how filthy they are, OK? Especially, espe-cially when you get down to Grand Central or Times Square or you go on into Coney Island, OK? Have you ever been down to that train station? That is so filthy it's unbelievable. And with so much manpower, I can't understand why they can't keep it clean. . . . OK, you can just leave New York and just leave New York City and go upstate and it's such a difference, I mean one hundred percent change, OK? I just can't understand with so much manpower in this city, OK? And the sanitation department making a good salary, why can't they clean up the city, OK? I have seen the proprietors of grocery stores and the pizza shops around my area, they themselves have to go with a broom, OK? and something to pick it up with, you know? and just clean up all the dirt, even wash down the streets and the sidewalks because they—it's just unbelievable the dirt that—and so much money that they spend on equipment to clean the streets and all they do is just pick up the loose dirt and everything else stays. . . . And we got a big 15 inches of snow and you know that we used to get 14 or 15 inches of snow and—and in one week it was cleaned up. Now my God, everybody goes into a tizzy when you get 1 inch of snow.

#8. Male, 22, African American, grew up in Manhattan. Currently a student in a high school equivalency and job training program.

Seems like I always run into rush hour, yes, every time. It seems like it never fails, and the train be's packed, it be so packed you got to squeeze in through people. And it seems like nobody's getting off at the stop that—where I be at to catch the train. And it's hard, it be difficult for me sometimes. But the longest I ever had to wait to get on the train was about 15 minute, that's as long as I waited today. Took me 15 minutes to get here from where I [xxx] at. Sometimes it's difficult, but I can't complain about it I guess, if it gets here on time. . . . It [a device] hold the train so the train can't be moved because all the conductor do is steer the train. No, not really steers the train, all he just do is push the button to make sure the train goes. And certain times, he got to look at certain lights. When the red light come on, that means the train is ahead of you in the next station, and it has to be standing still in order to make sure the train doesn't be moved by the conductor, this is a little precaution they have, by tilting it over to the side. Without electrical power, the train can't move. And then when the light turns yellow, that means the train ahead of them is being moved forward and now this train can go up forward. . . . They had a guy one time, right? that was walking around pushing people off the track. A crowd of people seen him push a girl on a train and they finally caught him. They was looking for this guy I believe for about three months. And then they had a guy in Penn Station, they called him the subway sniper. He would—you know—they caught him. But for about a month and a half he was like—uhhh—like a sharpshooter, shooting people out of nowhere. Nobody knew where he was, you know, and this guy was just picking people off.

#9. Female, 50, Polish-American, Bronx born and raised. Church secretary.

When I took the bus to Fordham, the—it's all right going, but coming home you have to cross the street like so far to get back to . . . and then when you wait for the bus to come back to this neighborhood, there's like five buses that stop there and you're lucky to find—I know. And now the buses are going up. . . . They drink on the bus, they sit in the back of the bus and they drink in the summertime on the bus. [BU: do you think the bus is better to take than the subway?] I do, because you're on the street. If anything happens you can just get out and run. No, but I really think the buses are safer than the subways today. You know, 'cause there's too much going on with stealing and harrassing. I took the train for years when I worked in Manhattan. It used to go so fast though, God you would think you were . . . [Someone] was killed down here last night again, on the central. He was crossing, there's a shortcut from, you know, the park. Last year a young boy from the school was killed. Fourteen years old. And now last night a forty-year-old man with no identification.

#10. Male, 21, Puerto Rican, grew up in Manhattan. Currently a student in a high school equivalency and job training program.

Well I had um—it wasn't in the train really, it was like in the station, somebody tried to take my jacket I have. Luckily for me the guy was drunk. [BU: So he didn't get a good grip?] No it was not that he didn't, I didn't let him get close enough to do anything else. I kicked him in the back of his knees and he just stumbled down so I just walked away from him there. I got away pretty easy for that. I don't like—you know what I don't like is when the people be, when they start leaning on you? The train's not even that full and there was this guy leaning on me. He got me so mad, he was leaning all the way over the bridge, you know how long it is that ride. It's about a seven-minute ride just to get over that bridge and the guy's leaning on me. And I pushed back like three or four times and he's still—he still was leaning on me. So when I came to the door open, I just—I pushed him out because I knew he was getting off at that stop anyway. And then he looked at me like what'd I do wrong? . . . Somebody's planted a firebomb inside—inside a token, one of those token booths. I don't know how they managed that considering the door's always supposed to be closed.

#11. Female, 35, WASP, grew up in Manhattan. Professional writer, medical media.

Have you ridden on the el? The new trains, they're—these are the graffiti-proof trains, so they're very clean on the outside, they're you know very chrome and paint does not stick to them. And they do actually look nice. The el used to be just about the worst line and it's gotten a lot better. Umm, I think the A train has gotten really bad now. That's the one where—that is chronically delayed, particularly going in and out of the final stops. But they get delayed there 'cause they have the train yards there where they put the trains to bed for the night and they tend to delay the incoming trains during rush hour so that they can take trains out of service, they've decided that this is an efficient way to run things so that you are stuck between stations for twenty minutes. That's usually when the air-conditioning conks out.

#12. Male, 36, white, Jewish, grew up in Queens. Lawyer for public agency.

Well, probably the most horrible thing which ever happened to me was this little old woman who was leaning on her umbrella on the subway and I stood up, gave her my seat and she hit me with the damned umbrella and said, "it's about time, stupid." . . . What is the authority's fault is they never fix anything. They don't fix stairways, they don't fix gratings. The trains themselves will run until they run into the ground. And what's more is that there probably is no hope whatever of it getting better. F train's kind of a nice train. I used to take it home from high school. There never was a new Canarsie train, they built them old, out of rusted material. But they ran, and they never had delays. And the F train would break down and the E train would break down. The Canarsie didn't break down.

#13. Female, 20, African American, grew up in Manhattan. Currently a student in a high school equivalency and job training program.

Today was it. Today was like—oh, this morning it was—I waited like a half-an-hour for the F. It was crazy, I mean, that made me late. And yesterday going home I waited from 5:15 until like twenty to six for a C on West 4th Street. And it was—yecch. . . . It was like—OK, I was—I had borrowed something of someone's one day, right? it was like a Walkman. And there was a homeless person in the train, you know, and the train smelled very bad. And I would—there was a lot of people around and I was looking at these people like, you know, open that door, don't just smell this person, let some air in here, right? So I stumbled to the door and I opened the door, and I had umm, this person's Walkman on my bag. And once I opened the train door, the Walkman just like jumped off my bag and jumped down. Yup! and it was brand new and I felt horrible the whole day. And that just recently happened. And that's the most awful thing that ever happened in the train. [BU: You mean that crack between the doors?] And this man tried to grab it and it was like it just jumped out of his hand and it just wanted to just kill itself, I don't know. It was crazy! But that was awful.

#14. Male, 30, Dominican, came to New York at age 20. Office worker, attends evening college classes.

I been living in this city for the last ten years. And I used the subway only during my first year, and I was held up by someone and in that time I decided to buy my car and I said well I'm not going to take the subway anymore. I—And I said that I feel very unsafe in the subway. And another thing is the smell in the subway, I can't stand it. [Break] Let's see, uhh, three weeks ago my—one of my brothers was here and we came to the subway. And I looked very suspicious to many people because of the fear that I was going to get mugged, so say, like everybody seemed to be strange for me and I was very afraid of being mugged again. So, and he noticed, you know, and he said to me what happened to you, you look like, you know, you're afraid, what happened? Everything's fine here. You know, I enjoy this. This is the first time I see a subway but you know it's nice, it's just something different. I said well this place is not safe, you know, we'd better get out of here soon. And we took the subway to go to downtown and on the way back we took a taxi. We said no, let's take a taxi this time.

#15. Female, 55. Irish, moved to New York age 15. Housewife in Bronx.

There used to be a frankfurter stand there and while I was waiting I'd go in for a frankfurter . . . Exactly, that was the time that the bus came. That was the end of the frankfurter. Or if I bought the frankfurter, and I was coming out with it I'd of put it in my bag. . . . people in the bus and you're crushed up? I wouldn't enjoy my frankfurter. Because one time I bought it and 'twas squashed in my bag, for when I got home, *fffff*, into the garbage. . . . Well, I'll say the transportation is better because as crowded as you are in the bus, or on the train rather, the bus when it's crowded, you can't see where you go. [You can't] see [204th] Street, I'm [not going to] wait [in front of] Harnick's. So I'm crowded, I'm short, I can't see out, I don't know. The only time I don't like the train—the transportation, is when it goes underground. That's when I pray, underground. When I see the darkness, ahh, or when it goes express. Forget it! I am praying for that train to get into where I can see the light. . . . Do you stand in front of the train and look out at the very front? You don't notice it as much as if you're sitting down in the train and looking out the window and all I say is, God forbid if that should jump the tracks.

#16. Male, 23, Dominican, came to New York age 14. Working his way through college.

What about taking a three—two-and-a-half hour trip that should take fifteen minutes regularly? This started out—got out of work at 12:30, should have caught the train at 12:32, I ran down, I was there on time, the train was there on time. Then it got stuck between 168 and 181 for half an hour. So it finally gets going and I figure I'm going to get home 45 minutes later. And it got stuck between 181 and 191 for an hour and you couldn't get out of the train, you couldn't do anything about it. Just stuck in there. Then after it gets moving again it gets stuck between 191 and Dyckman for another half an hour. By the time I got home, it was 3:30 in the morning. I had to be at work at 8:00 in the morning, I had to get up at 7. The next day I went out to the bank, took out all my money and bought a car. . . . Just—just, when that ever happened to me, I never got left behind, I always just jump over the side. If you gotta get someplace, it doesn't matter, you do what you have to do. I got stopped I think three times for jumping the train and two of those times what I had done was, I just dropped a dollar in the—in at the—where the token booth is? The guy that sells tokens? I put a dollar there, the train was there, the guy takes forever to give you tokens, when the train is coming especially, so I just said forget it, I just jumped over. The cop stopped me and I pointed toward the guy, and the guy said OK. Because no way. I mean, they don't care, they really don't. They just—it's their job to sit there.

#17. Female, 20, Dominican, came to New York (Brooklyn) age 5. College student.

I hate the pushing. I mean, they're constantly pushing pushing. I don't know where they think you're going to go. I mean, they push you and push you and push you. I don't know what they want you to do, sit on other people? You know, [where people are] sitting, they want you to go like on top of them or whatever? I hate the pushing I can't stand that. Especially, when they leave it's so crowded, in other words a lot of people, and everybody wants to get on the train, everybody, no matter what time it is.

OK, when I was working where I used to work there was this lady with two kids and the sorriest person you ever seen in your whole life. You see her in the train station axing and begging for money, cigarettes and what have you. She would go into the [railway car?] and axe for money, I mean, all around. But then you would go to lunch, got to MacDonald's and she's there stuffing her face, and [xx xx] what's up?

You would think, give your kids something. No, the kids have their little french fries and a roll, a little bit of this and a little bit of that, but she has the Big Mac. I mean, that really pissed me off. I mean here I am giving you money and you're talking about it's for your kids, and then here are your kids starving to death and you're eating a big stupid meal. That really killed me. And after that I'm like, no. No! [I hate] to see that. I mean, I don't understand. I mean, you're begging for your kids, give your kids some food.

References Cited

Alvarez, Celia. 1988. "An Interpretive Analysis of Narration in Social Interaction." In *Speech and Ways of Speaking in a Bilingual Puerto Rican Community*. Investigators: Celia Alvarez, Adrian Bennett, Mel Greenlee, Pedro Pedraza, Alicia Pousada. Center for Puerto Rican Studies Language Policy Task Force. New York: Hunter College, City University of New York, pp. 139–192.

Anderson, Benedict. 1983. *Imagined Communities*. London: Verso.

Appadurai, Arjun. 1991. "Global Ethnoscapes: Notes and Queries for a Transnational Anthropology." In Richard Fox (ed.) *Recapturing Anthropology: Working in the Present*. Santa Fe NM: School of American Research Press, pp. 191–210.

———. 1986. "Introduction: Commodities and the Politics of Value." In Arjun Appadurai (ed.) *The Social Life of Things: Commodities in Cultural Perspective*. New York: Cambridge, pp. 3–63.

Attinasi, John. 1979. "Language Attitudes in a New York Puerto Rican Community." In Raymond Padilla (ed.) *Bilingualism and Public Policy: Puerto Rican Perspectives*. Center for Puerto Rican Studies, City University of New York, pp. 10–63.

———. 1983. "Language Attitudes and Working Class Ideology in a Puerto Rican Barrio of New York." *Ethnic Groups* 5:55–78.

Austin, J.L. 1962. *How to Do Things with Words*. Cambridge: Harvard University Press.

Baron, Dennis. 1992[1987]. "Federal English." In James Crawford (ed.) *Language Loyalties: A Source Book on the Official English Controversy*. Chicago: University of Chicago Press, pp. 36–40.

Barth, Frederick (ed.). 1969. *Ethnic Groups and Boundaries*. Boston: Little, Brown.

Basso, Keith. 1979. *Portraits of the Whiteman: Linguistic Play and Cultural Symbols Among the Western Apache*. New York: Cambridge University Press.

Bateson, Gregory. 1972. "A Theory of Play and Fantasy." In *Steps to an Ecology of Mind*. New York: Ballantine, pp. 177–193.

Bauman, Richard. 1977. *Verbal Art as Performance*. Prospect Heights IL: Waveland.

Baver, Sherrie. 1984. "Puerto Rican Politics in New York City: The Post-WW II Period." In James Jennings and Monte Rivera (eds.) *Puerto Rican Politics in Urban America*. Westport CT: Greenwood Press, pp. 43–72.

Bean, Frank, and Marta Tienda. 1987. *The Hispanic Population of the United States (for the National Committee for Research on the 1980 Census)*. New York: Russell Sage Foundation.

Benveniste, Emile. 1971[1956]. "The Nature of Pronouns." In *Problems in General Linguistics*. Coral Gables: University of Miami, pp. 217–222.

———. 1971[1958]. "Subjectivity in Language." In *Problems in General Linguistics*. Coral Gables: University of Miami, pp. 223–230.

Berger, Peter, and Thomas Luckmann. 1967. *The Social Construction of Reality*. Garden City NY: Doubleday.

Berk-Seligson, Susan. 1990. *The Bilingual Courtroom: Court Interpretation in the Judicial Process*. Chicago: University of Chicago Press.

Bernstein, Basil. 1971. *Class, Codes and Control*, vol 1. London: Routledge and Kegan Paul.

Bodnar, John. 1992. *Remaking America: Public Memory, Commemoration and Patriotism in the Twentieth Century*. Princeton: Princeton University Press.

Bonilla, Frank, and Ricardo Campos. 1981. "A Wealth of Poor: Puerto Ricans in the New Economic Order." *Daedelus* 110:133–176.

———. 1985. "Evolving Patterns of Puerto Rican Migration." In Steven Sanderson (ed.) *The Americas in the New International Division of Labor*. New York and London: Holmes and Meier, pp. 177–205.

Bourdieu, Pierre. 1977a. *Outline of a Theory of Practice*. Cambridge: Cambridge University Press.

———. 1977b. "The Economics of Linguistic Exchanges." *Social Science Information* 16:645–668.

———. 1991. *Language and Symbolic Power*. Cambridge MA: Harvard University Press.

Brown, Roger, and Albert Gilman. 1960. "The Pronouns of Power and Solidarity." In Thomas Sebeok (ed.) *Style in Language*. Cambridge: Massachusetts Institute of Technology Press, pp. 253–276.

Carr, Raymond. 1984. *Puerto Rico: A Colonial Experiment*. New York: Vintage.

Chan, Sucheng. 1990. "European and Asian Immigration into the United States in Comparative Perspective, 1820s to 1920s." In Virginia Yans-McLaughlin (ed.) *Immigration Reconsidered: History, Sociology and Politics*. New York and Oxford: Oxford University Press, pp. 37–75.

Chock, Phyllis Pease. 1989. "The Landscape of Enchantment: Redaction in a Theory of Ethnicity." *Cultural Anthropology* 2:347–368.

———. 1991. "'Illegal Aliens' and 'Opportunity': Myth-Making in Congressional Testimony." *American Ethnologist* 18:279–294.

———. 1994. "Porous Borders: Retelling America in the Illegal Alien Crisis." *Political and Legal Anthropology Review* 17 (2):45–56.

———. 1995. "Culturalism: Pluralism, Culture and Race in the *Harvard Encyclopedia of American Ethnic Groups*." *Identities*. 1(4):301–323.

City of New York Department of City Planning, Herbert Sturz, Chair. 1979. Manhattan Portfolio Planning District #3.

———. 1979. Bronx Portfolio Planning District #4.

———. 1983. Demographic Profile: a Portrait of New York City from the 1980 Census.

Conk, Margo A. 1986. "The 1980 Census in Historical Perspective." In William Alonso and Paul Starr (eds.) *The Politics of Numbers (for the National Committee for Research on the 1980 Census.)* New York: Russell Sage Foundation, pp. 155–186.

Conley, John M., and William M. O'Barr. 1990. *Rules versus Relationships: The Ethnography of Legal Discourse.* Chicago: University of Chicago Press.

Crawford, James (ed.) 1992. *Language Loyalties: A Source Book on the Official English Controversy.* Chicago: University of Chicago Press.

Darder, Antonia. 1992. "Problematizing the Notion of Puerto Ricans as 'Underclass': A Step Toward a Decolonizing Study of Poverty." *Hispanic Journal of Behavioral Sciences* 14(1):144–156.

Davis, Mike. 1986. *Prisoners of the American Dream.* London and New York: Verso.

DeMott, Benjamin. 1990. *The Imperial Middle: Why Americans Can't Think Straight About Class.* New York: William Morrow and Company.

Díaz-Duque, Ozzie F. 1989. "Communication Barriers in Medical Settings: Hispanics in the United States." *International Journal of the Sociology of Language* 79:93–102.

Dietz, James. 1986. *Economic History of Puerto Rico: Institutional Change and Capitalist Development.* Princeton: Princeton University Press.

di Leonardo, Micaela. 1984. *The Varieties of Ethnic Experience: Kinship, Class and Gender among California Italian-Americans.* Ithaca NY: Cornell University Press.

Dittmar, Norbert. 1983. "Descriptive and Explanatory Power of Rules in Sociolinguistics." In Bruce Bain (ed.) *The Sociogenesis of Language and Human Conduct.* New York: Plenum, pp. 225–255.

Dorian, Nancy. 1981. *Language Death: The Life Cycle of a Scottish Gaelic Dialect.* Philadelphia: University of Pennsylvania Press.

———. 1982. "Defining the Speech Community to Include Its Working Margins." In Suzanne Romaine (ed.) *Sociolinguistic Variation in Speech Communities.* London: Edwin Arnold, pp. 25–34.

Douglas, Mary. 1966. *Purity and Danger: An Analysis of the Concepts of Pollution and Taboo.* London: Routledge and Kegan Paul.

Epstein, Erwin. 1970. *Politics and Education in Puerto Rico.* Metuchen NJ: Scarecrow.

Erickson, Frederick. 1975. "Gatekeeping and the Melting Pot: Interaction in Counseling Encounters." *Harvard Educational Review* 45:44–50.

Estades, Rosa. 1980. "Symbolic Unity: The Puerto Rican Day Parade." In Clara Rodríguez, Virginia Sánchez Korrol and José Oscar Alers (eds.) *The Puerto Rican Struggle: Essays on Survival in the U.S.* Maplewood NJ: Waterfront Press, pp. 82–89.

Fabian, Johannes. 1979. "Rule and Process: Thoughts on Ethnography as Communication." *Philosophy of the Social Sciences* 9:1–26.

———. 1986. *Language and Colonial Power.* Berkeley: University of California Press.

Falcón, Angelo. 1984. "A History of Puerto Rican Politics in New York City: 1860s to 1945." In James Jennings and Monte Rivera (eds.) *Puerto Rican Politics in Urban America.* Westport CT: Greenwood Press, pp. 15–42.

———. 1988. "Black and Latino Politics in New York City: Race and Ethnicity in a Changing Urban Context." In F. Chris Garcia (ed.) *Latinos and the Political System.* Notre Dame: University of Notre Dame Press, pp. 171–194.

Falcón, Luis, and Charles Hirschman. 1992. "Trends in Labor Market Position for Puerto Ricans on the Mainland: 1970–1987." *Hispanic Journal of Behavioral Sciences.* 14(1):16–51.

Fernandez, James. 1986. "The Mission of Metaphor in Expressive Culture." In *Persuasions and Performances: The Play of Tropes in Culture*. Bloomington: Indiana University Press, pp. 28–72.

Fields, Barbara Jeanne. 1990. "Slavery, Race and Ideology in the U.S.A." *New Left Review* May/June: 95–118.

Fishman, Joshua, Robert Cooper, and Roxana Ma. 1971. *Bilingualism in the Barrio*. Bloomington: Indiana University Press.

Flores, Juan, John Attinasi, and Pedro Pedraza. 1981. "*La Carreta* Made a U-Turn: Puerto Rican Language and Culture in the United States." *Daedalus* 110:193–217.

Flores, Juan, and George Yudice. 1990. "Living Borders/*Buscando* America: Languages of Latino Self-formation." *Social Text* 8(2):57–84.

Foley, Douglas. 1990. *Learning Capitalist Culture Deep in the Heart of Tejas*. Philadelphia: University of Pennsylvania Press.

Foner, Nancy. 1987. "The Jamaicans: Race and Ethnicity Among Migrants in New York City." In Nancy Foner (ed.) *New Immigrants in New York City*. New York: Columbia University Press, pp. 195–217.

Fordham, Signithia, and John Ogbu. 1986. "Black Students' School Success: Coping with the "Burden of 'Acting White'." *The Urban Review* 18:176–206.

Foucault, Michel. 1972. *The Archaeology of Knowledge and The Discourse on Language*. New York: Pantheon.

Fox, Richard. 1991. "Introduction: Working in the Present." In Richard Fox (ed.) *Recapturing Anthropology: Working in the Present*. Santa Fe NM: School of American Research Press, pp. 1–16.

Friedrich, Paul. 1979[1966]. "Structural Implications of Russian Pronominal Usage." In Anwar Dil (ed.) *Language, Culture and the Imagination: Essays by Paul Friedrich*. Stanford: Stanford University Press, pp. 63–117.

———. 1979[1978]. "The Symbol and Its Relative Non-Arbitrariness." In Anwar Dil (ed.) *Language, Culture and the Imagination: Essays by Paul Friedrich*. Stanford: Stanford University Press, pp. 1–62.

———. 1986. *The Language Parallax*. Austin TX: University of Texas Press.

Fuentes, Luis. 1984. "Puerto Ricans and New York City School Board Elections: Apathy or Obstructionism?" In James Jennings and Monte Rivera (eds.) *Puerto Rican Politics in Urban America*. Westport CT: Greenwood Press, pp. 127–143.

Gal, Susan. 1979. *Language Shift: Social Determinants of Linguistic Change in Bilingual Austria*. New York: Academic Press.

———. 1987. "Codeswitching and Consciousness in the European Periphery." *American Ethnologist* 14:637–653.

García, Ofelia, Isabel Evangelista, Mabel Martínez, Carmen Disla, and Bonifacio Paulino. 1988. "Spanish Language Use and Attitudes: A Study of Two New York City Communities." *Language in Society* 17:475–511.

García, Ofelia, Joshua Fishman, Michael Gertner, and Silvia Burunat. 1985. "Written Spanish in the United States: An Analysis of the Spanish of the Ethnic Press." *International Journal of the Sociology of Language* 56:85–98.

Geertz, Clifford. 1984. "Common Sense as a Cultural System." In *Local Knowledge*. New York: Basic Books, pp. 73–93.

Genishi, Celia. 1981. "Codeswitching in Chicano Six-Year-Olds." In R. Durán (ed.) *Latino Language and Communicative Behavior*. Norwood NJ: Ablex, pp. 133–152.

Goffman, Erving. 1961. *Encounters: Two Studies in Social Interaction*. Indianapolis: Bobbs-Merril Educational Publishing.

Goffman, Erving. 1981. *Forms of Talk*. Philadelphia: University of Pennsylvania Press.

———. 1974. *Frame Analysis*. New York: Harper and Row.

González, Eddie, and Lois Gray. 1984. "Puerto Ricans, Politics and Labor Activism." In James Jennings and Monte Rivera, (eds.) *Puerto Rican Politics in Urban America*. Westport CT: Greenwood Press, pp. 117–125.

Gordon, David, Richard Edwards, and Michael Reich. 1982. *Segmented Work, Divided Workers: the Historical Transformation of Labor in the U.S.* New York: Cambridge.

Gould, Stephen J. 1979. "Why We Should Not Name Races: A Biological View." In *Ever Since Darwin: Reflections in Natural History*. New York: Norton, pp. 231–236.

———. 1981. *The Mismeasure of Man*. New York: Norton.

Gramsci, Antonio. 1971. *Selections from the Prison Notebooks*. New York: International Publishers.

Greenburg, Dan. 1979. "The Ninth Precinct Blues." *New York Times Magazine* 21 January 1979, pp. 31ff.

Greenhouse, Carol. 1986. *Praying for Justice: Faith, Order and Community in an American Town*. Ithaca NY: Cornell University Press.

Gumperz, John. 1968. "The Speech Community." In *International Encyclopedia of the Social Sciences*. London: Macmillan, pp.381–386.

———. 1982. *Discourse Strategies*. Cambridge: Cambridge University Press.

Gumperz, John, and Robert Wilson. 1971. "Convergence and Creolization: A Case from the Indo-Aryan/Dravidian Border in India." In Dell Hymes (ed.) *Pidginization and Creolization of Languages*. New York: Cambridge University Press, pp. 151–167.

Halle, David. 1984. *America's Working Man*. Chicago: University of Chicago Press.

Handler, Richard. 1988. *Nationalism and the Politics of Culture in Quebec*. Madison: University of Wisconsin Press.

Hannerz, Ulf. 1980. *Exploring the City: Inquiries Toward an Urban Anthropology*. New York: Columbia University Press.

Haugen, Einar. 1969. *The Norwegian Language in America*. Bloomington: Indiana University Press.

———. 1972. "The Ecology of Language." In Anwar Dil (ed.) *The Ecology of Language: Essays by Einar Haugen*. Stanford CA: Stanford University Press, pp. 325–339.

Haviland, John. 1977. *Gossip, Reputation and Knowledge in Zinacantan*. Chicago: University of Chicago Press.

Hayakawa, S. I. 1992[1985]. "The Case for Official English." In James Crawford (ed.) *Language Loyalties: A Source Book on the Official English Controversy*. Chicago: University of Chicago Press, pp. 94–110.

Heath, Shirley Brice. 1992[1976]. "Why No Official Tongue?" In James Crawford (ed.) *Language Loyalties: A Source Book on the Official English Controversy*. Chicago: University of Chicago Press, pp. 20–30.

———. 1983. *Ways with Words: Language, Life and Work in Communities and Classrooms*. New York: Cambridge University Press.

Hechter, Michael. 1975. *Internal Colonialism*. Berkeley: University of California Press.

Heller, Monica. 1982. "Negotiations of Language Choice in Montreal." In John Gumperz (ed.) *Language and Social Identity*. New York: Cambridge University Press, pp. 108–118.

———. 1988. "Strategic Ambiguity: Codeswitching in the Management of Conflict." In Monica Heller (ed.) *Codeswitching: Anthropological and Sociolinguistic Perspective*. Berlin and New York: Mouton de Gruyter, pp. 77–96.

Herbstein, Judith. 1983. "Politicization of Puerto Rican Ethnicity in New York 1955–75." *Ethnic Groups* 5:31–54.

Herrell, Richard. 1992. "The Symbolic Strategies of Chicago's Gay and Lesbian Pride Day Parade." In Gilbert Herdt (ed.) *Gay Culture in America: Essays from the Field*. Boston: Beacon Press, pp. 225–252.

————. 1994. "Gay Americans: In the (National) Life." *Political and Legal Anthropology Review.* 17 (2):37–44.

Herzfeld, Michael. 1987. *Anthropology Through the Looking Glass*. New York: Cambridge University Press.

Hill, Jane, and Kenneth Hill. 1986. *Speaking Mexicano: Dynamics of Syncretic Language in Central Mexico*. Tucson: University of Arizona Press.

History Task Force, Center for Puerto Rican Studies. 1979. *Labor Migration Under Capitalism: The Puerto Rican Experience*. New York and London: Monthly Review Press.

Horsman, Reginald. 1981. *Race and Manifest Destiny: The Origins of American Racial Anglo-Saxonism*. Cambridge: Harvard University Press.

Huddleston, Walter. 1992[1983]. "The Misdirected Policy of Bilingualism." In James Crawford (ed.) *Language Loyalties: A Source Book on the Official English Controversy*. Chicago: University of Chicago Press, pp. 114–118.

Huerta-Macías, Ana. 1981. "Code-Switching: All in the Family." In R. Durán (ed.) *Latino Language and Communicative Behavior*, Norwood NJ: Ablex, pp. 153–168.

Hymes, Dell. 1973. "Speech and Language: On the Origins and Foundations of Inequality Among Speakers." *Daedalus* 102(3):59–85.

————. 1974. *Foundations in Sociolinguistics*. Philadelphia: University of Pennsylvania Press.

————. 1980. *Language in Education: An Ethnographic Approach*. Washington D.C.: Center for Applied Linguistics.

Iglesias, César Andreu (ed.) 1984. *Memoirs of Bernardo Vega*. New York: Monthly Review Press.

Institute for Puerto Rican Policy Inc. 1987. "Puerto Rican and Other Latino-Owned Businesses in the U.S., 1982." *Datanote on the Puerto Rican Community* #6.

Interfaith Adopt-a-Building, Inc. 1978. *A Portrait of Loisaida*. New York: Interfaith Adopt-A-Building.

Irvine, Judith. 1989. "When Talk Isn't Cheap: Language and Political Economy." *American Ethnologist* 16:248–267.

Jakobson, Roman. 1960. "Linguistics and Poetics." In Thomas Sebeok (ed.) *Style in Language*. Cambridge MA: Massachusetts Institute of Technology Press, pp. 350–377.

Janowitz, Morris. 1967[1952]. *The Community Press in an Urban Setting*. Chicago: University of Chicago Press.

Jennings, James. 1984. "Puerto Rican Politics in Two Cities: New York and Boston." In James Jennings and Monte Rivera (eds.) *Puerto Rican Politics in Urban America*. Westport CT: Greenwood Press, pp. 75–98.

————. 1988. "Future Directions for Puerto Rican Politics in the U.S. and Puerto Rico." In F. Chris Garcia (ed.) *Latinos and the Political System*. Notre Dame: University of Notre Dame Press, pp. 480–497.

Kasinitz, Philip, and Judith Freidenberg-Herbstein. 1987. "The Puerto Rican Parade and West Indian Carnival: Public Celebrations in New York City." In C. Sutton and E. Chaney (eds.) *Caribbean Life in New York City: Sociocultural Dimensions*. New York: Center for Migration Studies, pp. 327–349.

Katz, Michael. 1989. *The Underserving Poor*. New York: Pantheon.

Klein, Flora. 1980. "A Quantitative Study of Syntactic and Pragmatic Indications of Change in the Spanish of Bilinguals in the United States." In William Labov (ed.) *Locating Language in Time and Space*. New York: Academic Press, pp. 69–82.

Labov, William. 1982[1966]. *The Social Stratification of English in New York City*. (Third Printing). Washington: Center for Applied Linguistics.

———. 1972. *Sociolinguistic Patterns*. Philadelphia: University of Pennsylvania Press.

Lambert, Wallace, Richard C. Hodgson, Richard C. Gardner, and Samuel Fillenbaum. 1960. "Evaluational Reactions to Spoken Languages." *Journal of Abnormal and Social Psychology*. 60(1): 44–55.

Language Policy Task Force, Center for Puerto Rican Studies. 1980. "Social Dimensions of Language Use in East Harlem." *Working Paper No. 7*. New York: Center for Puerto Rican Studies, Hunter College, City University of New York.

———. 1982. *Intergenerational Perspectives on Bilingualism: From Community to Classroom*. Investigators: John Attinasi, Pedro Pedraza, Shana Poplack, Alicia Pousada. New York: Center for Puerto Rican Studies, Hunter College, City University of New York.

LaRuffa, Anthony. 1988. *Monte Carmelo: An Italian-American Community in the Bronx*. New York: Gordon and Breach Science Publishers.

Lauria, Anthony. 1964. "Respeto, Relajo and Inter-personal Relations in Puerto Rico." *Anthropological Quarterly* 37(2):53–67.

LePage, R. B., and Andrée Tabouret-Keller. 1985. *Acts of Identity: Creole-based Approaches to Language and Ethnicity*. Cambridge: Cambridge University Press.

Lewis, Oscar. 1966. *La Vida*. New York: Random House.

Lieberson, Stanley. 1980. *A Piece of the Pie: Black and White Immigrants Since 1880*. Berkeley: University of California Press.

———. 1985. "Stereotypes: Their Consequences for Race and Ethnic Interactions." In Cora Bagley Marrett and Cheryl Leggon (eds.) *Research in Race and Ethnic Relations: A Research Annual*. Greenwich CT and London: JAI Press, pp. 113–137.

Limón, José. 1979. "The Folk Performance of *Chicano* and the Cultural Limits of Political Ideology." *Working Papers in Sociolinguistics No. 62*. Austin TX: Southwest Educational Development Laboratory.

Lipsitz, George. 1986. "The Meaning of Memory: Family, Class and Ethnicity in Early Network Television Programs." *Cultural Anthropology* 1:355–387.

López, Iris. 1987. "Sterilization Among Puerto Rican Women in New York City: Public Policy and Social Constraints." In Leith Mullings (ed.) *Cities of the United States: Studies in Urban Anthropology*. New York: Columbia, pp. 269–291.

Lyons, John. 1977. *Semantics*. New York: Cambridge University Press.

Maldonado, Edwin. 1979. "Contract Labor and the Origins of Puerto Rican Communities in the U.S." *International Migration Review* 13:103–121.

Mannheim, Bruce. 1991. *The Language of the Inka since the European Invasion*. Austin TX: University of Texas Press.

Marshall, David. 1986. "The Question of an Official Language: Language Rights and the English Language Amendments." *International Journal of the Sociology of Language* 60:7–75.

Massey, Douglas. 1981. "Hispanic Residential Segregation: A Comparison of Mexicans, Cubans and Puerto Ricans." *Sociology and Social Research* 65:311–322.

Massey, Douglas, and Brooks Bitterman. 1985. "Explaining the Paradox of Puerto Rican Segregation." *Social Forces* 64:306–331.

Massey, Douglas, and Nancy Denton. 1985. "Spatial Assimilation as a Socioeconomic Outcome." *American Sociological Review* 50:94–105.

Matsuda, Mari. 1991. "Voices of America: Accent, Antidiscrimination Law and a Jurisprudence for the Last Reconstruction." *Yale Law Journal* 100:1329–1407.

Meléndez, Edwin, and Janis Barry Figueroa. 1992. "The Effects of Local Labor Market Conditions on Labor Force Participation of Puerto Rican, White and Black Women." *Hispanic Journal of Behavioral Sciences* 14(1):76–90.

Merry, Sally Engle. 1990. *Getting Justice and Getting Even: Legal Consciousness Among Working-Class Americans.* Chicago: University of Chicago Press.

Miller, Kerby A. 1990. "Class, Culture and Immigrant Group Identity in the United States: The Case of Irish-American Ethnicity." In Virginia Yans-McLaughlin (ed.) *Immigration Reconsidered: History, Sociology and Politics.* New York: Oxford University Press, pp. 96–129.

Milroy, Lesley. 1980. *Language and Social Networks.* New York: Basil Blackwell.

Milroy, James, and Lesley Milroy. 1985. *Authority in Language: Investigating Language Prescription and Standardisation.* London: Routledge and Kegan Paul.

Model, Suzanne. 1990. "Work and Family: Blacks and Immigrants from South and East Europe." In Virginia Yans-McLaughlin (ed.) *Immigration Reconsidered: History, Sociology and Politics.* New York: Oxford University Press, pp. 130–159.

Morawska, Ewa. 1990. "The Sociology and Historiography of Immigration." In Virginia Yans-McLaughlin (ed.) *Immigration Reconsidered: History, Sociology and Politics.* New York: Oxford University Press, pp. 197–238.

Muñoz Rivera, Luis (ed.) 1915. *La Democracia.* Editorials.

Myles, John. 1988. "Postwar Capitalism and the Extension of Social Security into a Retirement Wage." In Margaret Weir, Ann Shola Orloff, and Theda Skocpol (eds.) *The Politics of Social Policy in the United States.* Princeton: Princeton University Press, pp. 265–84.

Nash, June. 1989. *From Tank Town to High Tech: The Clash of Community and Industrial Cycles.* Albany: State University of New York Press.

Negrón de Montilla, Aida. 1975. *Americanization in Puerto Rico and the Public School System.* Rio Piedras: Editorial Universitaria.

Nelson, Candace, and Marta Tienda. 1985. "The Structuring of Hispanic Ethnicity: Historical and Contemporary Perspectives." *Ethnic and Racial Studies* 8:49–74.

Newman, Katherine. 1988. *Falling From Grace: The Experience of Downward Mobility in the American Middle Class.* New York: The Free Press.

Omi, Michael, and Howard Winant. 1986. *Racial Formation in the U.S. from the 1960s to the 1980s.* New York and London: Routledge and Kegan Paul.

Orfield, Gary. 1986. "Hispanic Education: Challenges, Research and Policies. *American Journal of Education* 95(1):1–25.

———. 1987. "School Desegregation Needed Now." *Focus* July:5–7.

Ortner, Sherry. 1991. "Reading America: Preliminary Notes on Class and Culture." In Richard G. Fox (ed.) *Recapturing Anthropology.* Santa Fe NM: School of American Research Press, pp. 163–189.

Oscar Alers, José. 1978. *Puerto Ricans and Health: Findings From New York City.* New York: Fordham University.

Osuna, Juan José. 1949. *A History of Education in Puerto Rico.* Rio Piedras: University of Puerto Rico.

Pedraza, Pedro, John Attinasi, and Gerald Hoffman. 1980. "Rethinking Diglossia." In Raymond Padilla (ed.) *Ethnoperspectives in Bilingual Education Research: Theory in Bilingual Education*. Ypsilanti MI: Eastern Michigan University.

Pedraza, Pedro. 1987. "An Ethnographic Analysis of Language Use in the Puerto Rican Community of East Harlem." Working Paper #12. New York: Center for Puerto Rican Studies Language Policy Task Force, Hunter College, City University of New York.

Peirce, C. S. 1956. "Logic as Semiotic: The Theory of Signs." In J. Buchler (ed.) *The Philosophy of Peirce: Selected Writings*. London: Routledge and Kegan Paul, pp. 98–119.

Perin, Constance. 1977. *Everything in its Place: Social Order and Land Use in America*. Princeton: Princeton University Press.

Phelan, Thomas James. 1989. "From the Attic of the *American Journal of Sociology*: Unusual Contributions to American Sociology, 1895–1935." *Sociological Forum* 4(1):71–86.

Philips, Susan U. 1983. *The Invisible Culture: Communication in Classroom and Community on the Warm Springs Indian Reservation*. New York: Longmans.

Poplack, Shana. 1979. "Sometimes I'll Start a Sentence in Spanish *Y Termino en Español:* Toward a Typology of Code-Switching." Working Paper #4. New York: Center for Puerto Rican Studies Language Policy Task Force, Hunter College, City University of New York.

————. 1988. "Contrasting Patterns of Code-switching in Two Communities." In Monica Heller (ed.) *Codeswitching: Anthropological and Sociolinguistic Perspectives*. New York: Mouton, pp. 215–244.

Portes, Alejandro. 1990. "From South of the Border. Hispanic Minorities in the U.S." In Virginia Yans-McLaughlin (ed.) *Immigration Reconsidered*. New York: Oxford University Press, pp. 160–186.

Pousada, Alicia, and Mel Greenlee. 1988. "Toward a Social Theory of Language Variability." In *Speech and Ways of Speaking in a Bilingual Puerto Rican Community*. Investigators: Celia Alvarez, Adrian Bennett, Mel Greenlee, Pedro Pedraza, Alicia Pousada. New York: Center for Puerto Rican Studies Language Policy Task Force, Hunter College, City University of New York, pp. 13–92.

Pousada, Alicia, and Shana Poplack. 1979. "No Case for Convergence: The Puerto Rican Spanish Verb System in a Language Contact Situation." Working Paper #5. New York: Center for Puerto Rican Studies Language Policy Task Force, Hunter College, City University of New York.

Pratt, Mary Louise. 1986. "Fieldwork in Common Places." In James Clifford and George Marcus (eds.) *Writing Culture: The Poetics and Politics of Ethnography*. Berkeley: University of California Press, pp. 27–50.

Preston, Dennis. 1989. *Perceptual Dialectology: Non-linguists' Views of Areal Linguistics*. Providence: Foris.

Rapp, Rayna. 1987. "Urban Kinship in Contemporary America: Families, Classes and Ideology." In Leith Mullings (ed.) *Cities of the United States: Studies in Urban Anthropology*. New York: Columbia University Press, pp. 219–242.

Rieder, Jonathan. 1985. *Canarsie: The Jews and Italians of Brooklyn Against Liberalism*. Cambridge: Harvard University Press.

Ridge, Martin (ed.) 1980. *The New Bilingualism: An American Dilemma*. University of Southern California Transaction Books—Rutgers University.

Ríos, Palmira. 1985. "Puerto Rican Women in the United States Labor Market." *Line of March* 18:43–56.

Rivera, Monte. 1984. "Organizational Politics of the East Harlem Barrio in the 1970s." In James Jennings and Monte Rivera (eds.) *Puerto Rican Politics in Urban America.* Westport CT: Greenwood Press, pp. 62–72.

Rodríguez, Clara. 1979. "Economic Factors Affecting Puerto Ricans in New York." In Center for Puerto Rican Studies History Task Force (eds.) *Labor Migration Under Capitalism.* New York: Monthly Review Press, pp. 197–221.

———. 1989. *Puerto Ricans: Born in the U.S.A.* Boston: Unwin Hyman.

———. 1990. "Racial Identification along Puerto Ricans in New York." *Hispanic Journal of Behavioral Sciences* 12(4):366–379.

———, Aida Castro, Oscar García, and Analisa Torres. 1991. "Latino Racial Identity: in the Eye of the Beholder?" *Latino Studies Journal* 2(3):33–48.

Rodríguez, Havidan. 1992. "Household Composition, Employment Patterns and Income Equality: Puerto Ricans in New York and Other Areas of the U.S. Mainland." *Hispanic Journal of Behavioral Sciences* 14(1):52–75.

Romaine, Suzanne. 1982. *Sociohistorical Linguistics: Its Status and Methodology.* New York: Cambridge University Press.

———. 1984. *The Language of Children and Adolescents.* New York: Basil Blackwell.

———. 1989. *Bilingualism.* New York: Basil Blackwell.

Ryan, Ellen B., and Miguel Carranza. 1975. "Evaluative Reactions of Adolescents Toward Speakers of Standard English and Mexican American Accented English." *Journal of Personality and Social Psychology* 31: 855–863.

Sánchez Korrol, Virginia E. 1983. *From Colonia to Community: The History of Puerto Ricans in New York City, 1917–1948.* Westport CT: Greenwood Press.

Santiago, Anne. 1992. "Patterns of Puerto Rican Segregation and Mobility." *Hispanic Journal of Behavioral Sciences* 14(1):107–133.

Sapir, Edward. 1949. "Symbolism." In David Mandelbaum (ed.) *Selected Writings of Edward Sapir.* Berkeley: University of California Press, pp. 564–568.

Sassen-Koob, Saskia. 1985. "Changing Composition and Labor Market Location of Hispanic Immigrants in New York City, 1960–1980." In George Borjas and Marta Tienda (eds.) *Hispanics in the U.S. Economy.* Orlando FL: Academic Press, pp. 299–322.

———. 1989. "New York City's Informal Economy." In A. Portes, M. Castells, and L. Benton (eds.) *The Informal Sector.* Baltimore: Johns Hopkins.

Schneider, David M. 1980[1968]. *American Kinship: A Cultural Account* (Second Edition). Chicago: University of Chicago Press.

Schneider, Jo Anne. 1990. "Defining Boundaries, Creating Contexts: Puerto Rican and Polish Presentation of Group Identity Through Ethnic Parades." *Journal of Ethnic Studies* 18(1):33–58.

Schwartz, Barry. 1975. *Queuing and Waiting: Studies in the Social Organization of Access and Delay.* Chicago: University of Chicago Press.

Scotton, Carol Myers. 1988. "Codeswitching as Indexical of Social Negotiations." In Monica Heller (ed.) *Codeswitching: Anthropological and Sociolinguistic Perspectives.* New York: Mouton, pp. 151–186.

Sennett, Richard, and Jonathan Cobb. 1972. *The Hidden Injuries of Class.* New York: Vantage.

Sharff, Jagna. 1986. "Free Enterprise and the Ghetto Family." In E. Angeloni (ed.) *Annual Editions in Anthropology 1986–1987.* Guildford CN: Dushkin Publishing Group, pp. 139–143.

———. 1987. "The Underground Economy of a Poor Neighborhood." In Leith Mullings (ed.) *Cities of the United States: Studies in Urban Anthropology.* New York: Columbia University Press, pp. 19–50.

Shklar, Judith. 1991. *American Citizenship: The Quest for Inclusion.* Cambridge: Harvard University Press.

Shuman, Amy. 1986. *Storytelling Rights: The Uses of Oral and Written Texts by Urban Adolescents.* New York: Cambridge University Press.

Silverstein, Michael. 1976. "Shifters, Linguistic Categories and Cultural Description." In Keith Basso and Henry Selby (eds.) *Meaning in Anthropology.* Albuquerque: University of New Mexico Press, pp. 11–55.

———. 1977. "Cultural Prerequisites to Grammatical Analysis." In Muriel Saville-Troike (ed.) *Georgetown University Round Table on Languages and Linguistics: Linguistics and Anthropology.* Washington, DC: Georgetown University Press, pp. 139–151.

———. 1987. "Monoglot 'Standard' in America." Working Papers and Proceedings of the Center for Psychosocial Studies No. 13. Chicago: Center for Psychosocial Studies.

Singh, Rajendra. 1983. "We, They and Us: A Note on Code-switching and Stratification in North India." *Language in Society* 12:71–73.

———, Jayant Lele, and Gita Martohardjono. 1988. "Communication in a Multilingual Society: Some Missed Opportunities." *Language in Society* 17:43–59.

Slessarev, Helen. 1988. "Racial Tensions and Institutional Support: Social Programs During a Period of Retrenchment." In Margaret Weir, Ann Shola Orloff, and Theda Skocpol (eds.) *The Politics of Social Policy in the United States.* Princeton: Princeton University Press, pp. 357–379.

Smith, Neil. 1992. "New City, New Frontier: The Lower East Side as Wild Wild West." In Michael Sorkin (ed.) *Variations on a Theme Park: The New American City and the End of Public Space.* New York: Hill and Wang, pp. 61–93.

Smith, Neil, Betsy Duncan, and Laura Reid. 1989. "From Disinvestment to Reinvestment: Tax Arrears and Turning Points in the East Village." *Housing Studies* 4:238–252.

Stanfield, John. 1985. "Theoretical and Ideological Barriers to the Study of Race-making." In Cora Bagley Marrett and Cheryl Leggon (eds.) *Research in Race and Ethnic Relations: A Research Annual.* Greenwich CT and London: JAI Press, pp. 161–181.

Steinberg, Stephen. 1989. *The Ethnic Myth: Race, Ethnicity and Class in America.* Boston: Beacon Press.

Stevens-Arroyo, Antonio. 1980. "Puerto Rican Struggles in the Catholic Church." In Clara Rodríguez, Virginia Sánchez-Korrol, and José Oscar Alers (eds.) *The Puerto Rican Struggle: Essays on Survival in the United States.* Maplewood NJ: Waterfront Press, pp. 129–139.

Steward, Julian (ed.) 1956. *The People of Puerto Rico.* Urbana: University of Illinois Press.

Susser, Ida, and John Kreniske. 1987. "The Welfare Trap: A Public Policy for Deprivation." In Leith Mullings (ed.) *Cities of the United States: Studies in Urban Anthropology.* New York: Columbia University Press, pp. 51–68.

Szwed, John. 1975. "Race and the Embodiment of Culture." *Ethnicity* 2:19–33.

Tarver, Heidi. 1989. "Language and Politics in the 1980s: the Story of U.S. English. *Politics and Society* 17:225–245.

Tilly, Charles. 1990. "Transplanted Networks." In Virginia Yans-McLaughlin (ed.) *Immigration Reconsidered: History, Sociology and Politics.* New York: Oxford University Press, pp. 79–95.

Trouillot, Michel-Rolph. 1990. "Good Day Columbus; Silences, Power and Public History (1492–1892)." *Public Culture* 3(1):1–24.

————. 1991. "Anthropology and the Savage Slot: The Poetics and Politics of Otherness." In Richard Fox (ed.) *Recapturing Anthropology: Working in the Present*. Santa Fe NM: School of American Research Press, pp. 17–44.

Tumin, Melvin, and Arnold Feldman. 1961. *Social Class and Social Change in Puerto Rico*. Princeton: Princeton University Press.

United States Bureau of the Census. 1983. *1980 Census of Population and Housing: Census Tracts* New York, NY-NJ, Washington DC: U.S. Government Printing Office.

————. 1993. *1990 Census of Population and Housing: Population and Housing Characteristics for Census Tracts and Block Numbering Areas*. New York–Northern New York. Washington DC: U.S. Government Printing Office.

Urciuoli, Bonnie. 1991. "The Political Topography of Spanish and English: The View from a New York Puerto Rican Neighborhood." *American Ethnologist* 18:295–310.

————. 1993. "Representing Class: Who Decides?" *Anthropological Quarterly* 66(4):203–210.

Valdés, Guadalupe. 1981." Codeswitching as Deliberate Verbal Strategy." In Richard Durán (ed.) *Latino Language and Communicative Behavior*. Norwood NJ: Ablex, pp. 95–108.

Varenne, Hervé. 1977. *Americans Together: Structured Diversity in a Midwestern Town*. New York: Teachers College, Columbia University Press.

————. 1984. "Collective Representation in American Anthropological Conversations about Culture: Culture and the Individual." *Current Anthropology* 25 (3):281–299.

————. 1986. "Drop in Anytime." In H. Varenne (ed.) *Symbolizing America*. Lincoln: University of Nebraska Press, pp. 209–228.

Vásquez, Olga, Sheila Shannon, and Lucinda Pease Alvarez. 1994. *Pushing Boundaries*. New York: Cambridge University Press.

Vásquez-Calzada, José. 1978. "La Población de Puerto Rico y su Trajectoria Historica." *Escuela de Salud Publica, Recinto de Ciencias Medicas*. Rio Piedras: Universidad de Puerto Rico.

Waldinger, Roger. 1985. "Immigration and Industrial Change in the New York City Apparel Industry." In George Borjas and Marta Tienda (eds.) *Hispanics in the U.S. Economy*. Orlando FL: Academic Press, pp. 323–349.

Walsh, Catherine. 1991. *Pedagogy and the Struggle for Voice: Issues of Language, Power and Schooling for Puerto Ricans*. New York: Bergin and Garvey.

Warriner, John, and Francis Griffith. 1963. *English Grammar and Composition*. New York: Harcourt, Brace and World.

Weber, Max. 1978. *Economy and Society: An Outline of Interpretive Sociology*. Berkeley and Los Angeles: University of California Press.

Weinreich, Uriel. 1953. *Languages in Contact: Findings and Problems*. The Hague: Mouton.

Williams, Brackette. 1989. "A Class Act: Anthropology and the Race to Nation Across Ethnic Terrain." *Annual Review of Anthropology* 18:401–444.

————. 1991. *Stains on My Name, War in My Veins: Guyana and the Politics of Cultural Struggle*. Durham NC: Duke University Press.

Williams, Raymond. 1977. *Marxism and Literature*. New York: Oxford University Press.

————. 1973. *The Country and the City*. New York: Oxford University Press.

Wilson, William Julius. 1987. *The Truly Disadvantaged: The Inner City, the Underclass and Public Policy*. Chicago: University of Chicago Press.

Wilson, Kenneth, and Alejandro Portes. 1980. "Immigrant Enclaves: An Analysis of the Labor Market Experience of Cubans in Miami." *American Journal of Sociology* 86(2):295–319.

Wolf, Eric. 1982. *Europe and the People without History*. Berkeley: University of California.

Wolfram, Walt. 1973. "Objective and Subjective Parameters of Language Assimilation Among Second Generation Puerto Ricans in East Harlem." In Roger Shuy and Ralph Fasold (eds.) *Language Attitudes: Current Trends and Prospects.* Washington, D.C.: Georgetown University Press, pp. 148–173.

———. 1974. *Sociolinguistic Aspects of Assimilation.* Arlington VA: Center for Applied Linguistics.

Woolard, Kathryn. 1985. "Language Variation and Cultural Hegemony: Toward an Integration of Sociolinguistic and Social Theory." *American Ethnologist* 12:738–748.

———. 1989. *Double Talk: Bilingualism and the Politics of Ethnicity in Catalonia.* Stanford: Stanford University Press.

Yarrow, Andrew. 1988. "Theatrical Life on the Lower East Side." *New York Times* 1 May 1988.

Zentella, Ana Celia. 1981a. "Language Variety Among Puerto Ricans." In Charles Ferguson and Shirley Brice Heath (eds.) *Language in the U.S.A.* New York: Cambridge University Press, pp. 218–238.

———. 1981b. "*Ta bien,* You Could Answer Me *en cualquier idioma*: Puerto Rican Code-switching in Bilingual Classrooms." In Richard Durán (ed.) *Latino Language and Communicative Behavior.* Norwood NJ: Ablex, pp. 109–131.

———. 1982. "Codeswitching and Interactions Among Puerto Rican Children." In Jon Amastae and Lucia Elías-Olivares (eds.) *Spanish in the United States: Sociolinguistic Aspects.* New York: Cambridge University Press, pp. 354–385.

———. 1988. "Language Politics in the U.S.A.: The English-Only Movement." In B. J. Craige (ed.) *Literature, Language and Politics in the 80s.* Athens: University of Georgia, pp. 39–53.

———. 1990. "Returned Migration, Language and Identity: Puerto Rican Bilinguals in *dos* Worlds/Two *mundos.*" *International Journal of the Sociology of Language* 84:81–100.

———. 1997. *Growing Up Bilingual: Children in El Barrio.* New York: Basil Blackwell.

About the Book
and Author

Puerto Ricans in the United States, like other migrant minorities, face an array of linguistic judgments. They are told they don't succeed because they don't speak English. They are told their English is "impure" or "broken" because it has been "mixed" with Spanish. They are told that they sound inarticulate and that if they speak "correct" English, with no sign of Spanish influence—most particularly with no accent, they will get better jobs. In short, Puerto Ricans in the United States are told that the origins of their economic and social problems are linguistic and can be remedied through personal effort, when in fact their fundamental problems stem from racial and class exclusion.

Concepts like "mixed" or "broken" languages, and "good" and "bad" English are cultural constructions and therefore are about more than language. In the Puerto Rican experience of devaluation and prejudice in the United States, the institutionalization of racial exclusion and class location are mapped onto English and Spanish in complex and highly politicized ways. Formal linguistic studies of bilingualism rarely engage this process in a significant way. But the place, function, and meaning of cultural constructs within the politicized communicative economy must be understood in terms of the intersections of race, class, and language that shape the lives of working-class Puerto Ricans. Working from ethnographic studies and interviews done on New York's Lower East Side and in the Bronx, this book examines that intersection in detail.

Bonnie Urciuoli is an associate professor in the Department of Anthropology at Hamilton College.

Index

Printed in the United States
43747LVS00005B/20